Rae & Dennis Croft

Literature in Ireland

Studies
Irish & Anglo-Irish

Thomas MacDonagh

A New Edition

Introduction: Gerald Dawe   *Profile: Nancy Murphy*

First published in 1916 by The Talbot Press, Dublin

Published in 1996 in this redesigned edition by
RELAY Books
Tyone, Nenagh, Co. Tipperary, Ireland
Tel: (067) 31734

*The book is published with the financial assistance of
An Chomhairle Ealaíon/The Arts Council, Ireland.*

ISBN 0 946327 16 5

British Library Cataloguing-in-Publication Data
A catalogue record for this book
is available from the British Library.

Cover Design: Deirdre O'Dowd

Typesetting: in house by RELAY

Typeface: Times, 11pt on 12 leading
Page size: 216 x 138 mm

Printed by Colour Books Ltd., Dublin

Contents

Publishers' Note to 1996 Edition   v
Introduction by Gerald Dawe   vii

Author's Dedication   xii
Author's Preface   xiii
1.   Introductory and General   1
2.   Anglo-Irish Literature   13
3.   Language and Literature   21
4.   Irish and English   29
5.   Anglo-Irish Authors   39
6.   The Irish Mode   45
7.   The Lyric of the Irish Mode   59
8.1   Irish Literature: Ancient Ireland   75
8.2   Irish Literature: To-day   97
      Poems of the Irish Mode   119

Translations:
Ceann Dubh Dílis (Sir Samuel Ferguson)   127
Cashel of Munster (Sir Samuel Ferguson)   127
Have You Been at Carrick? (Edward Walsh)   128
The Outlaw of Loch Lene (J. J. Callanan)   129
Pastheen Finn (Sir Samuel Ferguson)   129
The Coolun (Sir Samuel Ferguson)   131
Pulse of my Heart (Edward Walsh)   132
Nach Aoibhinn do na hÉiníní/Isn't it Pleasant for the
        Little Birds (Anon-Thomas MacDonagh)   133
Pearl of the White Breast (George Petrie)   134
The County of Mayo (George Fox)   134

The Fair Hills of Ireland (Sir Samuel Ferguson) 135
Lamentation of MacLiag for Kincora (James C. Mangan) 136
A Farewell to Patrick Sarsfield (James Clarence Mangan) 137
Kathaleen Ny Houlahan (James Clarence Mangan) 140
The Song of Gladness (James Clarence Mangan) 140
Eamonn an Chnuic (Eamon Ó Riain-MacDonagh) 142
A Dhruimfhionn Donn Dílis (Anon-MacDonagh) 143
Stuairín Na mBachall mBreágh Réidh/The Stars
    Stand Up in the Air (Anon-MacDonagh) 145
An Bunnán Buí (Cathal Buidhe MacGiolla Ghunna) 146
The Yellow Bittern (Thomas MacDonagh) 147

Ballads and Street Songs:
Shule Aroon (Anonymous) 148
The Croppy Boy (Anonymous) 149
The Streams of Bunclody (Anonymous) 150
The Groves of Blarney (R. A. Milliken) 151

Original Poems:
At the Mid Hour of Night (Thomas Moore) 153
The Starling Lake (Seumas O'Sullivan) 153
The Irish Peasant to his Mistress (Thomas Moore) 154
A Vision of Connaught in the Thirteenth Century (James
    Clarence Mangan) 154
Your Fear (Joseph Plunkett) 156
The Fairy Thorn (Sir Samuel Ferguson) 157
The Lark in the Clear Air (Sir Samuel Ferguson) 159
May Day (Thomas MacDonagh) 160
The Triad of Things not Decreed (Alice Furlong) 160

Notes 161
Bibliography 176

A Profile of Thomas MacDonagh by Nancy Murphy 179
Thomas MacDonagh by Francis Ledwidge 200
Caoineadh Thomáis by Máirtín Ó Corrbuí 200
Notes to the Profile 201

Index 205

Publishers' Note to 1996 Edition

There have been two incentives for this re-publication of Thomas MacDonagh's major work of literary criticism, which co-incides with the eightieth anniversary of his death:
• a long-standing interest in the man himself and the several intertwined and overlapping strands of his abbreviated life – this interest prompted the addition of a profile positioned at the end of his book;
• the enjoyment derived by general readers (conceding patches of very heavy going) from MacDonagh's insights written with gusto and flashes of humour, noting along the way the tributes paid to this pioneering panache by critics Ezra Pound, Robert Farren, John Jordan, and Patrick Power, the American authors of two biographies and, recently, Gerald Dawe – which prompted the latter's introduction preceding the book.

Three other additions have been made to the original 1916 edition:
• the original Irish versions of five notable MacDonagh translations;
• appended to the profile – the elegy, 'Thomas MacDonagh', by Francis Ledwidge, and its translation by Máirtín Ó Corrbuí for whose permission we are grateful;
• brief biographical notes of fourteen contemporaries whose work was adverted to here by MacDonagh, positioned at the end of his Notes;
• a few paragraphs of elaboration in the light of incremental knowledge, given within square brackets among the Notes, thus [ ],

Editorial amendments have been made as follows:
• his original Study VIII, 'Irish Literature', running to sixty-seven pages in the 1916 edition, has been divided for easier digestion into 8.1 and 8.2 at a clear point of transition;
• the original Gaelic lettering and spellings have been converted to

modern roman to facilitate a new generation;

• all of the footnotes printed in the text pages of the original have been re-positioned – in the Notes where they are simply explanations or source references; within the text itself where they were clearly his afterthoughts and do not interfere with the natural flow of the text;

• his notes, at the rear of the 1916 edition, to pp. 76, 100 (part), 132 and 143 have been incorporated in the text of Studies 6, 7, 8.1 and 8.2, respectively, as seemingly more appropriate there; likewise, a hefty afterthought at pp. 233-4 of the Notes has been brought forward to the end of his introduction to 'Poems of the Irish Mode';

• a slight re-arrangement of some poems, now noted after his introduction to that section.

The original text and selection of poems is otherwise unchanged.

We are grateful for the helpful input of Gerald Dawe, Mary Guinan-Darmody of the County Library, Thurles, Eibhlín Uí Morónaigh, Áine Ní Mhurchada, Deirdre O'Dowd, Robert Towers and Jonathan Williams as well as RELAY staff members Elaine Burke Houlihan and Fiona O'Brien.

The publishers gratefully acknowledge the financial assistance of An Chomhairle Ealaíon/The Arts Council. The publication has also been aided by Irish Educational Services, St. Paul, Minnesota. The publishers are grateful also for the generous aid by George O'Leary, of Beechwood in MacDonagh's native parish, and Tucson, Arizona, donated 'in memory of Labhrás Ó Floinn and Mrs Frances O'Meara who had a profound impact on my formative years in Kilruane National School in the 1940s.' Mr Michael Killeen, the surviving trustee of a 1966 MacDonagh memorial fund, kindly made available the small residue of that fund which aided research of the Profile of Thomas MacDonagh.

Introduction to 1996 Edition

The first time I read Thomas MacDonagh's collection of lectures and essays, *Literature in Ireland: Studies Irish & Anglo-Irish,* I was a student at the recently-opened University of Ulster at Coleraine. It was the early 1970s. At that time Northern Ireland was in the grip of 'the Troubles', although very few in those days had any idea that the recurrence of the political conflict in the north would last for *twenty-five* years. There was an intense need during the early '70s for those of us who were politically grappling with what was happening to sort out as well what possible role writing could play in all the mayhem.

Writing poems, that most wayward and speculative of arts, had somehow to be called to account in an atmosphere of daily bombings and assassinations which were themselves becoming commonplace. It was a mistake to think that anything we could write would have an impact upon what was happening in the streets and townlands of the north but the desire was nonetheless there to find some kind of redress.

In the main we looked abroad for answers: to the Russian poets like Mandelstam, Akhmatova; east European writers such as the Polish poet Zbigniew Herbert, Vasko Popa from former Yugoslavia, and the German Hans Magnus Ensensberger. We watched films like Wajda's *Ashes and Diamonds*, *Rome Open City* by Rossellini and Bergman's *The Shame*. Foreign shores are always greener.

Through lectures on literature in English, be they on Marlowe or Conrad, Coleridge or Larkin, it took some time before the cultural and intellectual ferment of what was happening, literally all around us, found an historical focus in Irish writing.

The centrality of history in Irish writing, in both languages, and the kind of example of writers and intellectuals earlier in the century, is now a critical truism taken for granted by the generation which emerged out of the shadows of the Troubles, north and south, in the '80s and '90s. During the same period, Irish writing has been seen world-wide as a laboratory within which the interpenetration of history, cultural nationalism and post-colonialism can be studied. Meanwhile, this history of political conflict and cultural attrition has become a theme-park many inside Ireland would prefer to pass by speedily. The murky old past is best left that way – in the past.

To discover in Thomas MacDonagh's *Literature in Ireland* a comprehensive, committed voice, calmly stating his position on the relationship between literature and history, was for this reader at least a revelation. The historical contexts of MacDonagh's own short life, detailed by Nancy Murphy in the Profile which follows, add poignancy to the writing such as one feels in regards to, say, the death of Wilfred Owen. Indeed, MacDonagh was well aware of what was taking place beyond his own political and imaginative life, as he remarks in the concluding paragraph of his own Preface:

> It is well to let it be known that some of the studies [in *Literature in Ireland*] were written before the summer of 1914. The present European wars have altered our outlook on many things, but as they have not altered the truth or the probability of what I have written here, I have not altered my words. As will be seen, I anticipated turbulence and change in the arts. These wars and their sequel may turn literature definitely into ways towards which I looked, confirming the promise of our high destiny here.

Dated January 1916, only a matter of months away from the Easter Rising for which MacDonagh, as a key figure and signatory, was condemned to death by British court-martial and executed by firing squad on 3 May 1916, the prophesy hangs upon those last few words with terrible irony: 'the promise of our high destiny here'. The terms of such utopian desire were sorely tested in the following decade and more: was the 'promise' of Irish cultural nationalism fulfilled? what 'high destiny' could attend a small island, exhausted economically and emotionally by years of constant expectation and ambition, a war of independence and civil war, and the eventual partitioning of the country into two self-insulated states? How would MacDonagh have responded, as a liberal intellectual, to the enactment of the shocking censorship laws of the new free state? Questions proliferate because of the sense of premature ending which surrounds the lives of the executed leaders of the 1916 Rising.

If the Rising was, in Declan Kiberd's words, 'a brave clean fight against an empire', what are we to do with its perverse legacy in the north where the majority of the citizens did *not* fight against 'the empire' but *for* it? What went so seriously wrong with the abundant idealism as there unquestionably was in 1916 (and later) that it should end in the grotesque parody of an imagined community, in the north, torn apart by self-inflicted and seemingly self-perpetuating violence? Was there something congenitally suspect in a nationalism which could not embrace the differences within the putative nation and was even to make a virtue out of refusing to imagine the problems it was storing up in the north? Must we still bear allegiance to that kind of official wish-fulfilment simply for the sake of 'History'?

Of course the answer is 'No' but, that said, there is in contemporary Ireland a reluctance to establish a clear idea of what the leaders of the Rising actually stood for; the cultural differences between them, and the (predominantly) secular and pluralist 'agenda' they pursued. What was their complex fate has been simplified both as marvellous self-sacrificing patriotic instinct and as the fatal gene of blood-lust. Only with the dubious benefit of hindsight are definitive lines of direct connection forged between their vision and the version of it which church and state connived at and ultimately achieved. These ideological and intellectual conflicts often appear claustrophobically obsessive and introverted in comparison with the airy, naive, enthusiastic and fascinating study, *Literature in Ireland*. MacDonagh's book radiates a seriousness and deft lyrical touch with handling poetry, as he cites *Poetry*, the Chicago journal, the Futurists, and other contemporary *vers libre* sources, to win the arch-modernist, Ezra Pound's approval.

Put at its simplest, MacDonagh sought to establish the linguistic and quasi-cultural factors (what he calls 'the Irish Mode') which will both establish and vindicate the separate identity of *Irish literature*. The idea for such an identity, its nature, prospects, antecedents, and so on were hotly debated throughout the previous decade and more by all kinds of writers, intellectuals, political figures and activists. That there *could* be an Irish literature ('a separate thing', as MacDonagh states) was as potent an issue as the legitimacy and validation of an Irish state.

Throughout *Literature in Ireland*, MacDonagh argues his case with insight and due regard for the notion of other literatures in English. Walt Whitman has an iconic status in MacDonagh's intellectual and artistic universe.

This is not the place to rehearse the various elements of the cultural debate with which *Literature in Ireland* is centrally concerned – the influence of the Irish language and folk tradition upon Irish writing in English; the notion of literature being 'national' in the first place; the issue of Race.

MacDonagh has important (and contentious) things to say about these and other issues. The rhetoric (in the strict sense) shifts register uncomfortably, and the range of literary reference is stretched beyond belief, but the key to this work is incontrovertible – his formulation of 'a movement that is important to English literature because it is in part *a revolt* from it' (my italics). Flowing from this premise, MacDonagh's task 'to examine the one aspect of literature in Ireland that can be examined and treated in terms of criticism', remains valid to this day.

In searching out some of the co-ordinants of 'a new literature, the first expression of the life and ways of thought of a new people, hitherto without literary expression, differing from English literature of all periods, not with the difference of age but with the difference of race and nationality', MacDonagh anticipated much of the current discussion about the relationship between poetry, cultural politics and post-colonialism.

Literature in Ireland, by a quirk of literary fate, became itself a part of the cultural assumptions underlying the post-independence state and dutifully disappeared from critical view. Its unavailability as a critical text and as a key to the 'internal' history of criticism in Ireland tells its own story. (Why has the original critical work of Irish literature such as the intrepid 'John Eglinton's' *Anglo-Irish Essays* or Daniel Corkery's *Synge and Anglo-Irish Literature* also disappeared?) The language of the stereotypes which MacDonagh often calls upon certainly needs astringent deconstruction:

> In spite of the self-consciousness of the age, in spite of the world influences felt here, in spite of all our criticism, the Irish poets and writers (those that are truly Anglo-Irish) are beginning it all over again in the alien tongue that they know now as a mother tongue. They delight not in the ink-horn terms

of the English literary succession but in the rich living language of a people little affected by book-lore, a people standing but a little way on the English side of the crossways, remembering something of the syntax or the metaphor of Gaelic, much of the rhythm, inventing mostly for itself its metaphor from the things of its life, things known at first hand.

In terms of literary history, such a passage neatly summarises the main assumptions which became standard in the critical reception for, and expectation of, Irish writing at home and further afield. *Literature in Ireland* is a classic of stating the case for the separateness and integrity of national literary and cultural traditions. Whether or not we agree with MacDonagh his collection of studies has an historical significance in the development of what is known world-wide as 'Irish literature'.

MacDonagh strikes me as the most reluctant of heroes. The much-quoted story of his last class at University College Dublin on Jane Austen, or the unattributed anecdote, retold by Terry Eagleton, to the effect that 'MacDonagh was one of the first men to be seen wheeling a pram in the streets of Dublin' suggest an individualist rather than one of those misguided fantasists we are so often given. Now is probably the time when Thomas MacDonagh can be seen for what he actually was, along with all the other men and women who believed as he did in Irish nationalism. In unpicking the strands which go to make up *Literature in Ireland* the reader will also find along the way the literary ambitions and critical understanding of one of present-day Ireland's founding fathers.

Gerald Dawe
Trinity College, Dublin, 1996

Bibliography
Gerald Dawe, *Stray Dogs and Dark Horses* (1996)
Theo Dorgan and Máirín Ní Dhonnchadha, *Revising the Rising* (1991)
Terry Eagleton, *Heathcliff and the Great Hunger* (1995)
Declan Kiberd, *Inventing Ireland* (1995)
Richard J. Loftus, *Nationalism in Anglo-Irish Poetry* (1964)
Edna Longley, *The Living Stream* (1994)
Desmond Ryan, *The 1916 Poets* (1963, 1995)

Author's Dedication

Author's Preface

THESE STUDIES in Irish and Anglo-Irish literature are frankly experimental. In them I have tried to clear away certain misconceptions, to fix certain standards, to define certain terms. I trust that as a result the Irish Mode will be better understood and appreciated than the Celtic Note for which I substitute it.

My exclusion from the scope of these inquiries of the Hiberno-English writers of the eighteenth century has already provoked protests from my friends. They do indeed form a band apart in English Literature, with the common characteristic of adventurous and haughty individualism. But to me, who look rather from the Gaelic stand-point, the attitude of Swift, Steele, Sheridan, Burke, Goldsmith and the rest, for all that they have in common and for all that they owe to their Irish birth or upbringing, is an attitude rather of dissent from an English orthodoxy than of consent in an orthodoxy of their own or of Ireland's.

Æ has claimed, in conversation with me about this, that all these emigrants, down to Oscar Wilde and Shaw, have that Irish mien of aristocracy that marked our great in the days of the clan system – an aristocracy not of the talents merely, but of character, of self-confident and often self-made leadership. I would not deny their claim. I would not abate their praise. But the two literatures of my choice here have other claims and are worthy of other praise. If I have done a little wrong to the emigrants in one of my Studies, this will undo it.

My subject is Literature in Ireland. My business as regards Gaelic is simple – to show the value of the old literature, the prospects of the new. To this business I have devoted the last and longest of these Studies [divided into Studies 8.1 and 8.2 in this 1996 edition] and portions of others. My theses as regards Anglo-Irish are these three, restated in Study 5 and dealt with in detail in the rest of the book:

1. That an Anglo-Irish literature, worthy of a special designation,

could come only when English had become the language of the Irish people, mainly of Gaelic stock, and when the literature was from, by, of, to and for the Irish people.

2. That the ways of life and the ways of thought of the Irish people – the manners, customs, traditions and outlook, religious, social and moral – have important differences from the ways of life and of thought which have found expression in other English literature.

3. That the English language in Ireland has an individuality of its own, and the rhythm of Irish speech a distinct character.

To illustrate my text I have put together at the end a selection of poems in English, examples of the Irish Mode – poems which show in their form the influence of Gaelic versification, of Irish music or of the Irish way of speech. In my introductory note to these I explain the limitations of the selection.

I have throughout used italics in printing words and quotations from other languages than English. I have, however, used Gaelic type for quotations from modern Irish. [See Publisher's Note to this 1996 edition] For other explanations of this nature I refer readers to the notes at the end.

It is well to let it be known that some of the studies was written before the summer of 1914. The present European wars have altered our outlook on many things, but as they have not altered the truth or the probability of what I have written here, I have not altered my words. As will be seen, I anticipated turbulence and change in the arts. These wars and their sequel may turn literature definitely into ways towards which I looked, confirming the promise of our high destiny here.

University College, Dublin
January, 1916.

Study 1

Introductory and General

'*No great poet has really put new wine into old bottles ...*
These studies are then a first attempt to find standards for criticism
in Irish and Anglo-Irish literature, more especially in Anglo-Irish
poetry ...'

1

I N LITERATURE it will be found that the characteristic contribution of each great master is two-fold. The new message comes in a new form, the new wine in a new vessel. No great poet has really put new wine into old bottles.

To English Chaucer gave a fresh literature and a fresh mode of literary expression. One part of his gift was a narrative poetry never since surpassed. The vessel in which he presented a quantity of it, the couplet to which later was given that high title of heroic, was perhaps more rare and new than his other forms. So Dryden, with the first fine vintage of literary criticism, gave that modern prose of the living voice, made good at last for all the purposes of prose. So Milton, to take an example that may be at once accepted, that need not be explained and proved, with his epic poetry gave that epic blank verse of such different poise from the already perfect dramatic. So Pope, with the poetry of the intellect (to damn it with a paradox) gave the heroic couplet, wrought to a second perfection – perhaps for that alone a second-rate master. One need not drag in Shakespeare, from whose work you can prove anything; and one need not make a list of the masters of English or other literatures.

A new verse, a new style in prose – something that can be weighed and measured – a new manifestation that can be seen, comes always with that new imponderable, incommensurable, elusive something which one knows to be fine literature, but which cannot be tested by any such sure standards. I will say that poetry may be not only a criticism of life, as Matthew Arnold thought, but an interpretation of life, or, at its highest, an illumination of life. The ancient Irish critic of the *Triads*[1] had this for one of his marks of the poet, *imbas forosna*, knowledge that illumines.

I will say this. I know well enough what I mean by these terms. But when I come to apply them to some actual piece of literature, more especially of new literature, they help me little. This new thing is unlike all the fine literature that I know. Is it a criticism of life? Is it an interpretation? Is it an illumination? What really is life? When so illuminated does it change and become different from all that we know by experience? What right have we to limit it to experience? Are we looking only for the experience of the intellectual thing, forgetting the intuitive? Are not these terms of criticism only words of praise and no standards at all? And so – though with the old standard of beauty we have set aside the old standard of truth – so back to the tragic query, What is truth?

If, in the course of these studies, I have said that poetry is a criticism, or an interpretation, or an illumination of life, I use the terms with reference to work that has fallen back into perspective – not work in the near shadow of which we stand. To answer one of my questions just put, I use them as terms of praise, not as tests for the next poem that comes.

On the other hand one can really, if only in a negative way, judge the form of a new work. Forms change and become outworn though the essential stuff of literature may be the same from age to age. A five-act play, written now in just Shakespeare's verse, if such a thing could be done, would be something of a sham antique. Good Tennysonian blank verse betrays many pretentious poems. The imitators of Blake and Browning have not surpassed their masters. Whitman, however, the most confident of us cannot condemn so easily. He may be but another eccentric. He may be the great innovator.

The futurists may be charlatans, or fools, or lunatics. They may be prophets. The difference of their manner from the good old ways does not prove their rightness or their greatness; but the hostile critics of their works use words and weapons so like those used against other work that survived attack and afterwards became right and great and good, that one cannot lightly join them. Most writers who made daring departures in form merely wandered off and were lost. Yet the new path of some pioneer to-day may prove the right turning for all. The path of glory in literature has not been, as many appear to think, the broad and easy way. It is now beaten broad enough – up to a certain point, reached a generation ago – by the feet of many who have followed in the tracks of men who discovered things in the heavens and on earth, not keeping their eyes on their feet, and of men who ran hither and thither after splendid adventures, and of men who fared far to the east and to the west lured by the voices of strange peoples. It is not the obvious straight path that leads from height to height.

As with the masters, so with what we have still to call the movements. The Renaissance, in whose mode we are still, or have been till now, had its new wine and its new vessels. The so-called classic and romantic movements within it have theirs, each stage of each remembered by the double gift of a master. The gift to literature of the writers whom I count as of the Irish Mode – putting this term of mine in the place of that vague and illogical Celtic Note – is likewise double. For the reasons which I here set forth, I criticise as much the form of the work as the import, though to me, of course, that import is its chief worth. I make experimental studies to satisfy myself that this is at least a mode, distinctive and apart.

The Renaissance, with the discoveries of Copernicus and Galileo, the discoveries of Columbus and his followers; later such things as the discovery of the law of gravitation, the Cartesian philosophy, the French Revolution, Darwin's theory of evolution: these have profoundly affected European literature. They have not similarly affected literature in Ireland. This is not to say of course that in Ireland writers are still likely to write of the earth as the centre of the solar system, of epicycles and the rest. It is to say that literature here has not had just that education which is common to the other literatures of western Europe. Those literatures have been, as I have said, up to these days, parts of the Renaissance. In them the authority of the ancients has held:

And Boileau still in right of Horace sways.

That word 'authority' holds a world of meaning in this matter. Another word of great content is 'intellectual.' Intellectualism is the Renaissance. When in the place of that clear standard we set those pillars of cloud and of fire known to the spiritual intuitions, the day of the Renaissance is done; the forms of Renaissance literature decay.

In Ireland some literature has kept the old way familiar to the Middle Age.

Let me not anticipate my conclusion. Let me make clear my meaning of things I have said above.

In his sonnet, *On first looking into Chapman's Homer,* Keats has set together the three great influences of Elizabethan literature: the classic world, its art, its literature, its story, represented by Homer;

the new astronomy that raised adventure to the skies; the new discoveries that opened to the view new seas and lands beyond the peaks of Darien. Keats himself, who might have lived long enough for me a child to know him, owned the same influences. He touched in not too late a day the beautiful mythology of Greece; yet he felt other influences too. *La Belle Dame Sans Merci*,[2] though he may have disdained it, shows that another wind blew on him at hours. So too with the other arts in his time. They derived from Italy, and through Italy from Greece.

To our eyes even the Romantic era has a classic quality, a sense of repose almost, compared with the disturbance now taking place in all the arts. All the forms are suffering change. It would seem that the mind (its outlook and its inlook, if one may say so) is suffering change and demanding different forms of expression. This, since the establishment of Impressionism, is more easily admitted in painting than in literature, as indeed since Wagner it may be more easily admitted in music too; but to anyone conversant with modern literature the same change of order is evident here. Compare modern poems and modern novels, the claim of which to serious recognition cannot be denied, with similar works of the previous ages and you will at once perceive that the difference here too is due to the introduction of Impressionism and Wagnerism.

To us, as to the ancient Irish poets, the half-said thing is dearest.[3] The rhythm made by an emotion informs the poem and so recreates the emotion. As to the mystic, so to the lyric poet the unknown transcends the known. The purely rational, purely intellectual way of expression does not lead from it and so to it.

I am not writing here of European literature in general, or of English literature in particular. I am introducing a movement that is important to English literature, because it is in part a revolt from it – because it has gone its own way, independent of it, though using for its language English or a dialect of English. I am treating it as a separate thing; and all that I have said so far is said rather by way of comparison, to set it in its true light. It enters literature at a period which seems to us who are of it as a period of disturbance, of change. Its mode seems strange to the critics and to the prosodists of the old order. Its mode is not that of the Futurists or the writers of *vers libres*; but still, coming with the work of these, it stands as another element of disturbance, of revolution; it is comparatively free from the old authority imposed by the Renaissance, while the other elements in this disturbance are rebelling against that authority; it is the mode of a people to whom the ideal, the spiritual, the mystic, are the true, while theirs is that of people who seek, however blindly, for a truth beyond the easy truth which is the beauty of the romantics, who will not admit that this identification of a rational truth and a rational beauty is all they know on earth or all they need to know.

Beyond this I would not urge the parallel; but this it is necessary to note in order to understand the reception given to the Irish Mode. It has come in its due time. Mangan and Callanan in the first half of the nineteenth century tuned the harp that is now ringing to the hands of many. Ears that in the older days would not have listened to the rarest music of that harp are now attentive to every tone. The poets of this mode have till now been ignorant of the parallel movement; they have taken little or no note of the new writers of free verse or of the futurists. Yet their work to the coming age may appear one with the work of these. And indeed there is a near kinship. The freedom being sought now elsewhere has long been enjoyed here. One might reasonably argue that Macpherson, so great an influence in the Romance, was the first of the free verse men – that his work marks the beginning, not merely of the Romantic Era of European literature, but of that freedom of the new time set against the old Authority of the Renaissance (one finds free verse in Mangan, too – in Kidder.)

In such a train we should come to regard the Romantic Era as the dawn of Freedom, not the noon of Liberty under Law. Should we follow such a train we should not at the same time forget that, as the work of each great author may be an epitome of a whole literature, with parts representing all the stages – as, in English literature, we find in Shakespeare, in Milton, in Wordsworth, in Keats, both the classic and the romantic, both the meditative and the lyric – parts which are monuments of the central tradition, obedient to Authority, and parts which are the promise of the Freedom to be, with examples of its mode, with stones for the building of its monuments, and even the first chambers of its towers, as finely shaped and firmly built as any added in its full day; so the eras dovetail and interlace; so the colours shade into one another; so always side by side go reaction and radicalism; so the classic has not died and romance has but revived; and still there is nothing new under the sun and all novelty is but oblivion.

These things we should not forget; but these should not at the same time hold us from the perception of change: they are limitations of the law, not the law itself. The train which I have indicated would lead us to look for a transformation of literature similar, not to the transformation which we call the Romance (itself a beginning, a first stirring of this greater change) but to the Renaissance, the influence and authority of which it would end. Such a train would give a high importance to the Irish mode. In the Bible, English, as other West-European literatures, has had, since the Renaissance, a second great source of tradition and authority. A third might have been found in that so-called folk literature, the ballads, the wonder-tales and fragments of old prose epics that survived the change wrought in the schools. Various strands of the other two materials were caught by various hands and worked into the fabric of the literature. Strands of this material were caught at now and again – by Sir Philip Sidney, by Addison[4] – but missed and merely looked at, not held and woven in. The strands hung down beside the others with which all hands were busy. They have been used now these hundred years. Is the new fabric made of them so different from the old that it will tear away from it now that new weight of the stuff wrought in these days is added? For beyond that folk literature we might trace the Gaelic influence direct, never quite absent even under the Renaissance, now present and potent.

The work which I have set myself to do in some of these studies is rather to examine the one aspect of literature in Ireland than can be examined and treated in terms of criticism. To serve this I have dealt with the language, the Irish dialect of English, if it can be called a dialect. I have not with some modern writers made much ado about chance idioms. The absolute construction found in Charles Wolfe's poem, *On the Burial of Sir John Moore*:

And we far away on the billow,

has been traced by most writers on this subject to Gaelic origin, and flaunted as a modern Irishism. Of course the phrase translates word for word into Irish: 'agus sinne i bhfad ar an bhfairrge'; but then the idiom occurs in English too, easily enough and early enough.[5] I came across an instance of it the other day in Pepy's Diary, and to-day another in Jane Austen. Pepy's '1665, 20th July. The bell always going. This day poor Robin Shaw at Blackwell's died, and Blackwell himself in Flanders.' Jane Austen, in *Pride and Prejudice*, Chapter

VIII.: 'Yes, and her petticoat – I hope you saw her petticoat. Six inches deep in mud, I am absolutely certain, and the gown which had been let down to hide it not doing its office.'

More important than such phrases is word order. Though in Anglo-Irish speech we keep in the main the order of English, not of Irish, even in the most literal translations, yet the Irish way of emphasis is kept. The sentence, 'I came from town', may have four meanings according to the emphasis, or rather the voice stress. An Irishman may use this sentence as it stands for those four meanings too; but in general he introduces the verb which corresponds to the Irish verb of identity ('is')[6] and brings into the emphatic position after it the particular word of the four which he wishes to stress. Thus he will use such a sentence as 'It is from town I came', instead of the original stressed on the last syllable, and even such a Gaelicism as 'It is how I came from town,' instead of the original stressed on the second. It will be seen that in these substitutes the words do all the work. The voice does not exert itself. This goes with the even way of speech that ranks equal with Irish metrics and Irish music as one of the most important factors of the Irish mode of versification, in English. I merely indicate these matters here, as I have dealt fully with them in the studies which follow. Another matter worth indicating is the phonetic difference between Irish and English. This, of course, has to do with that Irish way of speech which I have set down as one of the three great influences on the versification of this mode.

So much then for the form: of the spirit, the genius, of this literature, and therefore of this people, I could not trust myself to speak: I could not trust myself to set out with certainty Irish characteristics, or to point out the probable trend of the literature. This is an age of beginnings rather than of achievements; for a hundred years now writers in this land have been translating, adapting, experimenting – working as the writers of the sixteenth century worked in many countries. The translations which have survived are those most in consonance with the genius of the country. An age of beginnings: what the next age or the ripeness of this may bring, one can only guess at.

Does some one say that I shirk work necessary in one portion of my field – that criticism can deal surely with national characteristics? Whimsicality is an Irish characteristic as definite as any – that drollery so different from wit proper, so different from humour proper, going waywardly with an inconsequence that one knows to be natural. Yet what is one to say of it? To collect samples would be stupid work, and the result as stupid as any book of bulls. 'You're cosy and easy up there, Johnny', I heard a man say at a football match in Dublin to a friend who watched from a tree. The day was windy. 'Aye, begad', said Johnny, 'blown about by every breeze, like a bee on a posy.' In this, to be sure, I might find certain graces of diction, the half-rhyme of 'cosy' and 'easy,' with the echo of it in 'posy,' and the alliteration of Johnny's bs, to say nothing of the rhythm. These things are to be found in almost all Irish speech of a humorous turn. 'Come into my arms, you bundle of fun', is the more delightfully humorous for its obvious rhythm. But that examination would again be of the sound rather than of the sense, and would be to me gruesome work.

Different from such is the great informing soul of a large body of our lyric poetry, of our oratory, and of much of the rest of our literature – 'the cause that never dies', the ideal held always by the Gaelic race that once dominated Europe – now held by the heir and successor of that race here, the Irish. The calamities of our history have given a voice to that cause. The constancy of our race has given pride to that voice.

It is easy, says a contemporary good critic,[7] to be patriotic in the days of a country's adversity; for then patriotism means something very personal. Its root is personal, no doubt, although that does not prevent the emotions transcending the bounds of a merely selfish personal motive. But the fact that the sentiment is emotional and personal, rather than abstract and rhetorical, is what constitutes its living force. When a country is in adversity, then this emotion is continuously active. It is a passion which absorbs all the energies. So much so that it completely enlists the services not only of men of action and practical life, but also of the contemplatives, the poets, the dreamers, for whom this emotion, like others, becomes transmuted into something beyond the personal emotion. ...

It is easy for us to appreciate the Irishman's zealous love for Ireland, the celebration of Bengal by the great East Indian poet, or the passionate spirit of the Roumanian folk-songs. Not only have these the direct motive of adversity, the minor note of which has been so much in sympathy with the spirit of the last

century's literary movement, but they are all deep-rooted in
the tradition which has had its earliest expression in folk-songs
and legends – always an enduring basis for subsequent poets
and artists, and an integral part of the blood and bone of the
people.

This writer has stated almost sufficiently for me the case of Irish
patriotism as an inspiration. It is never far off. Many strong workers
in the national movements are good poets too; no Irish poet or dreamer
knows the day when he may be called into action in the ancient fight.
More than that, nearer here than elsewhere seems the day that Ruskin
desired for his own country when her soldiers should be her tutors,
and the captains of her army, captains also of her mind;[8] for here the
professional barriers do not keep life and letters apart, and the national
cause survives politics.

I have heard a friend of mine state on the authority of one of the
new philosophers, that hunger and sex are the two wheels of progress.
If so, no doubt progress here must be set down to the account of
hunger. Sex counts for little enough in Irish or Anglo-Irish literature.
Mr Synge's people talk more of it than others, but even they do not
give it the importance that it has in most modern literature; they do
not talk of it in the decadent, suggestive way, however morbid the
analysis of their creator. They talk of it rather like the Irish peasantry,
whose language is at times coarse enough while their conduct is
almost impeccably proper. Such progress as there is would in this
philosophy be set down to hunger; but that seems to me a mean way
of judging life.

Our ideals, national and religious, are powerful and holy. Such a
matter-of-fact politician as Parnell exhorted us to national effort, not
in terms of hunger and profit, but in terms of tradition and the sacred
gift of the ideal for which we have stood against tramplings and
settlements these thousand years: 'Keep the fires of the nation
burning.' This 'terrible and splendid trust', this 'heritage of the race
of kings', this service of a nation without a flag, but 'with the lure of
God in her eyes', has endowed some of our poetry with meanings
that must be lost to all but those baptized in our national faith. To
some lyrics of Thomas Moore the heroism and death of Robert
Emmet, his early friend, gave a quality of emotion far deeper than
the sentiment that usually fills his verse. George Brandes, in his *Main*

Currents of Nineteenth Century Literature, has shown the importance of this poetry of revolt in Anglo-Irish.[9]

In Gaelic there is a symbolic poetry of patriotism that rises far higher. Lyrics like *Eamonn an Chnuic, Druimfhionn Donn Dílis* and a hundred other such are without parallel in any literature that I know of – and this too though, or perhaps because, the Gaelic poetry of the later centuries is but a wandering voice.[10] The old courts of the kings and the halls of the chiefs were in the earlier times centres of culture – of art, of learning, of song. These gone, the profession of poet lost dignity. There was no metropolitan life in Gaelic Ireland. The Gaelic language had not the fixing and centralizing of the printing press, a loss or absence which, given other advantages, is an advantage in itself, here only a thing to note as counting for something. From this Gaelic source Anglo-Irish inherited a folk poetry at times of almost indescribable tenderness and beauty, but narrow in range and of little variety.

As in other countries, the drama in Ireland is a foreign introduction, and an introduction of too recent date, speaking nationally, to be yet subject for criticism. It is probably certain that some of the drama of the present day in English will stand higher in literature than any of at least the last century. There has been a revival of the poetic drama. The new drama of ideas, of criticism of life, is a serious and important form of literature. Like almost all other forms, it has been influenced by, and is in part a development of, that most popular of all forms, the novel. In prose, satire is perhaps the form surest of enduring appreciation. The drama of modern Ireland, in English, is in the main poetic and satiric. It seems indeed not free from the faults of its time, or rather of the time just gone by in some on the continental countries – not free from the faults of impressionism, of quasiscientific Ibsenism, of unreal gloom and of shallow cynicism. It is its virtue to have shown the way back to the life of the people and back to poetry.

One inspiration of literature remains to mention in this cursory introduction. That mysticism, which in all literatures is the promise and earnest of great poetry, has come here in these days. The bulk of the mystical poetry I cannot claim for Anglo-Irish on account of the limitations of form and language which I have set to these studies. It is, nevertheless, the growth of this soil, of the passivist, contemplative character of this people, so long enduring and so certain of the right – the good. Of the science of mysticism, so to call it, these Irish poets know little by study or instruction, though one is tempted to think that with two or three of them, writers of fame, mysticism is an exteriority, a garment borrowed from the grammarians of this science of the saints. It is, unfortunately, not difficult to give to vague nothings set in verse an appearance of the mystery of St. John of the Cross.[11] But St. John, since I mention him, would not approve of this perhaps uncharitable judgment; and indeed in no matter more than this is criticism vain.

These studies are then a first attempt to find standards for criticism in Irish and Anglo-Irish literature, more especially in Anglo-Irish poetry. The good critic must judge a work or a creature in relation to its nature, its aim or purpose, its aspiration – in terms of what it is, not of what it might have been if otherwise designed and made. It is vain to blame the angel for not showing the steady utility of the cow, and to blame the cow for lacking the light and service of the angel. But, before coming even to the right way of judgment, the critic must discover the nature of the work or creature. I try to discover the nature of some literature produced in Ireland.

Study 2

Anglo-Irish Literature

' *Anglo-Irish literature is then different in its origins, in its history, in its tradition, ...*

... the term Anglo-Irish ... is worth having as a term only to apply to the literature produced by the English-speaking Irish, and by these in general only when writing in Ireland and for the Irish people. '

2

WE SPEAK OF ANGLO-IRISH LITERATURE as we speak of Elizabethan literature, of the literature of the Restoration age, or another, as a province of English literature, confined in the place of its production as those others in their periods, and with that difference between place and time, between race and succession. A better analogy than those that I have mentioned, Elizabethan and Restoration, would seem to be Scots literature, but I have avoided that at the beginning in order to avoid the confusion that constantly follows such comparison. The writers of the Restoration period of English literature succeeded in natural order to those of the Elizabethan. Dryden refers to Shakespeare and Ben Jonson as 'the writers of the last age.' Scots literature was born own brother to English, the literature of men of the lowland race; and the blood relationship has proved a strong bond. The literature produced in the English language in Ireland during the nineteenth century had no such rights of succession to previous epochs of English literature as had the work of Dryden to the work of Ben Jonson; it had no such claim of kinship to any as had the work of King James I of Scotland, of William Dunbar and of Gavin Douglas to the work of Chaucer. And Scots writers have from the beginning recognised that kinship. In his lovely *Lament for the Makaris*, after having bewailed the insecurity of life:

> No stait in Erd heir standis sicker;
> As with the wynd wavis the wicker,
> So wavis this warldis vanite: –
>   *Timor Mortis conturbat me,*

and mentioned those of all 'Estatis' who go unto death:

> He takis the campion in the stour,
> The captain closit in the tour

The lady in bour full of bewte,

Dunbar enumerates the dead poets, beginning:

He has done petuously devour
The noble Chaucer, of makaris flour,
The Monk of Bury and Gower, all three:
 Timor Mortis conturbat me,

and proceeding with a long list of Scots poets, some of them else unknown. To the Scots poets Chaucer was as Dunbar says in another poem,

As in oure tong ane flour imperial.

Anglo-Irish literature is then different in its origins, in its history, in its tradition, from Scots. At its weakest and poorest it is a weak and poor imitation of the poor contemporary work of Englishmen. At its richest and strongest it has qualities of its own not to be found in the work of any Englishmen of the time. And it is distinctly a new literature, the first expression of the life and ways of thought of a new people, hitherto without literary expression, differing from English literature of all the periods not with the difference of age but with the difference of race and nationality.

That race is the Irish race, now mostly English-speaking. That life, those ways of thought expressed in the new literature, are the life and ways of the Gael,[1] modified by the change of language from Gaelic to English and by the things that brought about that change, but still individually Gaelic, spiritually, morally, socially (in all the ways that matter in literature), filled with memories of the old Gaelic literature, moving to the rhythm of Irish music (a thing that matters very much to the metric of the new poetry), rich in fresh metaphor, very different from the petrified boughs of imagery that do duty for green branches in many admired works of this age.

The people are agricultural people, fresh from the natural home of man, the fields and the country, busy with the oldest and simplest things of life, people who have not grown up in the streets of towns among the artificialities of civilisation, with traditional memories of brick and plaster.

The Anglo-Irish literature that matters has not come from the English spoken for hundreds of years in the Pale, in Dublin and its surroundings, by the English garrison in Ireland, but from the new English speakers of the country whose fathers or grandfathers spoke only Irish.

In later studies I shall have to deal on the one hand with the character and growth of the English language in Ireland and on the other hand with many aspects of the Gaelic language and literature. Here I wish simply to show, without stating an opinion as to the benefit or the pity of it, that an Anglo-Irish literature of individual value, a literature of worth in English, expressing or interpreting or criticising life in Ireland was possible only when the people whose life was the subject matter spoke the English language and spoke it well, and when Irish writers had attained what may be called the plenary use of the English language – such use as had decidedly not been attained by some of the Gaelic writers who wrote occasionally in English also – when, in a word, Irish writers and Irish readers were able to practise and to appreciate the art of English poetry and the art of English prose. When this point had been reached by new writers who were themselves of the people, the English-speaking Irish people, then this literature appeared and not till then.

The so-called Anglo-Irish literature of the eighteenth century was no such thing. Certain Irishmen, going to England, adopted English manners, expressed English or European life, referred to themselves as Englishmen.[2] They occasionally introduced into their work what would now be called a little local colour, tinted with memories of their early Irish days; but for the rest they were as much out of Ireland in spirit as in body. Occasionally too they introduced to their readers English-speaking Irishmen, but these were either caricatures or were obviously only half articulate in their new speech.

At the same time Gaelic literature continued, but with the repression by law of Irish learning, the language fell towards the position of a patois, and its later literature is mostly of folk tales and folk poems, sometimes very beautiful, but in general poor by comparison with the monuments of previous epochs.

At the same time also some Irish writers who did not leave their own country, or at least lived mostly in Ireland, emulated their emigrant brethren and became English authors, never indeed of great importance, but frequently very ingenious, writing in English either of a life that they did not know at first hand or of a life that they could not express in this language, and so always something out of joint.

One small body of poems has the timber and the sap of true literature, but wants the shaping and the higher graces. This consists of the street ballads, almost altogether of Dublin origin. If one can have regrets in such a matter as literary criticism and history, if one can wish that things had ever gone otherwise, one must regret that Dublin did not, in the eighteenth or early nineteenth century produce an Irish Villon, a University wit capable of writing a poem like *The Night before Larry was Stretched*. The capital produced none such; and the ballads, religious and ribald and rebelly, are fragmentary and spasmodic: they created no fine literary tradition. No author arose of the more urbane or of the more rural forms of literature who was at once sufficiently Gaelic to express the feeling of the central Irish tradition and sufficiently master of English style to use it as one uses the air one breathes. George Darley's references to Irish history, his use of Irish clan names, are weak and colourless. Curran's Irish phrases are ungrammatical. Drennan, at his simplest a fine poet, in his eloquent poems stammers twenty book-words to fill the place of one true epithet.[3]

I would not be taken as wishing in any way to belittle the intentions of these writers or of those others mentioned above, who were, as I have said, something out of joint. They lived according to their lights. They did the work they found to their hands. They were not Gaelic, or at least they were not in touch with the Gaelic tradition. They thought they knew a better thing and followed it. Most of them recognised as their kith only the small English-speaking fragment of Ireland; and that fragment had not the culture, the enthusiasm or the intensity of life that breaks into poetry or eloquence.

Some of the early Anglo-Irish writers, not the emigrants like Goldsmith, Swift and Sheridan, anticipated the cohesion of the English-speaking Irish race, and began to translate, adapt and imitate Gaelic literature. Irish music was one of the most powerful influences in the work of Thomas Moore. Others adopted the sentiments of the only articulate popular politics of their day, the politics of Grattan and the sympathetic Protestant patriots, the patriotism of the Pale, a very different thing from the national feeling of the real Irish people; but these, such of them as Charles Macklin, on his return to Ireland appealed still only to Dublin audiences.[4]

The day of Anglo-Irish literature had not arrived, because the

Anglo-Irish author could not yet be the poet of his little clan. The old inspirations that had moved poets in this land were not breathed into the souls of those men of alien speech.

I have so far used without definition the term Anglo-Irish. Like many terms of the kind, it is misleading and awkward, yet so well established by usage that it can scarcely be dispensed with. It can be applied only to language, and so to literature. There is, of course, no Anglo-Irish race, though many Irishmen have English blood in their veins. The invaders who came at the end of the twelfth century, under Strongbow and his fellows, were Flemings and Welsh, not English. The English who were planted in Ireland under Mary, Elizabeth, James, Cromwell, and their successors, formed a small portion of the people, and though they brought the language which is now spoken by the majority of the Gaelic people, they made little enough impress on the race that they dispossessed and drove westwards. With the language, the Anglo-Irish dialect, English as we speak it in Ireland, to use Dr Joyce's phrase,[5] I shall deal in a later study.

Here it is well at once to make clear that the term Anglo-Irish literature is applied very rarely to the meagre writings of the planters; it is worth having as a term only to apply to the literature produced by the English-speaking Irish, and by these in general only when writing in Ireland and for the Irish people. We shall find some few writers such as Lionel Johnson and Nora Chesson of the last generation who, born and living altogether out of Ireland, were yet so much in love with Ireland, in sympathy with the Irish Mode, in consonance with the Irish rhythm of life and literature, in converse with Irish people and out of converse with others, that they must be counted of the number who come within the narrowest definition of our term. So also one or two of the best Gaelic writers of our time have no personal knowledge of this country. On the other hand some of us who live in Ireland, of Gaelic stock, even of Gaelic speech, are for all that more Greek than Gael.

It is difficult to fix the zone; but by the time we have analysed some characteristics of Irish literature in the two languages and verified the qualities of the Irish Mode, though we shall probably have shortened the list of Anglo-Irish authors, it is to be hoped that by doing so we shall have enhanced its value. For the rest, Ireland can now afford to contribute of her new wealth to the common literature of the English language, keeping this characteristic literature of her own apart.

Before proceeding to this analysis and verification it is well to examine origins, tradition, history and other influences, beginning with the question of language and literature.

Study 3

Language and Literature

3

'OUR MORNING STAR', wrote old Archbishop Trench, 'Chaucer yet ushered in no dawn which was on the point of breaking.' The well of English undefiled was indeed for just two hundred years alone the one rich source of English literature. Then many waters broke from the ground of the English language and the stream flowed strong.

The date of the beginning of the *Canterbury Tales*, 1386, is a useful one to count by. English, for a quarter of a century the language of the Courts of Law, had then just replaced French as the language taught in the schools. Chaucer's important contemporary, Gower, was on the point of turning from the French and Latin of his previous works to the English of his third poem, *Confessio Amantis*. The promise of an English literature must have appeared fair. Yet the language had to wait long for its fulfilment. It had to go to school again, and to a different school; it had to unlearn and to learn. It had to mellow its voice in silence; it had to train its members in patience, before it could attain the utterance and the gesture of its new youth and its prime. The language of Chaucer had not in his day become the national language. His contemporary, Langland, used a different syntax. The Anglo-Norman people, of which Chaucer was a good type, had to mingle and to weld before its thought and emotion could find expression in the modern English of the last three hundred and fifty years. The literature of a dialect is tuneful only to the accompaniment of a central literature.

It is significant that no English poet of importance has followed in Chaucer's way. He is the best, indeed the only, true narrative poet of the language. He is in a certain sense the least lyric of the great English poets. In this one quality of his work he is so much akin to French poets that one is tempted to set it up with other barriers and divide him from English literature proper.

I urge this matter here with instance because I wish to make clear the connection in Ireland between language and literature, to show that though in the seventeenth and eighteenth centuries an Irish

Chaucer might have arisen, turning from the Gaelic of his clan to the English of the Pale, he would have been only a morning star too, not the rising sun. Of course there are differences in the conditions and the rest, but the main consideration is that a literature with the seeds of succession in it comes in the mother language of the teller and of the listener, of the singer and of those who take up the refrain. The simple fact is that, as, according to a certain Scot, there must always be two parties to a joke, the man who makes it and the man who sees it; so, surely, there must be two parties to the making of a literature; and the second party must be capable of full appreciation. The poet is, no doubt, as I have said elsewhere is this volume, his own first audience. His poetry is a matter between himself and himself. If others afterwards come and share his joy, the gain is theirs.

But he is sensitive to the emotions and sympathies of his country and time. He is, whether he like it or not, the heir of the ages, in possession of the passing period and of the future. He himself is the poet and himself the auditor; but his second self is a critic, and to be a critic is to know other men and to appreciate the tastes of other men, and these others almost of necessity his countrymen. He is most blessed when his countrymen are fresh for literature – which is not to say that a writer, whatever his genius, could initiate a separate literature merely by seeking and finding a people, even his own people, without a modern literature. His doing so depends on the people, on the state of their culture, and more particularly on the state of their ideals, national, religious, mystical. And when he finds them with all these qualities, he must speak not merely of his people, but to them and for them, discovering them to themselves, expressing them for themselves.

William Carleton made the mistake, during one part of his career at least, of writing about Ireland for a foreign audience. He hoped, as he says in a letter from London to his daughter, to reach a popularity equal to that of Dickens or Thackeray, 'and consequently to have the English publishers at my feet and willing to come to my own terms.'[1] Carleton knew Irish, and might possibly, some think, have been the Gaelic Mistral – if he had been a patriot. As it was he fell between two stools. The Irish people proper were deaf to his word: the English people listened while moved by the horrors of the Famine of 1847, and then turned a deaf ear too. A Molière that cannot interest his washerwoman will not interest the passers by.

English literature has had some difficulty in getting rid of the phraseology, the inversions, the poetic words, the cumbrous epithets, the mannerisms, of its pastoral and of its genteel days. It has, indeed, not yet got quite rid of them. The English reading of the early Anglo-Irish writers filled their memories with those old, stale things; but the individual Anglo-Irish literature of which I write has no such lumber. It is the record of the speech of the people, the living word – sometimes, no doubt, heightened, to use the old phrase, but of a directness that Wordsworth would have adored. Indeed it would seem that the desire of Wordsworth for a literature written only in the common language of the people is best fulfilled in the work produced in Ireland. His own work rarely attains the level balance of such poems as *Michael*: the weak prose of some of his peasant verse errs as much on one side as does the heightened diction of such a poem as *The Affliction of Margaret* on the other. Of course the very latest of the Anglo-Irish writers have had something of Wordsworth's difficulty. Mr W. B. Yeats, who, for all the unearthliness of much of his work, has used in his lyrics the most direct colloquial phrase, confesses this in some of his poems. And in a letter to the writer he has said: 'I remember as an important event getting rid of the word "rife."'

In passing, one may remark that this striving after colloquial directness has its dangers too. The latest poems of Mr Yeats show that he has failed to recognise an important fact of English grammar, the function of the conventional word order.[2] Admit that poetic licences should be no more allowed than other licences, but examine poetry's charter of liberty before you tear it up. It is an older charter than that of prose.

One of the distinctions of this Anglo-Irish literature that marks it off from the mere epochs of English literature proper is its independence of obsolete species. It matters nothing to Irish writers of the day that English has had in due succession its lyric, its dramatic, its epic, its didactic poetry and then the new lyric of romanticism, inspired by the Celtic breath (I am here claiming the influence rather of Macpherson than of Blake and others); that the Elizabethan prose writers, even Bacon, set no standard, made no lasting moulds, were again morning stars and not day stars; that prose went on many anvils before it was fit for all its uses; that it has to-day become at once keen and flexible only after that long tempering.

In spite of the self-consciousness of the age, in spite of the world influences felt here, in spite of all our criticism, the Irish poets and writers (those that are truly Anglo-Irish) are beginning it all over again in the alien tongue that they know now as a mother tongue. They delight not in the ink-horn terms of the English literary succession, but in the rich living language of a people little affected by book-lore, a people standing but a little way on the English side of the crossways, remembering something of the syntax or the metaphor of Gaelic, much of the rhythm, inventing mostly for itself its metaphor from the things of its life, things known at first hand.

Once more this is not to say that the literature can grow and progress now as if nothing had ever happened in the world before – as if, for instance, the Renaissance had never been and as if the Romantic Revival had not changed the literatures of Europe. On the contrary, the things that have happened, especially indeed the things that have affected English literature, must powerfully affect our literature. Indeed it has its beginnings partly in the Romantic Revival. To find a literature that had none of its timbers out of a previous edifice one would have to go back to that raised in lamentation by Adam and Eve on the loss of Paradise or of their son.

This Anglo-Irish literature knows the poetry of Romance. It gains thereby. It continues it, and has a chance of continuing in a higher mood, given new freshness of ideas, freshness of race, independence of book tradition, and the advantage of experience shared in common with other English literature. It departs from Romance, and still has had the advantage of using it.

But with all this, and by all this, it is a new beginning. Some of its writers, *docti sermones utriusque linguae*, cannot, it would seem, fail to be under current influences. Does this detract from its claim to newness or make it but the going on of an older literature, whether Gaelic or English? Chaucer's work, to cite it again, must have seemed a going on in his day – part of it a continuation in English of the work of French poets, and part a continuation of the work of the writers of the old chivalrous romances and the like – with a new power and a new note. To some who could best appreciate the work of Langland he must have appeared a man who 'writ no language', as Spenser, in a different light, appeared to Ben Jonson. (I have not forgotten that in the matter of vocabulary Langland is almost as much under French influence as Chaucer.)

Chaucer stands in England at the end of the Middle Ages. Between him and Spenser intervene the barbarous Wars of the Roses, Amurath succeeding Amurath, for all that Shakespeare said. The gay time of the Canterbury Pilgrims was gone, when in the words of one of Chaucer's editors, those classes whose training fitted and disposed them to take an interest in books were in a state of gaiety at once the sequel of protracted military glory and the foster mother of artistic productivity; when songs and pretty things were prized supremely; when luxury was new and not quite understood; when people wore their glories upside down; when the ceremonial of Chivalry still retained the ostentation of devoutness and self-sacrifice. The succeeding time, so barren in literature, was, for all its ugliness, really literature in the making. The last English epic is the group of Histories in which Shakespeare dramatised the century 1385-1485.

In Ireland a period intervened between the last days of the Gaelic literature that mattered and the beginning of the new literature in the English tongue, between the hope and admiration that captured the imagination of the people in the days of Hugh O'Neill and Hugh O'Donnell, then of Eoghan Ruadh O'Neill, then of the Jacobites, and the new hope and anticipation that dawned in the last century and is widened to morning in this. The old Gaelic polity and culture having lost their force and their integrity, Gaelic literature became decadent in the time of the Penal Laws.

Whatever the fate of the Gaelic language and literature now may be – whether its long sickness end now in death without issue, or, as some of us confidently hope, in revival and vigorous life, with renewal of the same personality, a second youth, or in the birth of a new language to utter a new literature, destined to take after its Gaelic mother only in some parts, and for the rest to bear the name of bastard in its childhood and of true-born heir in its age, a well of Irish undefiled – whatever is to be in the unknown future, it would be folly to deny the sickness, the decadence, of the immediate past.

And while Irish was decadent, English was not yet able either to carry on the tradition or to syllable anew for itself here. The English-speaking population in Ireland had none of the qualities – social cohesion and integrity, culture, enthusiasm, joy, high and brave emotion – to stammer and then to utter clearly the new word. That word came to the call of the country. It came in the new language and was heard in the new day. The Renaissance that stirred England to its greatest literature brought the mingling of the cosmopolitan with the national. Here the waters have been stirred by the breath of freedom: the alien language has stirred to expression on the lips of the native people.

The revival of nationalism among the Irish subject majority following the days of the Irish Volunteers, the United Irishmen, the independent Parliament; this nationalism, strengthened by O'Connell with Catholic Emancipation and the franchise; this nationalism, hardened by the austere independence of Parnell, by the Land War and its victorious close; this, brought to full manhood by the renewed struggle for legislative freedom and the certainty of triumph and responsibility; this, free from alien hope and fear, craving no ease, hearing always the supreme song of victory on the dying lips of martyrs; this produced the unrest, the impetuous, intrepid adventure that shouts the song of joy for the sad things and for the glad things of life.

The song in the new language demanded an intellectual effort that gave it a worth apart. English had to be broken and re-made to serve that song. The language that had been brought to perfection for English use, and then worn by that use, that had had the fixing of the printing press and had set the printer's word above the spoken, that language, in order to serve the different purpose of the new people, had to go back to the forge of the living speech. King Alfred, in the first days of English prose, wrote long awkward strings of words for sentences, with little syntactical order. The modern English author writes well-balanced, well-ordered sentences. But the Saxon King expressed more truly his thought; in him the word order imaged more truly the thought order.[3] The modern writer uses counters where he used coin. The modern writer cannot distinguish between his idea and the set phrase that does duty for its expression, though its terms have other meanings. He alludes to things. His prose is a hint, perfectly understood no doubt by others who know the code, but not for all that a true language. Almost perfectly it does duty for a true language to the people with whom it has grown; better than perfectly in its poetry, which gains in suggestiveness more than its loss in concreteness.

Compare the prose of this language with the superior prose of French. Compare its poetry with the far inferior poetry of French. It was, in a word, the English language, good for the English people, redolent of English history, even of the vagaries and absurdities of the history of the English people, with practical jokes and puns and stupid grammatical blunders smelling sweet with the aroma of some splendid verse – with golden lads and girls that come to dust, as chimney sweepers, and with deeds of derring-do. This language, now a courser of ethereal race, now a hack between the shafts of commercialism, serving Shakespeare and the stenographer, used efficiently in William Blake's lyrics and in telegrams; this differed in many of the ways of linguistic difference from the language of the Gael. In it the ideas of the Gael did not find easy expression.

But I have been led on a little too far. The language that was brought face to face with Irish in the eighteenth and nineteenth centuries was not the language of English commerce. The Gaelic people had for English tutors the descendants of the old English settlers, in whose mouths the language was still the language of Shakespeare. The transplanted slip of a language does not develop as does the parent tree. By comparison it rather ceases to develop.

The descendants of the earliest English colonists here were found, by a new Englishman of Elizabeth's time, using 'the dregs of the old ancient Chaucer English.' So in our day we find in the mouths of the people what such a progressive might call the dregs of the old ancient Shakespeare English. And this was the English that had to be knit into a different complication from the modern complication of the central English language.

For the rest, it is not only in Ireland that the phenomenon has occurred: analogous is the use of English by the American booster and by the mystic who has to express in terms of sense and wit the things of God that are made known to him in no language.

Study 4

Irish and English

'*... between Irish and English ... there are wide differences, which prove different mental habits, different social conditions, different literary traditions.*'

4

I MENTIONED IN THE LAST CHAPTER the possibility of the birth of a new language in this country, sprung from Irish and English. It is of course possible, but so unlikely as not to deserve further discussion. In Old English sentence structure was rudimentary. Long before the Norman Conquest the Germanic word-order at the first touch of French influence ceased to rule alone, yielding half its sway to the French. Here was a language ready for transformation. In Ireland at the present day things are very different. The syntax of the Gaelic language – and it is the syntax that matters rather than the introduction of foreign words – is fixed and in all important features not likely to undergo modification. The verb will precede its subject, the adjective will follow its noun to the end.

Similarly, English in Ireland will not conform to Gaelic rules. The sentence *Is the book there?* cannot be reconciled with *Tá an leabhar ann*; though the Irish sentence is a word for word translation of the English it means *The book is there*. But, while this is so and shall remain so, the effect of the thinking that expresses itself in the Gaelic modes has already affected and must continue to affect expression in English. *Is it the book that is there?* translates directly an Irish sentence of the same meaning.[1] (In Irish the first word will be the verb of identity.) More important are the use in Irish of the concrete as against the English use of the abstract; the use of the adjective in preference to the verb; the use of periphrasis to avoid trusting to voice emphasis the meaning of the sentence; the more elaborate system of verbal forms and the use of a periphrastic perfect, pluperfect and future perfect; idioms connected with the use of prepositions; the use of the absolute case in clauses introduced by *and*; the use of the one Irish word *féin* for *even* and *self*; the use of *do bheith ag* for *have*.

It would be tedious to give many examples of these differences. Passages quoted in subsequent chapters may be examined in this connection. Here a few will suffice. The English sentence, *That startled me*, translates into Irish: *That took a start out of me. I go to Cork,* translates according to the word stressed, *It is I that am going to Cork, It is going to Cork that I am, It is to Cork that I am going.* English, *I work here*, translates *I am (now) working here, I do be working here, I (usually) work here; I have, had*, or *shall have worked* (for so long) translate *I am, was,* or *shall be, after working*.

Irish has undergone no very violent change in any of its stages. Modern Irish is much more in line with Old Irish than is Modern English with Old English. This has saved Irish from the introduction of words that are rather labels than names, or, to use my former image, rather counters than coin of intrinsic worth. The name of a thing in Irish, to take the first and most obvious of all examples, is *ainm*. This word is used also in the sense of the English word *noun*. Of course grammarians know of the relationship of *ainm* with *name* and *noun* and *nomen* and *onoma*; but the people to whom such things matter more do not know. A child in an English-speaking school is taught – or used to be taught – that the name of the thing he knows as a hand must be parsed as a noun, and that a noun is the name of a person, place, thing, or idea. The Irish child, learning grammar in Irish, is told that the word *lámh* (hand) is a name (*ainm*), that the words *leabhar, mian, fuacht, Baile Átha Cliath, Eoin* (book, desire, cold, Dublin, John) are names. He deals directly with his trader: there are no middle-men with terms like *parse, noun* and the rest to make him pay double.

On the other hand Irish has on the whole remained unaffected by things that have very greatly affected almost all other modern languages – by the printing press, by modern commerce, by modern science and the rest. The result is that it has not been unified. It is still rich in dialects and in variant forms. No single literary, commercial or journalistic language exists; and, to use an Anglo-Irish phrase, there is no call for one. The vocabulary of the language is very large. It would seem that the people, thrown back on themselves and on nature, not forced to invent technical terms for the new things of civilization, have gone on with the minute study of the old things. They have named all the facets and distinguished all the moods. With this they have retained an ease for full expression that English does not know. Translation from English into Irish has more resemblance to rendering into Latin than into a modern language, like French, in spite of all the characteristic qualities of English. Take this passage of De Quincey:

> It adds much to these considerations that Southern Asia is and has been for thousands of years the part of the earth most swarming with human life, the great *officina gentium*. Man is a weed in those regions.

This is Beaudelaire's French version, almost a word for word translation:

> *Ce qui ajoute beaucoup à de tels sentiments, c'est que l'Asie meridionale est, et a été, depuis des milliers d'années, la partie de la terre la plus four-millante de la vie humaine, la grande* officina gentium. *L'homme, dans ces contrées, pousse comme l'herbe.*

Latin dispenses with the redundancies, the over-sayings, compressing a phrase into a verb:

> *Quod vero multo magis sentimus quia ex omnibus orbis terrae gentibus Asia meridionalis per multa milia annorum hominibus maxime redundat et semper redundavit; officina gentium, ut ita dicam, facta.*

When one comes to translate this into Irish one has to choose between a colloquial version, easily comprehensible to a people which has none but a literature of folk poems and tales, and an elaborate, emphatic version, more carefully balanced than the Latin, with ringing rhythms and assonances. To kill two birds with the one stone I shall give instead of the popular Irish version an Anglo-Irish rendering of it:

> There is that much sure. Along with that there are far more people in South Asia than in any other land of its size in the world, and that is how it has been for thousands of years now. A forge, or workshop of nations it is – *officina gentium,* as you would say – or, to say it in another way, men grow there like weeds.

To find a literary man with a style to set against De Quincey's one has to go back to Geoffrey Keating, the last classic prose writer. A friend of mine has rendered the passage into the Irish of Keating:

> *Agus ni beag d'adhbhar iongantais dúinn a mheas gurab i an Aissia theas tír is lia lánaitreabh agus is lusmhaire léirthionól agus is truime trombhuidhean do chríochaibh domhain ó chéin mhóir gus aniu, agus ní h-éigcneasta ghoirid ughdair dh'airithe officina gentium, mar atá, ceardcha ioltuath, di. Gá dtám ris acht ni fairsinge fás fiadhlosa i bhfearán fódbhog ioná urfhás na h-Ádhamhchloinne ar ithir na hInnia.*

(And not little reason of wonder to us its consideration that it is South Asia that is greatest of full house-holds and that is most plentiful of gatherings-up and that is heaviest of heavy companies of the territories of the earth from a long time ago till to-day; and not unbecomingly certain authors call it *officina gentium*, that is a forge of many races. Where are we then, but that not more generous the growth of wild plants in a soft sodded grassy place than the fresh growth of the Adam-clan on the arable soil of India?)

One fears to draw conclusions too general from particular points of difference between Irish and English, in vocabulary and in grammar. The one thing worth knowing in the matter, as far as we are concerned here, is that there are wide differences, which prove different mental habits, different social conditions, different literary traditions.

English writing is full of metaphor that cannot be understood without knowledge of historic events which have not affected Ireland: Shakespeare's plays are indeed, as has been said, nothing but strings of popular sayings. Irish has a different set of historic memories and of popular sayings. These have come into Anglo-Irish, but not in full force, and Anglo-Irish is the simpler for it. New images have to be supplied from current life in Ireland; the dialect at its best is more vigorous, fresh and simple than either of the two languages between which it stands. It is indeed by its colloquial directness that you will know the true Anglo-Irish work. Some of our best poems indeed have no word or phrase which alone could be labelled Irish.

On the other hand there appear at present quantities of so-called Celtic poems, plays, stories, which, for all their Irish phrases, and indeed because of them, are obvious shams. A writer of these could turn almost any sentence into his 'Celtic'. Where I have said 'Which are obvious shams' just now, he would say something like this: 'And, Johnny, I give you my hand on it this night, 'tis out and out humbugs they are surely.' One of the most powerful writers of recent years, the late J. M. Synge, was very often merely 'Celtic' in his phraseology, though far more often rich and right. His fault in the matter was that he crammed his language too full of rich phrases. He said that he used no form of words that he had not actually heard. But this probably means that he took note only of the striking things, neglecting the common stuff of speech.

In another matter Synge compares very favourably with his Irish contemporaries, his respect for the Gaelic language. He treats Irish as he would treat French or another language. Not so many of the best known Anglo-Irish writers, who treat Irish words as W. S. Gilbert and such writers for comic purposes used to treat French. As *monsieur* became *mounseer* or *mosha*, the Irish *Éire* is rhymed with *fire, mo bhuachailín* becomes *ma boucheléen, slán* and *sláinte* become *shlan* and *shlainte*, against all the principles of Irish phonetics. It would be tedious and not edifying to deal thoroughly with this matter. Irish has been regarded as fair game for almost any treatment. A language with an elaborate grammatical system, with delicate phonetic changes to indicate changes of sense, is treated as if it had no system and as if it could suffer nothing from barbarous mispronunciation. If the ignorance or carelessness of the writers who use it so mattered only to the Irish language, the Irish language could well afford to let it pass: it would affect it no more than does the fact that now, half a century after the time of O'Donovan and O'Curry, the Royal Irish Academy has for its president a man so grossly ignorant of the language that he is incapable of pronouncing the names of the books in its library.

But to the new generation of Irish readers who know the two languages, many otherwise fine books are spoiled or at least made a little foolish and ridiculous by the grotesque disguises under which Irish words appear in them. And this ignorance of the authors is like that of the old sham philologists. A modern writer who made an image from the derivation *lucus a non lucendo*, who referred to a wood as 'that which the Roman named from darkness', would be doomed to unintelligible obscurity or to absurdity.

What then of Mr W. B. Yeats who confesses that when he wrote the greater number of his poems, he had hardly considered seriously the question of the pronunciation of Irish words, who copied at times somebody's perhaps fanciful spelling, and at times the ancient spelling as he found it in some literal translation, pronouncing the words always as they were spelt?[2] That is, pronouncing the words as if they were English. Mr Yeats, however, is quite honest in the matter. He would not, he says, have defended his system at any time. If ever he learns the old pronunciation of the proper names he has used he will revise the poems. He is content to affirm that he has not treated his Irish names as badly as the mediaeval writers of the stories of King Arthur treated their Welsh names. But Mr Yeats is not living in the Middle Ages. Whether we regret it or not, we cannot ignore the knowledge of those to whom we communicate our works. In the lines:

> The host is riding from Knocknarea
> And over the grave of Clooth-na-Bare,

nothing is gained, surely, by that extraordinary perversion of the Irish name of the Old Woman of Beare, *Cailleach na Béara*. The word *clooth* is not Irish; it has no meaning. Even for others than Irish scholars the right word would have served as well. And – if it be not too philistine a question – would not:

> And over the grave of the Hag of Beare,

have been better in this poem in English? In his revision of *The Wind Among the Reeds*, Mr Yeats has changed Irish words into English, 'colleens' into 'women.' Lately he has set his face against all this use of Irish words and Irish stories; but he cannot undo his work. Let me admit, before passing from him, that his constant use of the form used before him by Ferguson, has fixed a new word in the English language. Danaan is impossible in Irish, which has Dannan (in *Tuatha De Dannan*) accented on the first syllable. Mr Yeats has, as he claims, the excuse that the words he uses are of the old language. Mr James Stephens has no such excuse when he translates Miss Murphy into *Ingin Ni Murachu,* sinning against Irish three times in three words.[3]

No modern writer treats Greek or Latin or French or German so. Irish goes down with the oriental languages, Owen Roe O'Neill with Morari Row, Usheen with Alladin. The pity of it is that it is in Ireland that Irish meets this fate.

One influence of Irish remains to be noted, perhaps the most important of all with regard to poetry, the effect of Irish rhythm, itself influenced by Irish music, on the rhythms of Anglo-Irish poetry.

English rhythm is governed by stress. In England the tendency is to hammer the stressed syllables and to slur the unstressed syllables. In Ireland we keep by comparison a uniform stress. A child in Cork, reading the word *unintelligibility*, pronounces all the eight syllables distinctly without special stress on any, though his voice rises and falls in a kind of tune or croon, going high upon the final syllable.

Early Irish verse is syllabic. The lines are measured by the number of syllables.

In modern verse, both Irish and English, the lines are measured by the feet, and commonly the feet differ from one another in number of syllables: each foot has one stressed syllable. In common English verse the voice goes from stress to stress, hammering the stress.

In most Anglo-Irish verse the stresses are not so strongly marked; the unstressed syllables are more fully pronounced; the whole effect is different.

Before proceeding to examples, it is well to draw attention to the fact that some other influence, probably French, has produced a similar effect on the verse of one or two English writers. Thus the poem of Ernest Dowson's, *Non Sum Qualis Eram Bonae sub Regno Cynarae*, which can owe, I think, nothing to Irish, has that level fall of syllables, found occasionally, as I have shown elsewhere, in the poems of Campion and one or two other of the Elizabethans,[4] but not again till the rise of Anglo-Irish poetry:

> I have forgot much, Cynara, gone with the wind,
> Flung roses, roses, riotously with the throng,
> Dancing, to put thy pale lost lilies out of mind,
> But I was desolate and sick of an old passion –
>   Yea, all the time, because the dance was long.
> I have been faithful to thee, Cynara, in my fashion.

The earliest Anglo-Irish poems that exhibit this note we can compare with their Irish originals or with Irish poems that sing to the same air – for they are almost always songs. I quote two good examples, Callanan's *Outlaw of Loch Lene* (Killarney) and Ferguson's

Cashel of Munster, giving the first stanza in each case. Callanan's poem can be read easily by the most formal:

> Oh, many a day have I made good ale in the glen,
> That came not of stream or malt – like the brewing of men.
> My bed was the ground; my roof, the greenwood above,
> And the wealth that I sought one far kind glance from my
>   love.

Ferguson's music is subtler:

> I'd wed you without herds, without money, or rich array,
> And I'd wed you on a dewy morning at day-dawn grey;
> My bitter woe it is, love, that we are not far away
> In Cashel town, though the bare deal board were our marriage
>   bed this day!

One sees where Moore learned the rhythm of *The Irish Peasant to his Mistress*:

> Through grief and through danger thy smile hath cheered my
>   way,
> Till hope seemed to bud from each thorn that round me lay;
> The darker our fortune, the brighter our pure love burned,
> Till shame into glory, till fear into zeal was turned.
> Oh! slave as I was, in thy arms my spirit felt free,
> And blessed e'en the sorrows that made me more dear to thee.

Sometimes we find the Gaelic internal rimes – or rather internal rimes in the Anglo-Irish poems where in Irish we should have assonances:

> If sadly thinking, with spirits sinking,
> Could, more than drinking, my cares compose,
> A cure for sorrow from sighs I'd borrow,
> And hope to-morrow would end my woes.

One easily notes the difference between poems of this kind with frequently recurring emphasis, marked by the rime, and poems like those of Callanan, Ferguson and Moore just quoted. In those there is that grace of the wandering, lingering, musical voice which I have noted in connection with my remark above on *unintelligibility*. Music is definitely rhythmic, with stress recurrent at regular intervals; but as I have said elsewhere, in certain Irish tunes, set to Irish words, the music goes out of its way, as it were, to follow the varying expression of the words, which in an Irish song are all important. Mr Carl Hardbeck of Belfast has shown this in his lectures. The tunes played by him in the ordinary way, without the words, are inferior in beauty to the tunes sung wandering with the wavering words of the old poems.

Modern airs, on the contrary, tend rather to drag the words out of their way of sense. Compare the Elizabethan setting of Shakespeare's *O Mistress Mine* with the modern setting generally sung on the stage now in performances of *Twelfth Night*. In the former, words and notes run happily, 'coupled lovingly together', to use Campion's phrase. In the latter, the striking air of which seems to have been composed for the violin, there is no love lost; the words have to adapt themselves to the tune.

Matthew Arnold in his essay *On the Study of Celtic Literature*, largely a work of fiction, has written interestingly of the Celtic Note, using the name is a sense of his own. He has been rather apprehended than understood; and with later writers the meaning has become vaguer. This is due, at least in part, to the vagueness of the two terms, ' Celtic' and 'Note'. I propose, in my study of the metrical effect of poems like *Cashel of Munster*, to use instead my term, the Irish Mode. With the rhythm goes a certain emotion, as distinctly Celtic or Irish, no doubt; but emotions alone are unsafe guides.

Study 5

Anglo-Irish Authors

'*What then will the historian of Anglo-Irish literature have to deal with? Who are the characteristically Irish writers that come within the scope of his study? What poets, what novelists, what dramatists, what essayists, what historians, what authors?*'

5

IN THE PREVIOUS ESSAYS I have tried to arrive at definite conclusions with regard to the language of Anglo-Irish literature. Some questions which to many have appeared more important I have avoided, because I recognise that in attempting to answer them I should run the risk of suggesting more than I could prove, of drawing conclusions too general from very particular cases, of losing the little that I can hold by grasping either at too much or at other little that is of its nature elusive – worse still of begging the question, of running in a circle, of choosing the lesson to suit the example to hand.

I have little sympathy with the criticism that marks off subtle qualities in literature as altogether racial, that refuses to admit natural exceptions in such a naturally exceptional thing as high literature, attributing only the central body to the national genius, the marginal portions to this alien strain or that. It may be quite true that John Keats owed the quality of his work to his half Cornish, half Welsh origin. I can say only that I find it difficult to prove – as difficult as to prove, for instance, that a man of quite other extraction might also have produced work of similar quality. French poetry on the whole has lacked the lyric note. One need not for that agree with a recent writer that the French poets who have the more intense lyric gift must have been of foreign extraction. Less still need one agree that a great lyric poetry may not come to France any day and from the lips of French poets.

My definite conclusions are three:

First, that an Anglo-Irish literature, worthy of a special designation, could come only when English had become the language of the Irish people, mainly of Gaelic stock; and when the literature was from, by, of, to and for the Irish people.

Second, that the ways of life and the ways of thought of the Irish people – the manners, customs, traditions and outlook, religious, social, moral – have important differences from the ways of life and of thought which have found expression in other English literature.

Third, that the English language in Ireland has an individuality of its own, and the rhythm of Irish speech a distinct character.

If, with some of the best modern critics, we divide literature into poetry and science, the one to be attributed to the intuitive faculties and the other to the intellectual, it may seem that my conclusions have reference only to the science, the logical and the intellectual. That is not quite so: but this work is itself a work of science in that sense; it is a study, an analysis, aiming at the logical, at a clear intellectual grasp of its subject; dealing with literature and language, literature and nationality, and the like, rather than with the wind that bloweth where it listeth or with the utterances, in terms of sense and wit, of mystic things.

It will be seen also that these conclusions bar out from my study the works of some Irish-born writers of the first importance, of Swift, of Goldsmith, of Sheridan – in short, of all but the more characteristically Irish authors of the nineteenth and twentieth centuries.

What then will the historian of Anglo-Irish literature have to deal with? Who are the characteristically Irish writers that come within the scope of his study? What poets, what novelists, what dramatists, what essayists, what historians, what orators?

The poets of the Irish Mode are evidently his quarry. Moore in the beginning is of them, Mangan, Ferguson. Callanan has a few good poems; Edward Walsh a few. The best of the later poets must be reckoned under this head, down to George Sigerson, Douglas Hyde, and W. B. Yeats, the elder poets of the present day.

Equally within his scope are the explicitly patriotic poets, many of whom have no other subjects than national ones, and yet who have not in our ears, for all their Gaelic words, the Irish accent of Ferguson. Such are Davis and the poets of the *Nation*. Such on the whole are, in our days, Gerald Griffin and William Allingham. Such in much of their work are Emily Lawless and Alice Milligan. There are a few poets, like Aubrey de Vere, whose main work cannot be referred either to the Irish Mode or to living Irish patriotism, yet who are definitely Anglo-Irish. There are a few, like Lionel Johnson and Nora Chesson who were born and who lived their whole lives out of Ireland, and yet are truly Irish.[1] Others, whose relations with Ireland and Irish life were slight, have been included in Anglo-Irish anthologies and the like – Edgar Allen Poe, Emily Brontë, Arthur O'Shaughnessy, Edward Fitzgerald. The connection of some of these with the subject is, however, too slender a link to depend on.

Poe, who was a student of Mangan, had an ear for the Irish Mode. Emily Brontë, on the other hand, seems to have thought that the difficulty she found in conforming to the conventional regulations of English verse was a defect of power in her. She thought that to her was denied, as she said,

> The glorious gift to many given
> To speak their thoughts in poetry.

And her editors, her sister Charlotte, Mr Clement Shorter[2] and Mr A. C. Benson, have thought so too. They have 'corrected' and 'regularised' her wavering rhythms, Mr Benson changing 'never' into 'ne'er' and 'even' into 'e'en,' and regretting that he cannot reduce 'being' to a monosyllable. A good critic in *The Times* in defending her from these men of law, quotes an exquisite poem, never hitherto correctly printed:

> Tell me, tell me, smiling child,
> What the past is like to thee,
> An autumn evening, soft and mild,
> With a wind that sighs mournfully.
>
> Tell me, what is the present hour?
> A green and flowery spray,
> Where a young bird sits, gathering its power
> To mount and fly away.
>
> And what is the future, happy one?
> A sea beneath a cloudless sun,
> A mighty, dazzling, glorious sea,
> Stretching into infinity.

'The poet of "With a wind that sighs mournfully", and of "Where a young bird sits, gathering its power," knew', he says, 'the value and the music of every word she wrote and was in no need of assistance in the counting or compressing of her syllables.' What a pity it is that she did not know, by more than an hereditary memory and feeling, the mode of her kinsman, the Gaelic poet Padraic Ó Prunta.[3] She might in Ireland, with Irish music around her and Irish speech, have come to confident maturity, a great lyric poet. As it was she failed to reach that confidence and that ripeness. 'Emily Brontë', says the anonymous critic from whom I have quoted just now, 'with no dialect (such as Burns had) to isolate and reflect her to her own eyes, was continually attempting the "English poem", unaware of her true vein.' So too with the other exiles and strays. We have to share in their loss.

The Anglo-Irish prose authors offer little difficulty; although their prose, except when it is a record of peasant speech, has nowhere the distinct characteristics of Anglo-Irish verse. The novelists are Maria Edgeworth, Charles Mathurin, William Carleton, Charles Lever, Samuel Lover, Gerald Griffin, J. Sheridan Le Fanu, the Banims and some more recent writers; the orators, Grattan, Flood, Curran, Robert Emmet (by virtue of his one speech), Daniel O'Connell, Richard Lalor Sheil, Butt and a few others; the historians of literary stature, Mitchel and Lecky. The few Irish dramatists of the nineteenth century, from Macklin to the foundation of the Irish Literary Theatre, have little importance in literature. The political essayists are Davis, Fintan Lalor and their fellows.

The names of these authors answer my question of six terms above. There is one other group of authors whose work is, in one sense of the word, more truly Anglo-Irish than that of any of the writers I have mentioned here, with the exception perhaps of such men as Mangan and Ferguson. I refer to the great translators, those pioneers of Irish studies who rendered the Old Irish poems and sagas into an English which gained from the originals a distinct power and beauty. The importance of the work of Eugene O'Curry, John O'Donovan, Whitley Stokes, Standish Hayes O'Grady, can scarcely be over-estimated. With these scholars stands George Petrie.[4] Apart from them, not a scholar like them, yet looking in the same direction, stands the strange imaginative Standish James O'Grady. The latest of the great scholar translators, Kuno Meyer, is a German, who, by his own work and that of his disciples, has added wealth of matter and grace of manner to the new literature.

Study 6

The Irish Mode

'... *Mr Yeats, for all his want of musical ear, owes, I believe, this peculiar musical quality of his early verse to that Irish chant which at once saves Irish speech from too definite a stress and from an utterance too monotonous and harsh. ... The most valuable and characteristic contribution to verse made by the Anglo-Irish poets, by Moore, Mangan, Ferguson, Hyde, Yeats and all, has been a contribution of melody.*'

6

Every syllable of a word has a vowel and may have one consonant or more. The vowel may have a short sound, as 'u' in 'nut' or a long sound, as 'o' in 'note'. A syllable may be stressed or unstressed, the stress depending on the pronunciation of the word, or, in the case of a monosyllable, on the meaning of the sentence in which it is placed. In the classical languages, which had a full inflexional system and could in consequence indicate meaning without the same use of word order that English has, we may take it that stress had no real place, either formative or combative, in the making of verse. Their metric was founded on the rhythm of long and short syllables – quantity. This system, in the case of Latin, was an adoption, but was none the less rigid.

In English, metrical quantity proper does not exist, though English verse uses for a grace all the varieties of vowels, short and long, and of consonants and consonant combinations, quick and slow, light and heavy. The recurrence of stress marks the rhythm. The voice is capable of uttering at one 'pressure', up to three syllables but not more. That is, between two stressed syllables there may be no unstressed, one unstressed or two unstressed syllables. If, as in the case of such words as 'superfluous' or 'memorial', more than three syllables seem to be uttered at one voice-pressure, it will be found that there is either elision, as in '–uous' of 'superfluous' (if pronounced superfl'ous) or the introduction of a consonantal *yod* sound, as in –ial' of 'memorial' (memoryal).[1]

English verse, then, is accentual, a rhythm of stressed and unstressed syllables. Irish verse is also accentual; but there is this occasional difference, that while what may be called central English verse, in order to emphasise the stressed, under-emphasises the unstressed, Irish frequently allows for the clear pronunciation of several syllables between stress and stress. Such Irish verse is not rigidly governed by the law of mono-pressures;[2] it is generally found in songs, the tunes of which have a good deal to do with drawing the metrical feet dancing out of their bars. This less pronounced hammering of the stressed syllables is more noticeable in Irish prose speech; and on account of it English as we speak it in Ireland has a much more deliberate way of pronunciation, a much more even intonation, than the English of the English. One of the ablest living English metrists, Mr T. S. Omond, complained some time ago, in a letter to the writer, that he could not make out the metre of a poem beginning with the doggerel lines:

> I once spent an evening in a village
> Where the people are all taken up with tillage.

An Irish reader would be content to pronounce the words as they come, to read the lines as prose reads:

> I once spent an evening in a village where the people are all taken up with tillage,

not at all hurrying over or slurring 'spent,' '–ening,' 'taken,' and not over-stressing 'in' and 'up.'

Two examples from different stages of Anglo-Irish literature will illustrate this tendency of our poetry. The reading of the first we know from its whimsical tune:

> The town of Passage
> Is both wide and spacious
> And situated upon the sea,
> 'Tis neat and decent
> And quite contagious
> To go to Cork on a bright summer's day.

The last line of this verse is always sung in such a way as to be almost spoken with rapid and even enunciation of all the syllables. The effect may be got by reading the line with little or no stress on the words, 'go', 'Cork', 'bright', 'day'. In the song this effect adds to the drollery of the words and the tune.

Very different is the well known *Lake Isle of Inishfree* of W. B. Yeats:

> I will arise and go now, and go to Innisfree,
> And a small cabin build there, of clay and wattles made;
> Nine bean rows will I have there, a hive for the honey bee,
> And live alone in the bee-loud glade.
>
> And I shall have some peace there, for peace comes dropping
>   slow,
> Dropping from the veils of the morning to where the cricket
>   sings;
> There midnight's all a glimmer, and noon a purple glow,
> And evening full of the linnet's wings.
>
> I will arise and go now, for always night and day
> I hear lake water lapping with low sounds by the shore;
> While I stand on the roadway, or on the pavements gray,
> I hear it in the deep heart's core.

In the line

> And I shall have some peace there, for peace comes dropping
> slow,

it would be as wrong to mark, as heavily stressed, the syllables 'I', 'some', 'there', as to scan it:

> And I | shall have | some peace | there ...

as some English metrists might read it.

Take the line frankly as if it were a line of prose, only with that beauty of vibration in the voice that goes with the fine grave words of poetry. (It is impossible to mark the reading by punctuation or the like). Read it so, and you will understand the true quality of this mode in Anglo-Irish poetry. It is wrong to scan this verse, to cut off the syllables according to the measure of a rhythm that rises and falls sharply and regularly. Even with some marks to indicate that, though unstressed, a syllable is slow and long:

> And Í shall have sóme peace thére

the scansion is wrong. There is a recurrence in this verse, but it is not the recurrence of the foot. I have been able to take half a line to illustrate my meaning. The first three lines of each stanza have a cesura in the middle. I believe that that is the only division to make in them, and that as a rule open to exception. In general the second part of the line has a more obvious recurrence of stress than the first, as:

> ... of clay and wattles made.

Of course, as in all musical verse, there are contrasts, exceptional first half lines that run with a regular scannible rhythm, and exceptional second half lines like:

> ... with low sounds on the shore.

This general movement, changing from a slow beat to an easy rise and fall, happens constantly. I sometimes think it expresses, whether in accentual verse or quantitative, the mingled emotion of unrest and pleasure that comes with the break up of winter, with the south wind, with the thought of the shortness of life and the need to make haste to explore its good and simple joys – the desire to leave the unlovely, mingled with a vivid conception of the land of heart's desire.[3] It is the rhythm of that fourth ode of Horace's first book. In the long lines the four solemn bars, dactyls or spondees, are followed by three light trochaic feet; and the short lines, after the unrest of one syllable taken alone, continue the movement:

> *Solvitur acris hiemps grata vice veris et Favoni,*
> *   trahuntque siccas machinæ carinas;*
> *ac neque iam stabulis gaudet pecus aut arator igni,*
> *   nec prata canis albicant pruinis.*

The system is:

$$- \smile\smile \mid - \smile\smile \mid - \smile\smile \mid - \smile\smile \mid - \smile \mid - \smile \mid - \smile$$
$$\smile \quad\mid - \smile \mid - \smile \mid - \smile \mid \smile\smile$$

It would be possible to treat the second line taken above as iambic, but, considering the dactyls and trochees in the first, it must be read as trochaic.

It may be objected that owing to the utter difference between accentual and quantitative verse, it is wrong to apply these remarks to the two. I have elsewhere drawn attention to the difference, for instance, between the dactyl (quantitative) and the triple falling accentual measure of 'merrily'. This difference does not affect the similarity between the contrast of first half line and the second half line in both *Inishfree* and this ode of Horace's. For the rest, a rhythm may be produced not only in music, in noise, in words and in other things heard, but in things seen and things felt. And not merely the words of verse express the emotion. In true poetry, as the meaning of the words comes second to their rhythm, and the rhythm expresses an emotion, it will be found that the words mean the expression of this emotion as well as the rhythm.

To read correctly Anglo-Irish poetry one must follow either Irish music or Anglo-Irish prose speech. My earliest conscious observation, and notation, so to call it, of this speech was in Cork city about ten years ago. In the house at which I stayed there were two children. One was continually looking for the other and calling all over the house. 'Is Maudie in the garden?' Jimmy would chant in a most wonderfully sweet voice, lingering on every syllable. Later I was delighted to note, when living in a little mountain lodge above Rathfarnham in County Dublin, that a blackbird which came to wake me every morning in the spring sang just the notes of Jimmy's chant – a blackbird with a Cork accent. One need not think that Jimmy was guilty of that sin of childhood never committed by the Anglo-Saxon Saint Guthlac, who 'did not imitate the various cries of birds.' Jimmy was not peculiar in his accent.

In such instance song and speech are not far apart; and Mr Yeats, for all his want of musical ear, owes, I believe, this peculiar musical quality of his early verse to that Irish chant which at once saves Irish speech from too definite a stress and from an utterance too monotonous and harsh.

At the same time one must not deduce from all this that Gaelic verse is a footless thing of sinuous windings. Nothing could be more clearly marked than most Gaelic measures. And these too have had their effect on Anglo-Irish verse. To do Mr Yeats justice, since I have quoted from him to show the serpent, I shall now quote, to show the eagle, the Musicians' song from *Deirdre:*

FIRST MUSICIAN
'Why is it', Queen Edain said,
  'If I do but climb the stair
To the tower overhead,
  When the winds are calling there,
Or the gannets calling out,
  In waste places of the sky,

There's so much to think about,
  That I cry, that I cry?'
SECOND MUSICIAN
But her goodman answered her:
  'Love would be a thing of naught
Had not all his limbs a stir
  Born out of immoderate thought;
Were he anything by half,
  Were his measure running dry.
Lovers, if they may not laugh,
  Have to cry, have to cry.'

THREE MUSICIANS (*together*)
But is Edain worth a song
  Now the hunt begins anew?
Praise the beautiful and strong;
  Praise the redness of the yew;
Praise the blossoming apple-stem.
  But our silence had been wise.
What is all our praise to them,
  That have one another's eyes?

This poem is really syllabic, seven syllables to the line, like one species of Debhidhe poems in Irish[4] – without, of course, the arrangements of assonance. I do not know if Mr Yeats is aware of this syllablic measure; but again and again in his poems and in the poems of many contemporary Irishmen I find this tendency. Indeed I should say that the effects of our more deliberate Irish speech on our verse are these two:

first, a prose intonation, not monotonous, being saved by the natural rise and fall of the voice, a remnant of the ancient pitch – a quality, as it were, of chanted speech[5] – and second, a tendency to give, in certain poems, generally of short riming lines, almost equal stress value to all the syllables, a tendency to make the line the metrical unit.

From the first of these effects comes a more reasoning, not to say conversational tone, which disallows inversions, quaint words and turns of speech. Not conforming in our way of verse to the regular English stress rhythm we have not the same necessity as the English poets to depart from the natural word order. We have not to manufacture a rhythm in that unnatural way. I take up the first book of verse to my hand, the poems of William Drummond of Hawthornden, Ben Jonson's friend. The first poem I open, the lovely *Phœbus Arise,* does not afford good examples of poetic inversions. The lines, varying in length, go on their way freely. The last three lines are a little flat by comparison with the rest:

> The clouds bespangle with bright gold their blue;
> Here is the pleasant place,
> And everything, save Her, who all should grace.

These lines are a 'regularisation' of the three that ended the poem in the earlier edition:

> The clouds with orient gold spangle their blue;
> Here is the pleasant place –
> And nothing wanting is, save She, alas!

The reasons for the changes are apparent, as is the loss of beauty. But how could the poet have conceived the fear that anyone would try to read 'spangle' with a stress on the second syllable, and to such a fear sacrificed his 'orient gold.'

The sonnet beginning 'I know that all beneath the moon decays', which follows *Phœbus Arise* in my edition, will serve me better with examples. Lines like

> And that nought is more light than airy praise;

or

> But that, O me! I must both write and love,

would be read without difficulty and without that danger of wrong emphasis which Drummond seems to have feared.
His lines are:

> And that nought lighter is than airy praise;

and

> But that, O me! I both must write and love.

An editor has declared himself in doubt as to whether Drummond was a poet whose inspiration was marred by learning or a scholar who owed his literary success to study. Anyone who has read his work will know a true poet in it. The pity is that he was not more learned, as learned as Milton, say, whose verse he anticipates – learned enough to know that true liberty is separated from licence by law, not sandwiched between the two.

The freedom of Irish writers from these inversions and from kindred artificialities and the resultant colloquial naturalness may also, as I have suggested, have to do with the newness of the English language here, with the fact that the people, whose speech is echoed in these poems, have no literary memories in English, that we are still at the simple beginnings, that our literature is still at lyric babblings. However that may be, I am sure that the Irish writers are more direct, more modern, than such writers as Robert Bridges, Henry Newbolt and William Watson, on whom have fallen the mantles of older English writers, or at least who fill their shoes.

I go for examples to the *Oxford Book of English Verse*. I take, as I am seeking natural diction, a poem with a story and the living words of a modern man, an excellent poem, Newbolt's *He Fell among Thieves*.

> 'Ye have robb'd', said he, 'ye have slaughter'd and made an
>   end,
> Take your ill-got plunder, and bury the dead,
> What will ye more of your guest and sometime friend?'
> 'Blood for our blood', they said.

The diction of this, more especially in view of the admirably direct narrative in the stanzas that follow, is stilted and wrong. That phrase, 'made an end', and the whole third line are born of pen and ink. Not so, though it is not yet common colloquial diction, is the language of Mangan's version of *O'Hussey's Ode to the Maguire* – to go back seventy years:

Though he were even a wolf ranging the round green woods,
Though he were even a pleasant salmon in the unchainable sea,
Though he were a wild mountain eagle, he could scarce bear, he,
This sharp, sore sleet, these howling floods.

Oh, mournful is my soul this night for Hugh Maguire;
Darkly as in a dream he strays! Before him and behind

Triumphs the tyrannous anger of the wounding wind,
The wounding wind, that burns as fire! ...
Hugh marched forth to the fight – I grieved to see him
    so depart;
And lo! to-night he wanders frozen, rain-drenched sad,
    betrayed –
But the memory of the lime-white mansions his right hand hath laid
In ashes, warms the hero's heart.

Having quoted so much of *O'Hussey's Ode* here I omit the poem
from the Poems of the Irish Mode at the end of the book, though it is
one of the finest examples of the Mode.

O'Hussey is not a modern man, yet though Mangan gives him
words and phrases that were scarcely ever colloquial, he gives him a
natural directness that goes with emphatic speech all the world over,
at all times. If this comparison be unjust, it is so rather to Mangan's
bard than to the Anglo-Indian with his revolver. I have quoted these
two poems for another purpose than the comparison of diction.
Newbolt's poem has lines like:

He did not see the starlight on the Laspur hills,

which, contrasting with the beat of the regular lines, has something
of the unstressed movement so often found in Irish poems. Here,
one may take it, it comes naturally in the enumeration of scenes and
sounds, as an escape and relief. Mangan's rhythms are much subtler,
much deeper and more resonant; his escape, as in the second of the
stanzas quoted, is from precipitate half-unmeasured music to a regular
tolling.

For another parallel to the passage from Newbolt I take a typical
passage from a typical Irish writer of narrative poems, Alice Milligan:

'If I was home at all',
She is musing now, 'I would go that way to-night,
I would walk that way alone in the care of God,
All doors are shut and no one comes abroad
Because they think the souls are out to-night;
So in the windows they set the candles three
To let the wanderers know, "We pray for ye
And love ye yet, but would look on ye with dread
Returning from the dead." '

The inversion 'candles three' is the only forced phrase in this.[6]

Syllabic verse, riming or assonating, develops, I think, internal rimes and the riming of monosyllables with the last syllables of long words. Of course the rules of rimes and the rest were never arbitrary. They were discovered. They are 'nature methodised'. The rimes are as accidental as anything in such a matter can be. The grace occurs first by that accident of the wind blowing where it listeth; and then, being observed, the grace is sought again. In Old Irish, syllabic verse reached great perfection. I give as an example the first stanza of a poem written by a monk, a scribe, of his cat:

> *Messe ocus Pangur ban*
> *cecthar nathar fria saindan;*
> *bith a menma-sain fri seilgg*
> *mu menma céin im saincheirdd.*

It will be observed that the lines are all of seven syllables, that the first and third end in monosyllables and the second and fourth, riming with them in couplets, in words of two syllables. The constant rule in this particular kind of verse was that the second riming word should be a syllable longer than the first.

That is enough here about that wonderfully intricate thing, Gaelic versification. I leave it all the more willingly at this, as a certain over-insistence on its rarity has led many to think it the only virtue of Gaelic poetry. That such is not the case can be seen by anyone who reads, even in unadorned prose translation, poems like the dialogue between the King and the Hermit or Finn's Song of Summer or the Lament of the Old Woman of Beare.

Next to the effects of Gaelic metre and of modern Anglo-Irish speech comes the effect of Irish music.[7] The characteristic rhythms of Irish music are noticeable everywhere in the lyrics of the Irish Mode. In a poem like Ferguson's *Fairy Thorn* one can hear the notes of the dancing air – in the first stanza the beating of the feet to the music.

Note the different effect – the swaying with the wild sweet twist of the song – in such poems as *The Outlaw of Loch Lene* and Ferguson's translation, *Pashteen Finn*.[8] I remember once hearing this latter song sung in Irish by a large number of people in the South of

Ireland. The singers swayed their heads slightly in a slow, drowsy way; and the song went on through its full length, verses and chorus, without a break. When I read the poem now, the original or Ferguson's version, I find in it – read into it perhaps – that continuous swaying. In the same way my reading of *Loch Lene* is affected by the way in which the air to the third line refuses to stop at the end, but having taken breath on the penultimate syllable hurries without a pause into the next phrase.

So with a great number of Irish poems and of Anglo-Irish translations, imitations and original poems in that mode. We hear through them that music of our own. I am no exception – who can be? Here as I sit writing this on a morning of spring, in a place under the jurisdiction of the Dublin Corporation, in a garden full of flowers and thrushes, a boy is passing on the other side of my garden wall whistling a gay, rambling Irish dance tune. There are words to that tune. I do not know them; but I know that, Irish or English, they have that rambling way with them. I know too that some poet who hears that tune to-day or to-morrow is likely to be so haunted by the rhythm of it that he will lay the ghost of it by singing a song to it.

The earlier Anglo-Irish poets in whose work this mode is most obvious are Mangan and Ferguson. In recent times almost everyone who has written songs and lyrics has it somewhere or other. It cannot be attributed altogether to the actual music. Several masters of it have no ear for music proper, but this, I believe, means only that while deaf to the tone of the notes they are keenly sensible of the rhythm. As Coventry Patmore has remarked, the tattoo of a knuckle upon the table will lose most, if not all, of its rhythm if transferred to a bell. 'The drum', he says, 'gives rhythm, but the clear note of the triangle is nothing without another instrument, because it does not admit of an imagined variation.'[9] With these tune-deaf poets the imagined variation may exist in a piece of music as in the rattle of a railway train.

The most valuable and characteristic contribution to verse made by the Anglo-Irish poets, by Moore, Mangan, Ferguson, Hyde, Yeats and all, has been a contribution of melody, a music that at once expresses and evokes emotion. In the whole body of their literature you find scarcely a true poem which, in the words of the book reviewers, treats adequately a serious subject. Of course this may be said of the purely lyric poets of all ages and countries. It is the epic and dramatic poets, to say nothing of the didactic, who write formal addresses to Light and to the Sun, who discuss at length the question of immortality, to be or not to be, the question of medicine for a mind diseased. Allusions to all these you will find in the Irish lyric – more than that, sudden illuminations, that illumination of knowledge which again is one of the marks of the true poet – *imbas forosna*.

> Three things through love I see,
>   Sorrow and sin and death –
> And my mind reminding me
>   That this doom I breathe with my breath.
>
> But sweeter than violin or lute
>   Is my love, and she left me behind –
> I wish that all music were mute,
>   And I to all beauty were blind.[10]

When Irish poets write the new epics of this nation and the new poetic drama of the coming years, we shall, no doubt, have plenty of those treatments of serious subjects. At present a search for the like would bring us only the moralizings of poetasters, the obvious and the devious, the things so plainly seen in our path that they so not need description or indication, or so out of the way, so far-fetched, that they recall nothing in our experience.

Study 7

The Lyric of the Irish Mode

‘*The literature of a race goes at first to the pails of those who have previously drawn from the well of life of its parent race. Chaucer is full of translations from the work of his own people, the Normans ... So we are expressing ourselves in translating from the Irish.*’

7

OR THE PRESENT the best poetry of the Irish Mode that we can find
is in lyric form, the expression of the individual emotion. Worth
notice in connection with this are the frequent fine use and the frequent
misuse of the dramatic lyric form. The form is almost as old in Ireland
as poetry itself, but only modernly, I think, has it had the intense
human thrill of individual subtle character. Early Irish poems of this
sort are more direct; they often begin with the simple announcement
of the speaker's name, and then tell in those vivid nervous lines of
the *dán díreach* clear and simple thoughts of passion or emotion –
poems that translate so literally into all languages that they appear
almost too simple.[1] The monologue of Eve published in *Eriu* by Dr
Meyer is a good example of this:

> Mé Eba ben Adaimh uill,
> Mé rosháirigh Íosa thall,
> Mé róthall nemh ar mo chloinn,
> Cóir is mé dochóidh's a crand.
>
> Roba lem rightegh dom réir,
> Olc in mithoga romthár,
> Olc in cosc cinad romchrín,
> Forír! ní hiodan mo lamh.
>
> Ní biadh eighredh in gach dú,
> Ní biadh geimreadh gaothmar glé,
> Ní biadh iffern, ní biadh brón,
> Ní biadh omun, minbadh mé.
>
> > *Mé*

> I am Eve, great Adam's wife,
> I that wrought my children's loss,

I that wronged Jesus of life,
Mine by right had been the cross.

I a kingly house forsook:
Ill my choice and my disgrace:
Ill the counsel that I took,
Withering me and all my race.

I that brought the winter in,
And the windy, glistening sky:
I that brought terror and sin,
Hell and pain and sorrow, I.

I

I quote and translate the first, second and fourth stanzas of this Old Irish poem of the tenth century (of its four stanzas I have omitted one which I think worthless): my translation is very close to the original. To indicate a departure I translate literally the last three lines: 'There would not be winter, windy, clear, there would not be hell, there would not be sorrow, there would not be terror, were not I.'

No poem of just that dramatic nature is to be found in any collection of Anglo–Irish poetry, in any such anthology as *The Dublin Book of Irish Verse*, 1728-1909. In the first part of the book there is indeed no poem at all resembling it. This dramatic lyric has had to evolve again in Ireland in this new poetry of the foreign tongue; something of it has come with the language in which it is now written, something from the Irish through translation and transmission.

The opening poem of the *Dublin Book* is Goldsmith's 'When lovely woman stoops to folly'. In his book on Browning, Mr G. K. Chesterton has an apt note on this:

In Palgrave's *Golden Treasury* two poems, each of them extremely well known, are placed side by side; and their juxtaposition represents one vast revolution in the poetical manner of looking at things. The first is Goldsmith's almost too well known *When Lovely Woman Stoops to Folly*. Immediately after comes, with a sudden and thrilling change of note, the voice of Burns – *Ye banks and braes o' bonnie*

Doon. They are two poems on exactly the same subject, and the whole difference is this fundamental difference, that Goldsmith's words are spoken about a certain situation and Burns' words are spoken in that situation.

Such too in general is the contrast between the poems of this representative anthology of Anglo-Irish verse and the poems at the end. The younger poets are personal, their poems are things 'felt in the blood'; their poems are not merely poetical songs; they sing out of the heart of the situation. And it is with this very merit that the fault comes, the abuse of personal, something which misses the justification of exuberance at its extreme, something which is too literally expressed to be other than literal, and which, if literal, is untrue. Within my limits it is impossible without injustice to deal with evident examples. In spite of all qualifications I should seem to generalise, to condemn some authors of this as a constant fault. So I go outside and to the past for an example of my meaning, and take a well-known English poem, that most frequently quoted of W. E. Henley's:

Out of the night that covers me,
    Black as the pit from pole to pole,
I thank whatever gods may be
    For my unconquerable soul.

In the fell clutch of circumstance
    I have not winced nor cried aloud,
Under the bludgeonings of chance
    My head is bloody, but unbow'd.

Beyond this place of wrath and tears
    Looms but the horror of the shade,
And yet the menace of the years
    Finds, and shall find me, unafraid.

It matters not how strait the gate,
    How charged with punishments the scroll,
I am the master of my fate,
    I am the captain of my soul.

This to many readers seems the cry of a strong man 'in the fell clutch of circumstance'; and when they know of the poet's sufferings and refer this to his actual life they admire it the more. I have talked with some who knew Henley, and know that they regarded him as a strong man with a great personality. But the poem, full of fine phrases and all as it is, is wrong and unworthy of a great personality – the poem thus personal, thus autobiographical in form, thus boastful. The poem, whether directly personal or dramatic, rings false. The strong man is strong in character and conduct, not braggart in words. If he claim for himself such courage and self-reliance, it is by way of protest and denial to one who has doubted these things in him. But a protest addressed to the unseen, unheard God – to 'whatever gods may be' – is vain, not meant to be heard by ears divine, but to be over-heard by human. It becomes the boast of a vain man, useless so made. The poem I believe to be the work of a weak, conventional, self-flattering mood of the poet's. And it might have been so good a poem in another form, a tribute so splendid if written of another man, so fine an honour to the poet himself as man and poet!

> In the fell clutch of circumstance
>   He had not winced, nor cried aloud,
> Under the bludgeonings of chance
>   His head was bloody, but unbow'd.
>
> It mattered not how strait the gate,
>   How fraught with punishments the scroll,
> He was the master of his fate,
>   He was the captain of his soul.

So in some of the dramatic lyrics of our younger Irish authors the statement as of personal experience and of personal feeling spoils the sincerity or at least spoils our pleasure. I would not be taken as denying in any way the claim of the dramatic lyric and the dramatic monologue to the justification of imaginative rightness. The poetic is rarely identical with the personal *ego*. Good poetry is rarely, if ever, an exact copy. Intuition gives more to a poem than the record of actual experience. The potential lover, if he may be called so, or the potential vagabond, being a poet, will write as fine love poems or as fine wander poems as the lover or vagabond of experience. If the lover or vagabond of experience do write fine poems wrung out of life, still the imagination is more at the expense of them than anything else – the imagination and the interpretative faculty. For, once more, poetry is an interpretation, an illumination, and not a narrative. It recalls, it recollects in tranquillity, it suggests, it brings a light, it brings a key. Born of joy, it happily and spontaneously communicates gladness. Born of sorrow, it raises sorrow to the crown of sorrow through sympathy, in exultation.

Poetry interprets by philosophy, wisdom in great words; by knowledge through the selection of experience; by knowledge through the gesture of life, dramatic; by knowledge through intuition always, the plenary vision; by a flash of expression that a word gives, that a rime brings, suggested by a whim of the mind, by a dream of the night, by a colour in the sky, by an air of music, by a mute animal, by a chance word, by a word half heard, by a word misread, by a mistranslation – suggested by such, but suggested to the poet who is the *vates*, the seer, the interpreter, and then the maker, the poet who is the voice of his time.

Those of our writers who bring this interpretation to sincere words, narrative or dramatic, will be the voice of this time; those who assume tones of actual record and then outrage credence will be no such thing.

My going to an anthology thus for examples is symptomatic of our critical attitude now. Palgrave's *Golden Treasury* has had a profound effect on the modern criticism of lyric poetry. But in the anthologies of Anglo-Irish verse we find the symptoms of another thing – the futility of culling and choosing yet. We have now two full-dress anthologies, the Brooke-Rolleston *Treasury of Irish Poetry*, made in 1900, and Mr John Cooke's *Dublin Book*, 1909, just mentioned. In addition we have Mr W. B. Yeats' *Book of Irish Verse*, a personal choice made in 1895, now very inadequate, and Mr Padraic Gregory's *Modern Irish Poetry*, which includes only the work of writers of the present day.

Let it be said at once that an anthology of poetry, especially a large anthology, represents the average man's choice – not that the compilation is in general the work of the average man, but that it is prepared for such. No anthology can absolutely please any lover of poetry but the compiler, and him only for a time; no lover of poetry is average. Anthologies are of two kinds; they are either books of poetry, poems chosen purely for the poems' sake, ' the best though a hundred critics say so', or else books of poets, in part records of literary history or of literary development. Mr Stopford Brooke in his introduction to the Brooke-Rolleston *Treasury of Irish Poetry* claims that such a book must necessarily be of the second class.

> When the book was first projected I wished to include nothing in it which did not reach a relatively high standard of excellence. But I soon discovered that the book on these lines would not represent the growth or the history of Irish poetry in the English language.

Similarly Mr Cooke's *Dublin Book of Irish Verse*, intended to be final, exhaustive and representative of the growth of Anglo-Irish poetry, must be judged by this standard. Of its five hundred and forty poems there are less than a hundred that I should include in my choice of the purest pure; but apart from that one must be glad that Mr Cooke has included a host of poems that have other claims – the street ballads and the humorous songs and the swinging poems of nationality. The book is, up to Douglas Hyde and the older living writers – that is, as far as any book can be – final, exhaustive and representative. No compiler will again, I hope, go over the early part of the work; that is so much definitely put in its place, and for that reason so much done for the future as well as for the past.

No such justification as Mr Stopford Brooke has claimed for his book can be allowed to an anthology of contemporary verse. Yet a book like Mr Padraic Gregory's would need even a better justification for its existence. Poems of little intrinsic value may have an historic value if they come early and prove to be originals of better work later. But contemporary poems of little intrinsic value should have no value to the anthologist. Mr Gregory has three worthless poems for every one worthy poem in his book, and so has failed to produce the good book that many had looked for. If his failure be a warning to others and save us for a time from anthologists, it may be well for poetry.

In connection with this subject it is only just to mention Miss Eleanor Hull's *Poem Book of the Gael*, a volume of translations from the Irish done by many hands. Though the book is full of faults, and some of Miss Hull's own translations are very bad, the book is a far

finer treasury of poetry than any of the Anglo-Irish anthologies. It is
drawn from the lyric poetry of a full literature, though to us a literature
in fragments.

Poetry does not bear kindly the shackles of the anthologist:
criticism is wronged by him. He sets up a standard of niceness. He
sets up a false standard of clarity. For the clarity of prose is not the
clarity of poetry; and poets must not be struck dumb by the catch-
cry, obscurity. The true poet will not indeed be struck dumb by any
catch-cry; but others may have their ears filled by such and may be
kept longer than they otherwise would be from listening to the poet's
word. 'There are two kinds of obscurity', writes Mr Joseph Plunkett,

> the obscurity of Art and the obscurity of Nature. They may be
> called the obscurity of mist and the obscurity of mystery. They
> have nothing in common. They are opposed as the poles.
>
> A thing may be hidden by Art in two ways. It may be overlaid
> with irrelevancies, or its expression may be restrained to the
> point of poverty. The effect is the same. The essentials are
> hidden. In Nature also (but by Nature we mean not so much
> apparent Nature as real Nature) there are two ways by which
> things may be hidden. They may become so common as not to
> be regarded, or they may be so uncommon as not to permit
> regard. They may be as universal as light or as unique as the
> sun. Observation involves comparison, and that which is
> entirely universal or absolutely unique – or both – cannot be
> compared with anything.
>
> An artist is one who has the power of unveiling Nature, only
> to substitute the veils of Art. Indeed it is by imposing the veils
> of Art that he is enabled to show the real qualities and relations
> of things. For the veils of Art need not be obscure. The vision
> of the artist if of such a kind that it penetrates these veils and
> thus can view the realities underlying them that otherwise could
> not be confronted. It is through his Art that the artist sees.
>
> The artist's task, however, is to make others see; for all Art
> is revelation. This he does chiefly by the great instrument of
> inspiration, Choice. He chooses the portion or phase of Truth
> that he is to reveal, and he chooses the veils that he must impose
> in order to make that Truth visible. Here it is that the artist is
> liable to obscurity. He is apt to lose the consciousness of his

purpose of revelation to others in the overwhelming devotion that the vision requires. Then is it that the quality of his inspiration decides the nature of the obscurity that is certain to result. If his vision be powerful and his inspiration deep he will choose to scale the topless peaks of beauty and attempt to set down the splendour of the spreading plains of Truth. He will fail to clothe his vision with the necessary veils. His work will have the obscurity of Nature. If, on the other hand, his inspiration be more subtle and superficial, running hither and thither in intricate mazes of wonder, he will multiply veils on detailed portions of his subject, adding one to another according as the various points of view and possible relations of parts come within his cognizance. His work will have the obscurity of Art.[2]

In his essay on Coleridge, Francis Thompson says: 'There is not one great poet who has escaped the charge of obscurity, fantasticalness, or affectation of utterance.' With Mr Plunkett we may ask, Is there one great poet who has not deserved the charge of obscurity? With him we may answer that if we limit the charge to that kind of obscurity that he has called the obscurity of Nature or of Mystery, then to our knowledge there is none.

For the purpose of criticism here I would say part of that in another way of the young poet. He takes for known and seen by others things apparent to him only. He begins by being the seer. He becomes the interpreter and so the maker, when he learns to express the creature of his vision as it must inevitably be expressed for himself, and in a code known to others too. But it is better that a young poet should have a vision and express it only for himself than that he should have only the conventional novel things worn by all the poetic of his time. He may set too high a value on the secret phases of his vision. The best is that which is universal. The poet finds himself when he gives himself.

And these obscure young poets are not all of one kind. Like many things that I have mentioned here, like all the men and matters of the universe, these poets may be divided into two classes. There are those who begin by being accomplished and come to power along the road which leads to straight simplicity, and those who begin by stammering, those who have slowly to master the craft. The former

sing in well-ordered words things known to them in all details,
unknown or strange to others. The latter are obscure because of their
incoherency, their difficulty of utterance.

I have dealt at this length with obscurity in order to set right in a
little way that wrong trend of our time to discuss easily as obscure
much very sincere good work of young poets in Ireland. In one other
way their work is almost of necessity obscure to all but students of
Irish literature and those brought up in the Irish tradition. To us there
is a world of memory in these lines of Padraic Colum's *Drover:*

> Then the wet winding roads,
> Brown bogs and black water,
> And my thoughts on white ships
> And the King of Spain's daughter.

Others might well ask, Which King of Spain? Why white ships?
and find nothing but suggestions of unpleasantness in the thought of
wet roads, brown bogs and black water. I suppose one has to be
baptised Irish to feel the right thing, as to be sure one should be
baptised Russian to feel rightly all the beauty of Russian song, or
changed into Chinese to accept seriously and simply the craft of the
Chinese stage.

And there is the other great cause of obscurity. I have spoken
earlier of the mystic element in Anglo-Irish poetry. Literature, and
in consequence, criticism, have been so long rationalistic that mystical
poetry is almost of necessity obscure to most readers. Most readers
of poetry expect clear plain statements to have to do only with what
they would call plain things, things known to the outward senses. If
a poet makes a clear plain statement about any other thing – if he
says that he saw eternity or heard the voice of God – which every
heart must hear – or felt in his hands the fruit of the tree of good and
evil, he is supposed to be poetising, to be saying in a hard way
something that he might have said in an easy way if he liked, or else
something that is mere nonsense and that should not be said at all.
He is asked for an interpretation. It scarcely ever occurs to readers to
credit the poet simply. And of course that is not wonderful. Since the
old days of 'Unknowing' in the fourteenth century,[3] the English
language has had little mystical use, and the terms of sense and wit

now are good in the main only for the expression of the intellectual, not of the intuitive, faculties. Most readers will find it difficult or impossible to enter the world of the mystic, as in that of all worlds it is only experience that teaches, and experience cannot be taught. There vanity is vain indeed; pride always has a fall. Every mystic has used things known to the outward senses as figures of the unknown unknowable with which the soul identifies itself in contemplation. For this he often uses that puzzling form, paradox: this identity, which is absolute knowledge not arrived at by reason, makes him know the unknown.

> The middle of the things I know
> Is the unknown, and circling it
> Life's truth and life's illusion show
> Things in the terms of sense and wit.
>
> Bounded by knowledge thus, unbound,
> Within the temple thus, alone,
> Clear of the circle set around,
> I know not, being with the unknown.
>
> But images my memories use
> Of sense, and terms of wit employ,
> Lest in the known the unknown lose
> The secret tidings of my joy.

It is for the sake of criticism that I make this plea for the credit of mysticism in our poetry, not for the sake of poetry or of the poets, to whom that credit does not matter at all. They have the illumination and the joy.

The failure of readers has been due to yet another cause than the mystery of these poets: I mean the rather similar use of language to a different end. Lord Dunsany, who writes a beautiful imaginative prose, wants to say that in the evening silence settles on the earth, and is broken only by the cries of the night birds and night beasts. He wants to say too that the law which governs this fall of silence and this breaking of the silence of the night is a mysterious and divine law. He says:

And when it is dark, all in the Land of Tirboogie (the Lord of Dusk) Hish creepeth from the forest, the Lord of Silence, whose children are the bats who have broken the command of their father, but in a voice that is ever so low Hish husheth the mouse and all the whispers in the night; he maketh all noises still. Only the cricket rebelleth. But Hish hath sent against him such a spell that after he hath cried a thousand times his voice may be heard no more but becometh part of the silence.

And when he hath slain all sounds Hish boweth low to the ground; then cometh into the house, with never a sound of feet, the god Yoharneth-Lahai.

But away in the forest whence Hish hath come, Wohoon, the Lord of Noises in the Night, awaketh in his lair and creepeth round the forest to see whether it be true that Hish hath gone.

Then in some glade Wohoon lifts up his voice and cries aloud, that all the night may hear, that it is he, Wohoon, who is abroad in all the forest. And the wolf and the fox and the owl, and the great beasts and the small, lift up their voices to acclaim Wohoon. And there arise the sounds of voices and the stirring of leaves.[4]

Now readers easily understand that. It means a familiar thing, though expressed in an unfamiliar way. They easily believe that a mystic poem is expressing a familiar thing too, but in a way so unfamiliar as to be baffling. They think that the poet invents his images, not discovers. At worst they think that the poet does not himself know what he means or that he means nothing at all, winning confirmation from the poet when he says that he cannot express the thing otherwise, that he cannot simplify it into prose terms, that he cannot limit it to this application or that significance. Lord Dunsany and writers like him make mystery in a gracious way about plain things. The mystic simply states some well-known mystery. He tells of God or of immortality or of eternity. He reveals attributes, beauty or knowledge or power. He shows the significance of some common things, knowing them as emblems and symbols of things and powers in eternity. He tells a revelation made to him of something like the fall of man. His telling may be difficult, but if it is true it will be in clear terms, and will be understood by many from the first. Most of our mystic writings have been and will be in verse. The rhythm of verse is in itself an expression different from the too intellectualised use of words in prose.

The mystic poet indeed sometimes fears too easy intelligibility. 'In the manner of your verse', wrote Coventry Patmore to Francis Thompson, 'you are gaining in simplicity, which is a great thing. In the matter, I think you outstrip me. I am too concrete and intelligible. I fear greatly lest what I have written may not do more harm than good, by exposing Divine realities to profane comprehensions, and by inflaming popular esotericism'. Patmore learned his lesson from Father Gerard Hopkins, himself a rare and to some of us an exquisite poet. He sent the priest his book of mystical poems, *Sponsa Dei*, in manuscript, and on receiving it back with the simple comment, 'This is telling secrets', burnt it.[5]

One word more remains to say – of the importance, even the necessity, of translation in this literature of ours. Some of our poems from the Irish are re-creations. This is due immediately to the difference of metaphor in the two languages, and fundamentally to that greater difference of tradition, which is at once the cause and the sum and the effect of all our differences here. A phrase like 'the star of knowledge' in Douglas Hyde's translation *Ringleted Youth of My Love* has a value that can rarely be given to such metaphors in English poetry.

> I thought, O my love! you were so
> As the moon is, or sun on a fountain,
> And I thought after that you were snow,
> The cold snow on the top of the mountain:
>
> And I thought after that you were more
> Like God's lamp shining to find me,
> Or the bright star of knowledge before
> And the star of knowledge behind me.

The phrase thus literally rendered is unexpected and exciting in a strange language of different metaphors and different logic. The translations are in a way finer than the originals. The 'star of knowledge' has been used too often in Gaelic poems to have that new magic now. And other lines in the poem,

> Like a bush in a gap in the wall
> I am now left lonely without thee,

which are commonplace in Irish, have here a winning grace.

The literature of a race goes at first to the pails of those who have previously drawn from the well of life of its parent race. Chaucer is full of translations from the work of his own people, the Normans, and from writers among other people from whom his people derived culture. Elizabethan literature is full of translations and adaptations from older literatures in consonance with the new national life of England, not from the too Eastern or the too Western literatures. Shakespeare 'stole' all his plots and translated many of his sonnets and songs. Later poets derive from Chaucer, from Shakespeare and his contemporaries, from Milton. With the exception of the returned refugees to the court of Louis Quatorze, they no longer to any great extent find their originals abroad.

Our characteristic ways of thought and ways of life in Ireland have been expressed in Irish: other ways, which we have in common with other peoples, have been expressed in other languages. Mangan and Padraic Colum go to Arabic as well as to Irish for their originals. All of us find in Irish rather than in English a satisfying understanding of certain ways of ours and the best expression of certain of our emotions. So we are expressing ourselves in translating from the Irish. When we translate from the French we express Ronsard, say, a man of a different climate at least and of a different complexity of civilization, a man who warns his lady that her maids long hence of a drowsy evening, carding wool, will start at the name of the poet who sings her praises now, warns her that she will regret her proud disdain while he, a pale phantom, will haunt the myrtle shades.[6]

This is a different world, even in the version of Mr Yeats, from that of Raftery the poet full of hope and of love, playing music to empty pockets, from the deck of Patrick Lynch's boat sailing from the County of Mayo, different from Cashel of Munster, different from the Hill of Howth, 'clear Ben above a sea of gulls', different the whole distance between comfort and the outlawry of our kith, from the world of that untranslateable *Eamonn an Chnuic*, which yet we would all translate.[7] The national rose of Ireland is *An Róisin Dubh*, the Little Black Rose, not the tender red flower to be plucked with the joys of life.[8]

At present a large amount of translation is natural. Later, when we have expressed again in English all the emotions and experiences expressed already in Irish, this literature will go forward, free from translation. Through the English language has come a freshening breath from without: with the Gaelic Renaissance has come a new stirring of national consciousness: these two have been the great influences in all new literatures. At that I can leave it, at that freshening and that stirring of it. It is well for us that our workers are poets and our poets workers. 'The more a man gives his life to poetry', said Francis Thompson, 'the less poetry he writes.' And it is well too that here still that cause which is identified, without underthought of commerce, with the cause of God and Right and Freedom, the cause which has been the great theme of our poetry, may any day call the poets to give their lives in the old service.

Study 8.1

Irish Literature: Ancient Ireland

'*Nothing could be more clear, more direct, more gem-like, more surely true to nature, full of natural piety, nothing of another kind greater in suggestion, however brief in form. ... No other early literature has such a nature poetry, poetry so full of delicate, joyous observation, so wrought with delicate, light touch .... that the verse-forms are full of subtle beauty, that they are of great variety, ...*'

8.1

W HEN CANONS OF CRITICISM have been drawn from the works of
one antiquity and applied from age to age to all work of similar
kind, when side by side with the 'maker' has gone the critic and the
historian, it is at least difficult for an heir of these ages adequately at
once to judge the work of a different antiquity. When, moreover, it
has become part of the common thought that the style is the man,
when the work of a writer is, in the common mind, almost indissolubly
linked with a known personality, a body of fugitive lyrics, the work
of unknown men, cannot win recognition without very valid claims
of intrinsic merit. Modern European criticism has adopted, with
whatever modifications, canons drawn from the works of Greek and
Latin literature. It founds its admiration on these works. In them it
finds its touchstones of criticism. It has not broken from the hypnotism
of their old convention.

Example is the best definition. Some odes of Horace, with no
philosophy and no emotional appeal, with nothing of the thrill of
lyric singing, are still traditionally admired. The admiration is in part
due to the influence of the conventional criticism, which drew its
canons originally from work of the tradition in which the poet wrote,
and which now applies these canons to that work. In part also it is
due to the influence of the known personality. For in such a case the
man is the thing just as much as the play, as much as the poem. The
anonymous songs have their place, but the literatures, as literatures,
are judged by the great names. To use again the example of Horace,
we know more of him and his time than we know of the life and
times of many modern poets. We think of him in terms of his *urbanitas*
and his *curiosa felicitas*; still he may prophesy as of old:

ego postera
crescam laude recens,

for always we admire his modernness, a quality which may as well
be shown in the interpretation of some ancient artificiality which

has lived on into our modern civilisation, as in the expression of some old natural emotion of the heart of man. So we go to our Horace, so we go to our Villon, the scapegrace; so we go to some or other 'marvellous boy', some 'sleepless soul.'[1] Consciously or unconsciously, we are influenced in reading Keats by the thought of his twenty-five years.

The Gaelic Renaissance is only beginning. It can never be of just the same importance and influence as the Classic. It goes back to a literature of a different kind from the Greek and Latin, a literature almost entirely anonymous, a literature without epic or dramatic verse, a literature, as far as poetry is concerned, of fragments – little personal poems, nature poems, religious poems, short dramatic monologues and dramatic lyrics interspersed in prose tales. And yet it has been claimed for this remnant of literature, and claimed by the best authority in the matter, Doctor Kuno Meyer, that as 'the earliest voice from the dawn of West European civilization, it is the most primitive and original among the literatures of Western Europe.' Most original, and of not least intrinsic worth. It is a fragment. It must not be judged as if it were a fragment of a literature of the Hellenic kind. The difference between Greek and Gael is no fiction. In the purely Gaelic-speaking places, the people to the present day have their ways of thought and life different from the ways of Hellenised Europe. The knowledge and the influence of Rome and, through Rome, of Greece has not been unknown, but the matter and the outlook and the manner of the old poems are native.

Native too is the reservation of the verse form for the use of lyric poetry. Because to say that the literature is without epic verse is not to say that it is without epic. The *Táin* is a literature in itself. The Gaelic imagination invented abundantly hero tales and tales of sorrow and humour such as others would have shaped into verse epic and tragedy and comedy. But prose was the natural vehicle for Gaelic narrative. In his essay, from which I have quoted (the introduction to his book of translations, *Ancient Irish Poetry*), Dr Meyer draws attention to the fact that in later centuries, when the Arthurian epics were done into Gaelic, they were all turned from verse into prose. This, if it prove anything, proves less a want of power than a sensitive sincerity. Verse epic and drama would have seemed to the Gaelic mind as founded on a convention of make-believe.

The Gaelic Renaissance means to us not only the revival of interest in this old Irish literature, the revival of interest in the civilization, the culture and the history of ancient Ireland, the enthusiasm, the adventure, the pride, the satisfaction, the emotion that are quickened by the discovery of the old monuments, but, added to these, the study of modern Irish as a language capable of literature, the interest in the fragments and traditions that have survived, the reconstruction of our new state on some of the old foundations, and so, patriotism. A recent writer has lamented that instead of the Classic there did not take place in the fourteenth century a Gaelic Renaissance. Of course, the lament and all discussion of it is futile. I listen dreamily to it. To the speakers of the Romance languages, to the readers of Romance literatures, the Classic Renaissance was such as to a strange people, who had seen only the statues of men of our race, would be the sight of the living models. The remarkable thing about the coming of the Classic Renaissance is not its coming in the fourteenth century, but its not coming earlier. The coming was inevitable. It was long prepared for.

And when we use the same word, Renaissance, for the Gaelic revival, springing from the rediscovery of the ancient language and literature, and branching now into a double literature in two languages, we do not claim that it is quite the counterpart of the Classic. The old literature that was to be discovered, the ancient Irish art, were not in such consonance even with what of literature and art we still held, as were Classic literature and art with those of mediaeval Europe, with the culture that still held allegiance to Rome and had memories of ancient Greece.

Still at the heart of that lament for a Gaelic Renaissance five hundred years ago is this truth, that if history had been different the ancient culture and the ancient literature of our people might have had a more powerful influence on the culture and literature of Europe. The Celtic peoples had kindred memories with ours though they had changed their speech. Of Gaelic influence in literature, in art, in music, there have always been the sure marks and the sure effects, as has been pointed out by Dr Sigerson and others;[2] but only during the last century has it come home and thriven.

This is not the place to attempt a history of the Revival. I propose here rapidly to survey portions of the literature of ancient Ireland and to come thence to the literature and the prospects of to-day. The poems of Old Irish are from eight to fourteen centuries old. There has been in the intervening period a steady enough stream of literature in Middle and Modern Irish; but my ignorance of all but a small amount of this and my sympathy with the way of the old time send me back to the beginning and then draw me home to the new age opening now.

The themes of Early Irish Literature are many of them the themes of modern romantic literature – in lyric poetry, nature and humanity:

nature: the joy of natural things; the joy of the earth's beauty, the woods and the birds in the woods; the delight of summer, season surpassing, grateful to dwellers in a northern land; the terror of the white winter when not a bell is heard and no crane talks, when shapes are all gone; the joy of the sea, the plain of Ler, with its witching song, the delightful home of ships, the image of Hell with its dread tempest;

humanity: men and women, love and destiny: humanity at odds with life: a king and a hermit; a girl who died for love; a warrior who kept his tryst after death; Deirdre, the predestined of sorrow, winning some joy from life before her fate falls; an old woman who has seen the passing away of her famous beauty, who sees the ebb-tide carrying away her years, who sees the flood-wave foaming in for others.

Later, after the English are settled in the land, not humanity but the nation, Kathleen Ni Houlihan, is our heroic theme. The manifestations of nationality are symbolised by man and nature. The silk of the kine goes lurking in the woods, weeping down tears, while her foe has wine on his table. The little shining rose is black. Ned of the Hill beats on the bolted door of the Nation; he is out under the snow, under the frost, under the rain, without comradeship, hunted with hail of bullets, desolate most of all at the thought that he must go east over the sea because it is there he has no kindred. No wonder that those who, lured by the felicity of gracious words, have learned to read with satisfaction in Shakespeare the easy hideous history of the English Wars of the Roses, half won to sympathy with ravening lust and barbarity, are perplexed by Gaelic Literature of the middle period. And so all Irish Literature is set down as vague, mysterious, obscure.

Nothing could be more clear, more direct, more gem-like, hard and delicate and bright, than the earlier lyric poetry, nothing more surely true to nature, full of natural piety, nothing of another kind greater in suggestion, however brief in form. Not till the advent of Wordsworth comes there anything like this intimacy with nature into other modern literature. Not till we listen to the voice of Shelley do we hear in other lyric poetry such prophecy of song as has come down through folk poetry in Irish, a lyric poetry which, as Mr John Eglinton said some years ago, 'has far more in common with the later developments of English poetry – with poems, for example, like Shelley's *When the Lamp is Shattered* or George Meredith's *Love in a Valley* – than anything produced by the wits of the London coffee houses.'[3]

The themes of the old sagas have been used by many in our day as the story of the Trojan war has been used by many nations that read Greek. Deirdre is to us

> the morning star of loveliness,
> Unhappy Helen of a western land.[4]

They have not been used as successfully as the Greek models. They are not the inheritance of this alien civilization. They require different standards. To quote Mr John Eglinton again: 'These subjects, much as we may admire them and regret that we have nothing equivalent to them in the modern world, obstinately refuse to be taken up out of their old environment, and be transplanted into the world of modern sympathies. The proper mode of treating them is a secret lost with the subjects themselves.'

It is possible, of course that, while I write, these *dicta* are being disproved. It would be vain, even if unluckily we wished it or could do it, to set bounds to literary genius, which is always breaking new soil, or rather always coming in a new manifestation. It is at its best and highest a new epiphany. Some in our day or after our day may make a great new literature in the tradition of this old world of Early Irish Literature.

But I rather expect that the literature of to-morrow will be in terms of the life of to-morrow, and that the old world is too different, too far apart. too much wronged now, I fear, by misrepresentation, by false praise that would make it good of another kind than of its way of goodness, by false blame that would call its culture barbarism, its strength brutality or impropriety, its mysticism magic, its austere sincerity in literature a defect of power and richness, its power and richness, when it has such, exaggeration.

We may admit that we cannot now feel those old emotions at first heart, so to put it. We have not reverence for the same things. We cannot pray to the old gods. We could not blaspheme the old gods. We are of a different day; a different light shines upon us. History is between us and our heroes. We cannot rid our memories of the glories and the calamities of our story, of the mighty things, of the futile things. Our thought is woven of the stuff of memory and elder thought and of a knowledge that has gained on this side and lost on that like an island in the sea. Our dreams are children dreams and parent dreams. A part of the old world lives in us; to a large part we are alien not in speech only but in feeling, in sense, in instinct, in vision.

We are true to the best of the old literature when we are true to that part of it which we inherit now in the twentieth century, when we discover in ourselves something of its good tradition, something that has remained true by the changing standards and measures.

I have quoted the phrase, 'the earliest voice from the dawn of West European civilization'; but I should not like to be taken as meaning that this old literature is a beginning in itself, a first stammering, a simple babbling of simple things on the lips of a people just articulate. It is probably nothing of the kind. These pieces are but stray survivors of stray written records of poems that strayed down for a long time by oral tradition. They were written in the Golden Age of Irish civilization, during the sixth, seventh and eighth centuries.[5] And even so only two or three poems have come down from those centuries in contemporary manuscripts. The records that we have are copies made long after. The language proves the earlier composition. Here then is still another point of difference between this lyric poetry and the classic of Greece and Rome.

And to point the difference we can take a parallel example from a different portion of the same literature. Professor Eoin MacNeill in the Introduction to his fine edition of the first part of *Duanaire Finn* (The Book of the Lays of Fionn) has shown that while one of the great Irish epics, the Ulidian cycle, became crystallised and assumed what may be called a classic form in the hands of the Milesian writers, the other, the Fenian cycle, remained always modern, constantly undergoing reformation, always popular.[6] For the full statement of this I must refer readers to the Introduction. To make clear my reference here I quote a few paragraphs.

> The Milesian writers, when they adopted the Ulidian hero-lore, adopted it as a classic, with all the extreme reverence shown by people new to any form of culture towards those from whom that culture is received, and by whom it has been developed. The Ulidian sagas, having once passed into the hands of the dominant race, became rigidly crystallized, and ceased to evolve. Most of the changes they afterwards suffered were due, not to invention, but to the limitations of the scribes.
>
> The early history of the Fenian hero-lore was quite different. The cycle remained in the possession of the subject races apparently until about the tenth century. As the Milesians, though masters of nearly all Ireland, never colonized more than about one-third of the country, the remaining two-thirds continuing in the occupation of the older races and under the rule of their native kings, it is evident that this epic of a subject race had an extensive public to whose sympathies it could present a strong appeal. Thus it must have spread from North Leinster, where it first took shape, through a large part of Ireland, ultimately reaching the furthest bounds of Gaelic speech. The period I postulate for this extension is the early centuries of Milesian domination, mainly between the years 400 and 700. During this time the Fenian tradition must have been purely oral, and therefore susceptible of local development to any extent. ...
>
> It may be asked why, if the Fenian cycle was thus spread over Ireland, and accessible to the Milesian writers at all points, it was not taken up by them in preference to the Ulidian cycle, which, until the seventh century, was confined to one remote district. The question has already been partly answered. The Ulidian cycle came armed with the great prestige of letters. But a still more potent reason must have operated. In the seventh century the Ulidians were a free race. ... A conquering and dominant aristocracy (the Milesians) would appreciate such a story of freemen coming from freemen. On the other hand, the Fenian epic was in form and essence the story of a vassal race ...

The history of the Fenian epic, as I have essayed to reconstruct it, offers an easy solution of several problems. It explains the form of the heroic narrative, and the peculiar role of the heroes. It explains the long-deferred appearance of the epic in written literature, and its forward state of development when at length it does appear. It explains also the almost exclusive popularity of the epic – its position for many centuries as the chief hero-lore of the Gaelic-speaking races of Ireland and Scotland.

The legend of the Fiana, as it spread from race to race, was constantly undergoing reformation, and at no time acquired, like the Ulidian story, a classic and final form. It remained always modern, not only in language, but in the sense of being entirely the property of each succeeding generation of story-tellers and ballad-makers.

Do I take from its honour in holding that we have not in Old, Middle and Modern Irish a complete, continued literature; that, excuse it as you may by the many good reasons of history, it is a literature thwarted and frustrate in many forms, and in the last two centuries or more a literature in decadence? Rather I think that I hold a higher hope in looking for a new literature from now. If the works of some of our contemporaries be not the first stammerings of a new literature that will have to go to school again, then they are the final senile babblings of one moribund.

To the eyes of criticism, Irish literature, after having suffered unparalleled persecution under the long terror of English rule, still suffers wrong even from its Irish admirers. It has in the first place been used as quarry by modern authors in English. The result, as I have pointed out, has not been fortunate. Deirdre, the subject of many plays, is an 'unhappy Helen' indeed.

Then it has suffered criticism from learned people who do not know the Irish language, who cannot tell their stories as eye-witnesses, who are at the mercy of faulty translators, faulty philologists, faulty expositors, and who thus give currency to mistakes, mistranslations and misconceptions. The great name of Matthew Arnold will save me from the anger of Miss Eleanor Hull whom I set down with him.

A third wrong that Irish literature has suffered is perhaps worse than these, being akin to the higher criticism. The old Irish hero-lore became to a degree fashionable at the same time as sun myths and the like. Now new religions are made out of half-understood passages of the old literature, India, of course, contributing whatever is not to be found in these. If anyone has a favourite theory of the invisible world, he can use the translation of an obscure old Irish poem for text. The English words used in the version are sure to lend themselves to the vague suggestion needed. In a similar way personages of the old tales are identified with gods of foreign mythologies; their strange acts and their strange motives are made stranger still, losing humanity. Life in some new redactions of the ancient sagas is not this familiar way that we all know, for all our differences of tradition and literature, this way of love, this way of wonder, this way of commerce.

A poet of the Irish Mode has declared that to Standish O'Grady he and his comrades owe their introduction to Celtic hero-lore.[7] The introduction then has been of a very special kind. Standish O'Grady is a poet who walks this earth as if it were another earth, who finds and proves it another. In him vision is more than sight. Such as he, in this mean time of compromise and commerce and materialism, may find it hard not to forget that all times are, for all we know, equally mean, and so, equally noble – mean to the low and noble to the high.

Poets in every generation regret the good times of a better past, seeing in the glass of death only the heavenly colours that the blessed have taken on, seeing sometimes in the glass of life only one commerce of their kind, the traffic of dross and the strife with hunger, and material utility in the mart out-bidding the ideal. Such a one may forget or may not believe that commerce, even this one commerce, has not only its material utility but also its glory, its intrepid adventure, its strangeness and richness of far-off lands and seas and peoples, and so, its culture of wonder and imagination, its fosterage of the arts. Such a one may forget or may not believe that this one commerce is the business set over against the dream, keeping the dream true. The shop-keeper of to-day is the father of the poet, of the hero, of the saint of to-morrow.

Standish O'Grady, too, searching for the ancient heroes, may have forgotten these and similar things, or may not have believed them. He is different from many who keep only them in mind. For the poets of the Irish Mode it was he that found the *dún* in which the wild riders of ancient Irish hero-lore were confined. It was he that let them forth, them or phantasies of them. Phantasies, some believe who have gone later into the *dún* and seen the riders there. The things that he let forth were viewed by alien moderns as Oisín was viewed by the convertites of Patrick, and by some that were pagan still. They were a wonder as they rode, and they sang in a strange tongue. The moderns who sought to set down in alien letters their semblance and their song told of vague romantic mystery about them. The others who have gone into the *dún* have known of no such mystery. They have listened to their song in its own language, and they hold that by the poets it has been misinterpreted quite. The poets have used the frame of Irish story as a frame whereon to weave the palpable stuff of their vision and their interpretation of the heroic in life. Their vision is a mistranslation; not for the first time has the world owed a beautiful thing to a mistranslation of genius. The original is a work of genius in another way of beauty.

And yet for all that I have said here, for all their error of half-heard words, the poets may be nearer to the rhythm of the ancient song than those of us who spell the words in full. Some of the ancient tales, some passages in the epics, are altogether incredible and impossible to our modern ways of thought and life here. May they not have other than their apparent meanings? They have the impossibility of the fairy tale. Perhaps they have the enduring truth of the fairy tale, of the parable, of the fable, which is truer than a history that owes so much to accident and whim and personality.

The characteristic qualities of the ancient Irish lyrics are those of good lyric poetry the world over. They have a simplicity which is never *simplesse*. They have a sincerity free from self-consciousness. Enemies of poetry as of truth are make-believe and pedantry and eloquence: essential to true poetry are sincerity and clarity. Newman defined literature as the personal use or exercise of language, for the expression, that is, of the personal vision or the individual emotion. Yet the vision and the expression of all but a few lack the distinction of poetry. The more distinct the vision, the more distinct the utterance of the emotion, the nearer is the utterance to poetry – granted always sincere distinction, not mere quaintness, above all not affectation or eccentricity. True freshness of outlook is rare in those who possess the use of reason; it is lost generally with the first teeth. And it is not only 'the light of common day' that destroys 'the vision splendid' seen in early youth; the hypnotists of convention throw over the eyes of all but a few a glamour of make-believe, and tune all tongues but a few in each age to their own accents.

As a rule posterity soon enough finds out sham in literature; ultimately it is sure to do so; but the hypnotism of a convention holds long at times; the spell of make-believe is not always as easily broken by the voice of a child as it was in Hans Andersen's tale of the Invisible Clothes. Words have a tradition that gives them a price and worth in currency apart from their weight and their intrinsic value. Those Odes of Horace, referred to by me at the beginning, inferior odes, have in them well done what a long line of poets has sought to do. But those odes to a fresh mind, not under the hypnotism, would seem merely fine words well set, and not poetry at all.

The ultimate great test I believe to be the test of translation or transmission. 'A thing well said', declares Dryden, 'will be wit in all languages.' The high things of the Scriptures, the words of Our Lord about considering the lilies of the field, are still poetry in all languages. When the language of their first expression is dead and the day of its most gracious felicities is over, they still live.

If Shakespeare's phrases refuse to translate beautifully into some tongues, it is that their beauty consists rather in felicity of words than in high poetry. All that is great in his dramatic power, in his creation of character, in his philosophy, will be great in other languages, only indeed less great for want of that Shakespearean diction. On the other hand, some things, in verse, are finer when translated into a language like English than in their original, finer in their translation by Arthur O'Shaughnessy than in their original French of Sully Prudhomme, finer on an occasion (as I have shown above) in the English of Douglas Hyde than in their original Irish.

But this new consideration would draw me aside from those essentials of true poetry which must be re-stated before we can duly criticize Irish poetry – and re-stated clearly, in terms which may seem almost too obvious. How otherwise may one state clarity?

The object of language is to express something. The clearer the expression, the more successful it is. All the great things of literature that live are clear, however obscure to a passing age, even their own, blinded by false knowledge. They are terse and sufficient, yet with great lucid beauty, with the authentic accent of true knowledge, of true feeling, of true interpretation.

Perhaps the clarity of some of them seemed in their first day a fault. A critic has written of the 'terrible simplicity' of Catullus. To some of his contemporaries the poetry of Catullus may have seemed bald and obvious, wanting in the graces of art. On the other hand, Matthew Arnold's famous 'touchstones',[8] though sometimes examples rather of felicity than of the high seriousness of poetry, have all this clarity.

But it is as unjust to take such single lines as it is difficult to find a complete lyric poem that has in all its lines the true accent. To go aside for a moment, one may say that the little prayer to the Blessed Virgin, quoted by Dr Hyde in *The Religious Songs of Connacht* is such, and such that old English carol of the Nativity to which it has so curious a resemblance. Though full of this gracious clarity, the two poems are for the rest slight. The English poet plays with a conceit:

> I sing of a maiden
>   That is makeless;
> King of all kings
>   To her son she ches.
>
> He came al so still,
>   There his mother was
> As dew in April
>   That falleth on the grass.
>
> He came al so still
>   To his mother's bour,
> As dew in April
>   That falleth on the flour.
>
> He came al so still
>   There his mother lay,
> As dew in April
>   That falleth on the spray.
>
> Mother and maiden
>   Was never none but she;
> Well may such a lady
>   Goddes mother be.[9]

This little carol is duly honoured in anthologies, and praised by critics as a matchless specimen of lyric simplicity, yet almost casually An Craoibhin[10] quotes a poem as simple and as exquisite, taken from the lips of a fisher-boy in Aran of Connacht:

> A Mhuire na nGrás,
>   A Mhathair Mhic Dé,
> Go gcuire tú
>   Ar mo leas mé.
>
> Go sabhála tú mé
>   Ar gach uile olc,
> Go sabhála tú mé
>   Idir anam is corp.
>
> Go sabhála tú mé
>   Ar muir is ar tír,
> Go sabhála tú mé
>   Ar lic na bpian.
>
> Gárda na n-aingeal
>   Os mo chionn,
> Dia romham
>   Agus Dia liom.

(O Mother of Graces, O Mother of the Son of God, put thou me on the way of my welfare.

Save thou me from every ill. Save thou me both body and soul. Save thou me on land and on sea. Save thou me from the flag of pains.

Be the guard of the Angels over my head, God before me and God with me).

This is a modern poem. Ancient Irish poetry has many such pieces, though in general the religious verses are more woven, so to say, like the Even-Song of Saint Patrick:

> May the holy angels, O Christ, son of the living God,
> Guard our sleep, our rest, our shining bed.

> Let them reveal true visions to us in our sleep,
> O high prince of the universe, O great Being of the mysteries.
>
> May no demons, no ill, no calamity or terrifying dreams
> Disturb our rest, our willing, prompt repose.
>
> May our watch be holy, our work, our task,
> Our sleep, our rest without let, without break.[11]

It is in the little quotations and poems of accident, as it were, that is least adorned that clear, sincere, colloquial statement. These for all of us express things with the strange rightness of lyric beauty, once and for all. In the *Thesaurus Palæohibernicus,* at the end of the long Glosses, one finds the little poem written on the margin of a page in the St. Gall *Priscian*:

> *Domfarcai fidbaidae fál,*
> *Fomchain lóid luin luad nad cél*[12]

The modern spirit has tried to invent in a manner a personality for the monk who wrote that, interrupting his copying or his study of Priscian to listen to the bird. Doctor Sigerson himself, usually most faithful of translators, has added something in the last lines:

> May God on high thus love me
> Thus approve me, all unseen.

Miss Eleanor Hull in her book uses not Doctor Sigerson's translation but one of her own, ending also:

> Within my wall of green
> My God shrouds me, all unseen.

There is no 'thus' and no 'all unseen' in the original. I give Whitley Stokes' translation of the eight lines:

> A hedge of trees surrounds me, a blackbird's lay sings to me –
> praise which I will not hide. Above my booklet, the lined one,
> the trilling of the birds sings to me. In a grey mantle the cuckoo

sings to me from the top of the bushes. May the Lord protect
me! I write well under the greenwood.

This is the poem stripped of all its grace of verse. If the great test
of poetry be, as I have suggested, translation or transmission, it is
still exquisite; but in Irish it has something that not even the best
verse translation into a modern language can give it. Alliteration in a
language like English is different from the alliteration of this. The
seven syllables to the line of an exact English version would not
have the fall of these seven. English rime would not give to the ear
these rigidly governed assonances.

This little poem is useful to illustrate points of criticism, but is
not a specimen of the best ancient Irish poetry, nature poetry. No
other early literature has such a nature poetry, poetry so full of delicate,
joyous observation, so wrought with delicate, light touch –

Summer is come, winter is gone; twisted hollies wound the hound.
The blackbird sings a full strain, to him the live wood is a heritage,
the sad angry sea sleeps, the speckled salmon leaps.   ...

The harp of the forest sounds music, the sail gathers – perfect peace;
colour has settled on every height, haze on the lake of full waters....

Cold till Doom! ... The fish of Ireland are roaming, not a town there
is in the land, not a bell is heard, and no crane talks.   ...

When the wind sets from the north, it urges the dark fierce waves,
surging in strife against the wide sky, listening to the witching song.

'It is characteristic of these poems', says Doctor Meyer, 'that in
none of them do we get an elaborate or sustained description, but
rather a succession of impressionist pictures and images. The half-
said thing to them is dearest; they avoid the obvious and the commonplace.' They do better – they avoid the devious, the out of the way,
and the thing of false imagination.

How satisfying, how familiar, and yet how new to us in literature
is that wonderful enumeration in the colloquy between Marbhan and
Guaire:[13]

Mád fri samrad   suairc snóbrat
    somblas mblas,
curar, orcáin,   foltáin glaise,
    glaine glas,

and the rest.

> When pleasant summer time spreads its coloured mantle,
>   Sweet-tasting fragrance!
> Pignuts, wild marjoram, green leeks –
>   Verdant pureness!
>
> The music of the bright red-breasted men,[14]
>   A lovely movement!
> The strain of the thrush, familiar cuckoos
>   Above my house,
>
> Swarms of bees and chafers, the little musicians of the world,
>   A gentle chorus:
> Wild geese and ducks, shortly before summer's end –
>   The music of the dark torrent.

Of a higher mood than the nature poems are such pieces as that
which Doctor Meyer calls *The Tryst after Death*, of a higher mood
too than the justly-praised old English ballads. It is a poem of the
ninth century. The spirit of the slain warrior keeps the tryst with the
woman for whom he has died:

> Hush, woman, do not speak to me! My thoughts are not with
>   thee.
> My thoughts are still in the encounter at Feic.
>
> My bloody corpse lies by the side of the Slope of the Two
>   Brinks;
> My head all unwashed is among the warrior-bands in fierce
>   slaughter.
>
> It is blindness for any one making a tryst to set aside the tryst
>   with Death:

The tryst that we made at Claragh has been kept by me in pale death. ...

Some one will at all times remember this song of Fothad Canann;
My discourse with thee shall not be unrenowned, if thou remember my bequest.

Since my grave will be frequented, let a conspicuous tomb be raised;
Thy trouble for thy love is no loss of labour.

My riddled body must now part from thee a while, my soul to be tortured by the black demon.
Save for the worship of Heaven's king, love of this world is folly.

I hear the dusky ousel that sends a joyous greeting to all the faithful:
My speech, my shape are spectral – hush, woman, do not speak to me!

Of one other old poem I shall speak at length. It is the *Lament of the Old Woman of Beare*, which one likens at once to *Les Regrets de la Belle Hëaulmière*. A detailed comparison of the two, however, would only show to us again the difference between the two civilizations.

La belle qui fut hëaulmière is a courtesan who looks back over a wanton life with a cry of:

Que m'en reste il? Honte et pechié!

and then contrasts all her lost loveliness with the disgrace of her body in old age, and so, with other old women, regrets the past:

Ainsi le bon temps regretons ...
Et jadis fusmes si mignotes
Ainsi en prent à mains et maintes.

The Lament of the Old Woman of Beare, written five hundred years before Villon, has lines very like the French poem:

> My arms when they are seen
> Are bony and thin.

But how different is the whole life of the poem, which is an allegory and a miracle. 'The reason why she was called the Old Woman of Beare' (I quote Kuno Meyer's translation again), 'was that she had fifty foster-children in Beare. She had seven periods of youth one after another, so that every man who had lived with her came to die of old age, and her grandsons and great-grandsons were tribes and races. For a hundred years she wore the veil which Cummin had blessed upon her head. Thereupon old age and infirmity came to her. 'Tis then she said:

> Ebb-tide to me as of the sea!
> Old age causes me reproach. ...
>
> My body with bitterness has dropt
> Towards the abode we know:
> When the Son of God deems it time
> Let Him come to deliver His behest. ...
>
> The wave of the great sea talks aloud,
> Winter has arisen:
> Fermuid the son of Mugh to-day
> I do not expect on a visit.
>
> I know what they are doing:
> They row and row across
> The reeds of the Ford of Alma –
> Cold is the dwelling where they sleep.
>
> 'Tis, O my God!
> To me to-day, whatever will come of it.
> I must take my garment even in the sun:
> The time is at hand that shall renew me.

All through the poem is kept the image of the tide:

> The flood-wave
> And the second ebb-tide –
> They have all reached me,
> So that I know them well.
>
> The flood-wave
> Will not reach the silence of my kitchen:
> Though many are my company in darkness,
> A hand has been laid upon them all.
>
> O happy isle of the great sea
> Which the flood reaches after the ebb!
> For me
> Flood does not come after ebb.

Many modern writers have attempted verse translations of the Lament; the best that I know is a fragment of eight lines quoted in an interesting little pamphlet, *A Talk about Irish Literature* by *An Gae Bolga* (Dublin: Gill, 1907):

> Ebb-tide to me,
> For with the ebbing sea my life runs out,
> Old age has caught and compassed me about,
> I mourn the glad youth passed away from me.
>
> The flood-wave thine,
> Mine but the swift back-flowing ebb-tide's call.
> Out of my hand the ebb-tide carries all,
> Towards thee the flood-wave foams across the strand.

In dealing with these poems I have avoided all reference to metrics. I might indeed have added metrical study of the poems to the things mentioned above as having wronged appreciation for the poetry. As I have said in an earlier study, too much ado has been made of Gaelic metres; or rather, for want of due criticism and appreciation, the good metrical consideration has won undue prominence. Many in consequence think that Gaelic poetry is all a *chinoiserie* of intricate word-weaving, with no message that matters. It is sufficient to say that the verse-forms are full of subtle beauty, that they are of great variety, and that, as Eugene O'Curry pointed out long ago, the rhythmical structure of many of them exactly corresponds with the structure of Irish musical compositions of the highest antiquity.

Of the old claim that to Ireland Europe owes rime I have written elsewhere,[15] also of the nature of assonance, which is in Irish, as the late Professor Atkinson of Dublin University said, 'not imperfect rime, but something far richer than rime, and admitting of a far more complex series of harmonies.'[16] I can the better omit consideration of this because the work has been so well done by many able hands in our day – by Meyer, by Hyde, by Sigerson, most notably. For the rest no one need fear not to appreciate the best of the old lyrics for ignorance of the rules of their verse. The one simple reading rule laid down by MacNeill in his Introduction to *Duanaire Finn* will suffice for these:

> The reader of Modern Irish should bear in mind, in reading Old and Middle Irish poetry, that the modern accentuation of one syllable in each word must be carefully avoided if it is desired to appreciate the metrical value and rhythm of the poems. All syllables, in whatever position, and however lightly accented in modern pronunciation, must be regarded as equally accented in the olden poetry. Thus in the first stanza of the *Duanaire,*
>
> *Eol damh sencus Feine Finn*
> *re ré toigheachta in Táilginn,*
>
> *Finn* and *Táilginn* should be read so as to rime fully. The second syllable in *Táilginn* should be accented as strongly as the first, not lightly passed over as in the modern pronunciation. The same applies to all syllables in every verse, no less than the riming syllables. Again, there are no slurred consonants making one syllable of two, as at present pronounced.

Most of the ancient lyrics have been gleaned from old manuscripts here and there in Europe, written on the margins of grammars and bibles, or copied, a few together, in books of miscellanies. Some of them are embedded in the prose sagas, which are the most important reliques of ancient Irish literature. In addition to the two epic cycles, that of the *Táin Bó Cuailgne* (The Cattle Raid of Cooley) and that of Oisín and the Fiana, there are great numbers of other tales and colloquies. To learn something of the setting of the lyrics go to that treasure-house of Old Irish, *Thesaurus Palæohibernicus,* edited by Whitley Stokes. Read the introduction to the first volume, and all the end of the second. I do not know a more fascinating book unless it be the *Silva Gadelica* of Standish Hayes O'Grady, or the *Duanaire Finn* of Eoin MacNeill, or the *Buile Suibhne* of J. G. O'Keeffe, or some other of the volumes published by the Irish Texts Society.

No mere description of the contents of these is possible. They introduce the reader into the old world of Ireland, Irish story, Irish poetry, Irish study. They introduce him, too, to the work of the men who in our time have brought great learning to the service of Irish studies. The writers mentioned hitherto in this essay and the workers of the periodical *Eriu* – men like Osborn Bergin and R. I. Best in this country and a great line of University professors of Irish on the continent, especially in Germany – sustain the high hope and promise of the future.[17]

Study 8.2

Irish Literature: To-Day

'*Propaganda has rarely produced a fine poem. A great hymn, whether of religion or patriotism, is rarely other than the cry of a poet calling to his God or his country as if he alone experienced the emotion that he sings ...*'

8.2

T HE FUTURE, however, from present signs, does not seem
likely to run on the wheels of old learning. I presided this evening
at a meeting of the Gaelic Society in University College at which
Syndicalism was discussed in Irish. The prose of the original paper
on the subject was a model of style, clear, free from all ambiguity,
with rhythm used for the purpose of emphasis – far finer than most
similar College society papers in English. The writer of this and the
best of the subsequent speakers dispensed with complicated and
derived terms and went to the root of the matter, making their meaning
plain enough to be understood by simple men. To me the most
interesting thing was the difference between the sentences of these
and the sentences of the other students, whose thought is still in
English. It was as if there were two ends to each statement, as if the
Irish thinkers took one and the English thinkers the other. In English,
voice stress is necessary to the meaning. The emphasis may be thrown
to the end of the phrase. The better Irish speakers in the debate this
evening might have dispensed with stress.

In speaking of a recent strike one speaker, whose thought was of
the English order, said *Do bhí na fir buailte* (the men were beaten),
literally, 'were, the men, beaten.' One of the Irish order said *Do
buadheadh ar an lucht oibre* (the men were beaten) literally, 'won
was it, on the workers', or rather 'victory was won, over the party of
labour.' The speakers of the Irish order said more directly and more
fully what they meant and they marshalled their thoughts in the more
natural sequence. Here then was a modern subject giving opportunity
to Irish speakers to express themselves freshly and strongly and yet
in the good traditional manner.

So, as I have said before, the literature of to-morrow will be in
terms of the life of to-morrow; and yet it is possible that here we
may resume a broken tradition and make a literature in consonance
with our past. Our nation is small. The deeds of a few men who see

clearly, who know surely, and who act definitely, count for much. We can be concentrated into a little clan; and he who makes music for his little clan makes music for all the world. The greatest danger is from our own criticism and from our own bilingualism.

It is unfortunate to a degree that while original literature in Ireland is still but stammering, criticism already speaks with full voice, almost too fluently, too loudly. It is more unfortunate still that this full voice should sometimes shout down the word of youthful enthusiasm and admiration.

Criticism here is of European stature. It sometimes takes advantage of its height to push through the ranks of the ungrown and to issue commands from the front. Its proper place is the rear. It comes duly and comes usefully in the wake of other forms of literature, of lyric poetry, of epic, of drama, even of prose fiction, of the essay and of oratory. The fact of the matter is that this criticism of ours is an alien, an immigrant, or at least a cuckoo.

An Irish poet, if he be individual, if he be original, if he be national, speaks, almost stammers, in one of the two fresh languages of this country – in Irish (modern Irish, newly schooled by Europe), or in Anglo-Irish, English as we speak it in Ireland, a language yet unspoiled by the over-growths of literature. Such an Irish poet can still express himself in the simplest terms of life and of the common furniture of life.

> Her household motions light and free,
> And steps of virgin liberty,

sings Wordsworth, apostle of simplicity in diction. (I quote at random).

> She carries in the dishes
> And lays them in a row,

sings W. B. Yeats.

> I look for ghosts, but none will force
> Their way to me,

cries the mother in Wordsworth's poem.

Mavourneen is going
From me and from you, ...

From the reek of the smoke
And cold of the floor,
And the peering of things
Across the half-door,

cries the mother in a poem of Padraic Colum's.

Of course Wordsworth has things as bald and as simple as any
Irish poet could write; but they are not the rule in his successful
poems; they are not always his best expression, his natural expression;
they are often the worse for being the cries of a conscious literary
reaction, of a revival, of a return to simplicity. In Ireland we are still
at simple beginnings.[1]

And we are beginning in Irish as well as in English. Compare
with Matthew Arnold's 'unplumb'd, salt, estranging sea' – a phrase
English, modern, typical, beautiful – these lines of an Irish folk-
poem, a century old or more, but still natural and of the same accent
as the latest word of Irish poetry:

Mo bhrón ar an bhfarraige,
Is é atá mór,

(My grief on the sea, it is it that is big).

All this shall be granted to you, says a critic, but Irish, Gaelic,
cannot go further, or at least cannot go aside from this, without
violating the genius and the sense of the language. This Gaelic League
Irish, says the critic, is full of awful barbarisms. Gaelic League,
Connradh na Gaedhilge! Connradh is an agreement, a league
between parties, not a league in the sense of a body of people banded
together with a General Secretary. The English words 'league' and
'covenant' came, in the phrase 'Solemn League and Covenant', to
be used of the organisation; but we must not let Irish drift into that
loose use of words. *Saol in Eirinn* is Father Dineen's translation of
'life in Ireland', and he ought to have known better than to use *saol,*
akin to the Latin *saeculum,* for 'life' in that sense. The grammarian
in me, the purist, approves of the critic crying this but another man

in me cries: O happy Chaucer! O happy all ye who used words as you could take them, testing them only by their current value!

And Anglo-Irish work does not escape. I hear already the mutter of anger against the very name, Anglo-Irish, and against the lines I have quoted from W. B. Yeats and Padraic Colum. Just narrow peasant English and nothing more, says someone – No, I wrong criticism. The criticism to which I have been referring just now has nothing to do with these opinions. There is a school of criticism in Ireland, a school that knows the work of the finest critics in the world, and knows too, what is more important, the finest literature in the world. This, when dealing with literature in general, adds to the store of fine critical work. This at times encourages and approves good original Irish work.

I think it unfortunate, however, that it should have grown with, or indeed before, the original work. Dealing with the monuments of the older literatures – English, French, and the like – this criticism knows its place, its bearings, its conditions. Dealing with a naissant literature or with two naissant literatures, with literature still at the lyric stage, it looks over its shoulder, as it were. Its neck is awry. Its eyes are twisted round. Its feet turn from their known way and stumble. When it does get a clear view of its object, it misses the shapes and forms it saw in other lands and expresses its disappointment.

Ireland is not the only country that suffers so to-day. America also has a full-grown criticism and a baby literature. Something of the same relation exists between the two there as in Ireland.

Of course criticism, this use or this abuse of criticism, is not going to change what seems to be the natural law of growth, development, progress, ever recurring. The new literatures will grow in the due way, criticism or no criticism. And indeed it may be said that the effect of criticism on the author is quite negligible. Its effect on the audience is not negligible. Growing naturally with a native literature, dealing with a native literature in terms of the life of which that literature is an expression, an interpretation, an illumination, it is good. Coming from abroad, full grown and intolerant of youth, it may here be a false prophet.

Poets – and it is with poets we are most concerned in a youthful literature – have in general to wait long for recognition: those that speak with a strange accent are not understood at once by all. It is a pity that the delay of this recognition should be lengthened unnaturally. The formulating of rules, even of just rules, the setting up of standards, even of true standards, the preaching of purism in language, the blame of innovation and all such things, do lengthen the delay.

I take for illustration of this danger of alien criticism a book of original Irish poems, published in 1914, *Suantraidhe agus Goltraidhe* by Padraic MacPiarais. I do not offer my criticism of criticism here as an apology for the book: the book needs no apology. It needs appreciation and praise; and on account of our present state of criticism it may go without both. I should like to clear the way for a new criticism, a simple criticism in terms of a new literature. I shall therefore merely offer samples of the poetry published in this book with the briefest of introductions. I think them good poetry and true poetry.

The book is one of the first books of the new literature. Irish has produced very little original personal work since the beginning of the revival, and the few good books that have appeared have met with an ungracious reception. As the adherents of the old Saxon mode must have looked on the English work of Chaucer, the adherents of earlier Irish look on work such as this. Written in English, it might well have had a sure success, like that of Padraic Colum's *Wild Earth*, from which I have quoted above. Being written in Irish, it is likely, on the one hand, to be blamed for having something of the note of recent Anglo-Irish literature, and on the other hand to be ignored by those who appreciate that same Anglo-Irish literature and who have remained ignorant of Irish. The book is not Chaucerian in volume. It is one of the shortest books of poems I know: a dozen lyrics in all. It is not, for all I have said on the point, so different from central modern Irish work as to incur the hostility of the purists; and indeed a part of its difference consists in its going back to some of the older forms of Irish verse and continuing them in modern speech.

The title, *Songs of Sleep and of Sorrow* (Lullabies and Keens), promises tender, serious poetry. The note of the book is sadness; but in the most solemn poems there is exultation too. For the rest, as a farce can scarcely be too amusing, too funny, or a tragedy too tragic, so a solemn poem or a book of solemn poems can scarcely be too solemn. As I am writing in English, to introduce a book of Irish poems in which there is not a word of English, I am going frankly to use English throughout, even to translate literally the poems which I quote. The language of the poems is so simple, the phrases so primitive in construction, that anyone who goes to the originals can easily, with the help of a dictionary, spell out the meaning. The verse forms are so straight and so strong that anyone can know the movement, the beat of the rhythm.

The lovely harp in the Fenian lay had three strings, a string of silver, a string of bright brass, and a string of iron whole. The names of the strings were *Geantarghléas, Goltarghléas, Suantarghléas*, the string of laughter, the string of sorrow, the string of slumber. Padraic MacPiarais has two of these strings to his harp.[2]

Lullaby of a Woman of the Mountain and *A Woman of the Mountain Keening her Son*, the first two poems, are in the tradition of the songs that have come down unwritten from mother to daughter. I translate from the former:

> O little head of gold! O candle of my house!
> Thou wilt guide all who travel this country. ...
>
> Be quiet, O house! and O little grey mice,
> Stay at home to-night in your hidden lairs!
>
> O moths on the window, fold your wings!
> Cease your droning, O little black chafers!
>
> O plover and O curlew, over my house do not travel!
> Speak not, O barnacle-goose, going over the mountain here!
>
> O creatures of the mountain, that wake so early,
> Stir not to-night till the sun whitens over you!

The monotonous repetition of the one rime throughout and the swaying flow of the verse help to make this poem a perfect lullaby.

With the fourth begins a series of personal or dramatic lyrics. Some of them do not well bear translation. Judged by present English standards, which are hostile to sentiment, the mere words would give a false idea of the originals. One, the shortest of all, runs another risk in translation. It is one of two poems to Death:

Long (seems) to me your coming,
   Old herald of God,
O friend of friends,
   To part me from my pain!

O syllable on the wind!
   O footstep not heavy!
O hand in the darkness!
   Your coming seems to me long.

Here is another of this series:

I have not gathered gold;
   The fame that I won perished;
In love I found but sorrow
   That withered my life.

Of wealth or of glory
   I shall leave nothing behind me
(I think it, O God, enough!)
   But my name in the heart of a child.

The last poem I translate in full. In English its title might be *Ideal*:[3]

Naked I saw thee,
   O beauty of beauty!
And I blinded my eyes
   For fear I should flinch.

I heard thy music,
   O melody of melody!
And I shut my ears
   For fear I should fail.

I kissed thy lips,
   O sweetness of sweetness!
And I hardened my heart
   For fear of my ruin.

> I blinded my eyes,
>> And my ears I shut,
> I hardened my heart
>> And my love I quenched.

> I turned my back
>> On the dream I had shaped,
> And to this road before me
>> My face I turned.

> I set my face
>> To the road here before me,
> To the work that I see,
>> To the death that I shall get.

One need not ask if it be worth while having books of such poetry. The production of this is already a success for the new literature.

In addition to this danger of criticism of which I have been speaking – an outside criticism – there is the danger to poets here now of too much self-criticism – a natural and good and even necessary thing in a mature literature. It brings a self-consciousness that gives pause to the impulse which creates, or which would create spontaneously without taking thought. Once the impulse pauses it misses its mark.

Then there is the danger of too easy a verse music. A language that is so musical in its words as Irish is difficult for the best verse. In languages like French and English, prose phrases are continually harsh to the ear, and words that sing of themselves are easily recognised as verse. This is one of the great advantages that verse has in such languages; it stands apart from prose; its words have a distinct music. Phrases like A. E. Housman's:

> In summer time on Bredon,

or Paul Verlaine's:

> Mon Dieu, mon Dieu, la vie est là,
>> Simple et tranquille;
> Cette paisible rumeur-là
>> Vient de la ville,

or even Shakespeare's:

> Light thickens, and the crow
> Makes wing to the rooky wood,

owe at least half their beauty to the fact that they are distinct verse
phrase, however direct, not to be mistaken for the prose expression
of the same ideas. In Irish prose there is still the richness of open
vowels and the rhythmic fall of words, not so full and beautiful,
indeed, as in the verse, but yet not so distinctly apart as in the
languages from which I have quoted.

The quality of form that most frequently raises Irish verse to the
height of poetry is not beauty of verse music, but restraint, the severe
grace. A song like Seaghan Lloyd's *Bean an Leasa* (*Cois leasa 's mé
go h-uaigneach*) is full of rich music, with rimes and chimes and
contrasts, but it is sheer waste of exuberant melody on a barren theme.
Sometimes masters of verse-craft in the harsher languages link words
in this luscious way of sweetness, but their verses are then clever
achievements rather than poems. Verlaine claimed, indeed, that this
is the function of verse – *De la musique avant toute chose* – and so,
no doubt, could murmur over and over with great satisfaction those
beautiful lines of his which imitate the sobbing of a violin:

> *Les sanglots longs*
> *Des violons*
>   *De l'automne*
> *Blessent mon coeur*
> *D'une langueur*
>   *Monotone.*

But these lines, gracious though they be and replete with one of
the sweet minor qualities of poetry, are no more fine poetry than
Bean an Leasa. This exuberance which becomes mere sound and a
waste of melody is a sin against the medium of poetry which is not
chanted song but expressive language. True poetry always finds its
expression in beautiful moving words. Its effect is marred if empty
phrases, however melodious, are added. To take a simple example,
the first two verses of the better version of *Is Truagh gan Mise i
Sasana* are essential poetry; the three that are tagged on in the song-
books are no such thing. Swinburne praises a lyric poet who knew
'to sing and not to say, without a glimpse of wit or a flash of

eloquence.' The poet of these eight lines had that knowledge:

Is trua gan mise i Sasana
Agus duine amháin as Éirinn liom,
Nó amuigh i lár na farraige,
An áit a gcailltear na mílte long.
An ghaoth agus an fhearthainn
Bheith 'mo sheoladh ó thuinn go tuinn –
Is, a Rí, go seolaidh Tú mise
Ins an áit a bhfuil mo ghrá 'n-a luí.

This is a perfect lyric, with the directness and sufficiency of poetry.

'Tis a pity I'm not in England
And one from Ireland there with me,
Or out where the ships in thousands
Are lost in the midst of the sea.

The wind and the rain of the ocean
To be guiding me over the waves of the deep,
And, O King! that Thou mightst guide me
To the place where my love doth sleep![4]

The three stanzas that follow say the conventional things, of a heart broken in a hundred parts and a dream of lost love. I believe they were added by some one who thought the song too short, and who found it easy in Irish to string on the sweet empty lines.

A kindred danger that has beset the Irish less perhaps than the Anglo-Irish poet is that of rhetoric, the expression of the collective emotion rather than the individual, that which has given a small number of the greatest odes to the world and most of the poorest poems.The collective is in general enemy of true sincerity. Propaganda has rarely produced a fine poem. A great hymn, whether of religion or patriotism, is rarely other than the cry of a poet calling to his God or his country as if he alone experienced the emotion that he sings, though poignantly mindful that many felt it in a better day. Gaelic Ireland will have a great anthem when, in some great stress, a poet, using Irish naturally in all senses, will feel his patriotism as if he alone felt it, and utter it unconscious of propaganda for himself.

The poet once again is his own first audience. His poetry is a matter between himself and himself. If others afterwards come and share his joy, the gain is theirs.

So much for the lyric poetry, or rather for scattered glimpses of it far and near. I have not, of course, attempted to do more than indicate points of interest and significance. Every century has had its poets and its schools and its movements. Of lyric poetry there has been a constant, though at times a narrow stream. The libraries of Europe are still giving up stores of poetry long forgotten. Old men and women all round the Gaelic crescent of Ireland are still telling out lovely lyrics of known and unknown authorship. The quest of such is adventurous and romantic, only less so perhaps than the quest of living but forgotten poets or of the traces of poets once of great fame in their clan and still remembered by the living.

Douglas Hyde has been able to discover not only the poems of Raftery, whose word seemed a wandering voice far off, but a man who assisted at his burial, and a whole body of tradition about him. Mr P. H. Pearse and others who undertook the publication of the poems of Colm Wallace, were able a few years ago to discover not only the work, but the man himself, thought dead for many years but actually living, a centenarian in Oughterard workhouse. Mr Pearse's committee took the poet out of the workhouse, but subsequently had to let him return to it as a paying patient at his urgent request. He died at the age of a hundred and ten. Robert Weldon, the poet of the Comeraghs, seemed to us in Dublin some years ago like a visitant from the old Gaelic world.

So much for the poetry.

Of the novel and the modern essay, of which we have had many examples of late, I dare not speak. Irish prose I believe to be a finer vehicle than English prose. The poise and the concision of the idiomatic Irish sentence makes our long series of words in English seem weak by comparison. But that is a matter of language. Of the actual work of the acknowledged master of Modern Irish prose, Canon Peter O'Leary, one does not know well what to think. His novels and his plays should not be subjected to this outside criticism. Of his use of his medium and of his descriptive power one can write nothing but praise and quote examples which must suffice for all. I give a translation of a passage from his novel *Séadna,* as more representative of the new literature than his sermons, his plays, or his adaptations of old tales.

It was a wedding feast. One of the pipers knew the Fairy Music. He would often play it to himself; but it was very hard to make him play it when asked by others. He said that it was not right to play it in the presence of mortals – it was too eerie. On this occasion, after much pressing by all the guests, the piper drank some of the wine of the king and consented to play the Fairy Music.

> He tuned his pipes. He filled the bag with air. The company listened as though they had neither soul nor breath. Soon there was heard, as it were, a soft, murmuring sound, circling the house without. Then the people thought a breeze was blowing, with the murmuring, and that it was the breeze which caused the murmuring and not the pipes. Thereafter passed a pleasant melody through the murmuring, and both melody and murmuring came into the house. The murmuring increased, and there arose, as it were, a trembling and a swaying in its sound. Soon a second sound was heard, trembling and swaying like the first, whilst the sweet melody was heard through them both, none of the three obscuring either of the other two, but each of the three aiding the others, so that the melody was the better for the murmurings and the murmurings all the sweeter for the melody. Anon there spoke a third sound, trembling and swaying with pleasant music through it of its own. That third sound startled all who were there. They would swear it was a human voice.
>
> Then came as it were a torrent of melody, the most delicious, the sweetest, the gentlest, the most soothing that the people there had ever heard, and it mingled with the murmurings and with the sound like the human voice and the sound that was like the blowing of the breeze, and all the elements commingled began to move around the house like a whirlwind. The sound kept increasing in volume, the union of its parts grew closer and closer, and the revolutions about the house became ever faster, until the people thought that the fairy blast was whirling about the house. It was now here, now there. It would spring away and leap back again. It would lie down close to the ground and sweep around beneath the floor. Then, with a bound, it was on high playing amongst the rafters, in such wise that the

people thought they heard the beating of birds' wings through the music.

Now the people believed they heard the sobbing of one in tears, and anon bursts of laughter. Again they thought they heard plainly, speaking through the music, the voice of a child. Then came another childlike voice to answer it, and both made answer to the melody. Then there spoke a third voice, as it were the voice of a young woman, but none of those who were there ever heard human voice so sweet, so beautiful, so pleasing. Soon another woman-voice came to answer it, and if the first was sweet, the second was sweeter far, and they kept speaking to each other and to the music in tuneful measure.

Then, as though some door were flung open, there came a swelling, a rising, and a strength into all the music. The movement grew faster, its rush increased, and a flood of joy poured into the notes. They rose and fell. They were below on the ground and above in the rafters, in this corner and in that, till fear began to creep over the people as they cast hasty glances over their shoulders to see if anyone had spoken.

Then the music increased yet more in strength, as though another door wider than the first had been flung open. Still greater grew the swelling and the verve of the music, as it twisted and writhed about the floor and over the walls and away up to the highest ridge of the ceiling, now lowing, now crying out, now weeping aloud, now wailing with grief, in such wise that it would cause even a stone to sob; now exploding in bursts of mirthful laughter, now bursting into cries of pride and power, so that one would think it could raise the dead from the clay. There were voices of women and children, talking and answering clearly, through the cries that were loudest, through the grief that was saddest, through the laughter that was merriest. And ever and anon through all the maze, there would come a long-drawn, strange, cruel cry, that sent the shudder of fear through all in the house.

And by-and-by came the muttering of thunder, rising and falling and rumbling, swaying and trembling. It went through the beams of the house, through the wood of the chairs, and through the bones of the people. It grew and grew in strength till it gathered to itself all the other sounds and swept them with it round the house like straws in a whirlpool. Ever louder and heavier grew the thunder, spinning round with increasing force, swaying and vibrating ever more through the timbers and through the people's limbs, until every heart was throbbing fast and every head was dizzy.

Then the child-voice passed away through the chimney, and then the woman-voice followed, and so with each other sound in the music, till naught was left of all but the thunder still rocking and trembling. Then the thunder grew less loud. Its swaying and trembling grew ever weaker, and its rush ever feebler. Its strength faded away till there was left of it but a murmur. The murmur died down till there was left of it but a breathing. And then it ceased.

Then the cock crew, and Báb of the Liss uttering a piercing cry fell down in a faint.

No one stirred. You would think that they sat enchanted. But at last the Big Tinker jumped up.

'Arrah, praises be to God!' said he, 'what's on ye? Come, women, two of you take hold of the girl, and carry her out in the air.'[5]

In drama, for all our efforts these ten or fifteen years, we are still waiting for a fine work, stronger and more enduring than such good little plays as Douglas Hyde's *An Naomh ar Iarraidh,* and *An Tincéir agus an tSidheog.* An organisation like the Gaelic League is scarcely calculated to produce literature. I believe that it would be better for Ireland and for the Irish language if, instead of the Gaelic League as it is, we had a different thing, a folk movement in the Gaedhealtacht, a movement coming from the West eastward, not an organisation with the official institutions of a political propagandist society, with its capital the capital of the Pale. It would, no doubt, be better still to have both things, the folk movement and the League, but there is little chance of that.

I do not think that my criticism or the criticism of others will now make the Gaelic League reform itself, and set about work in a different way, yet my criticism is not factious, as it would be if I thought that nothing might possibly come of it. The workers in the Gaelic League do the work to their hand; but they do little to foster the growth of a new literature in Irish. Most of us agree that if modern Irish had a fine literature – fine poetry, fine drama – very many who are not now seriously affected by the propagandist appeals to them to learn Irish would do so, not because it has patriotic claims or grammatical or philological claims, but in order to read and know Irish literature, as they learn Italian to read Dante and Carducci, or German to read Goethe and Heine – as some have learned the languages of Mistral and Ibsen to read and understand those writers at their true best.

Mr George Moore has said that if he had learned Irish the language would probably now be saved, as he might have written such masterpieces in Irish as readers in this and other countries could not neglect to study in their original versions. Even with knowledge of Mr Moore's work, and with the example of Mistral before me, I am not certain that alone he could have done all that, but his idea is a right idea. If a language have a good literature, it is certain to be recognised and to have students. Now the Gaelic League does little to foster the production of such a literature; it tries to do much, but fails. In the circumstances it could not but fail.

Since I have been interested in Irish I have come to see the possibility of truth in Gray's line about a 'mute inglorious Milton'. I had learned to believe that as all men now have as much chance of acquiring the culture from which literature comes as Burns had, and as some of the ancient writers had, genius would out. There are no rules for genius, but still there is force in that thought of Gray's, a force that weakens the argument in which I believed. Burns had behind him all the tradition of Lowland Scots literature, freshened by acquaintance with Shakespeare and the great writers of English, which is really the same language. So with the ancients in their different age – I will not now labour the points of difference.

But the people of the Gaedhealtacht have no models except the out-worn verse-forms of the later Irish poets, and such English literature as comes their way. In Ireland at present this model should be the drama, and the Gaelic League could, I believe, by giving dramatic models to young Irish writers, do more even towards making Irish attractive to English speakers and foreigners, than by giving many prizes at the Oireachtas for all sorts of essays and stories and plays. This would be doing the work indirectly, no doubt, but would be the better way in the long run. As Mr W. B. Yeats has shown, drama is the right form to foster. Writing in *Samhain* in 1904, Mr Yeats said:

There are two kinds of poetry, and they are co-mingled in all the greatest works. When the tide of life sinks low there are pictures, as in the *Ode on a Grecian Urn*, and in Virgil at the plucking of the Golden Bough. The pictures make us sorrowful. We share the poet's separation from what he describes. It is life in the mirror, and our desire for it is as the desire of the lost souls for God. But when Lucifer stands among his friends, when Villon sings his dead ladies to so gallant a rhythm, when Timon makes his epitaph, we feel no sorrow, for life herself has made one of her eternal gestures, has called up into our hearts her energy that is eternal delight. In Ireland, where the tide of life is rising, we turn, not to picture-making but to the imagination of personality – to drama, gesture.

The new Gaelic literature might have its centre in the drama. The drama may be a graft on the Gaelic tree, but that tree is all but barren now, and we want new fruit. In order to found and to foster a dramatic literature in Gaelic it is necessary to teach young writers what the drama is. One cannot, with all the good will and all the good money in the world, produce literature to order, but one can lay down canons of criticism, one can strive to keep the way clear for the coming of a good thing by correcting false impressions, and – what is more to the point in this matter – one can set up good models and display them, when the models are at hand and the pedestals empty.

Canons of criticism are not brain-spun and merely theoretic; they are, or should be, drawn from masterpieces. There are certain qualities in all true art, in all fine poetry, in all good drama. Writers of plays in Irish want to produce dramas of a certain kind – very distinctively Irish, very characteristic in the right sense, but still of the same kind as certain plays in other languages – to take the example nearest home, as certain plays about Ireland written in English. They want to produce such dramas, but they have not studied the models which have been followed by the writers of the plays in English. They have done little or nothing towards mastering their craft, and they have failed in their endeavour.

The pedestals on which the models may be set are empty. Judging from all but one of the plays sent in for the Oireachtas some years ago, when I was adjudicator, the authors have no conception of what a play is. It is unfortunate that the one exception, which was the work of a man who does understand the craft, and was in every way admirable, was of a cosmopolitan description, not at all so Gaelic in character as several plays written in English. The others were for the most part stories or essays written in the form of dialogues or catechisms. They had no dramatic sequence or balance. The situations did not flow from the characters, as they do inevitably in all good drama. There is such a thing as stage-craft. The dramatist must learn his craft as a dramatist over and above his craft as a writer, and before he begins he must have in him the makings of a dramatist and a conception of dramatic art. I believe that the people to whom we must look to produce a new Irish literature are young people of the Gaedhealtacht, not people who have lost their Gaelic edge in the Pale. I believe that there are enough young Gaelic writers of dramatic talent to make the beginnings of a distinguished dramatic literature in Irish. The difficulty is to make them master the craft.

If a small company of Irish-speaking actors were sent by the Gaelic League to take four or five very well-written, well-constructed plays (one-act plays to begin with) from village to village in the most Irish-speaking districts, I am sure that within a year we should have the beginning of a real Gaelic dramatic literature. Visits of a Gaelic company would have immediate results. For plays to send on tour one would use the best of the plays already written and translations of the most Irish pieces of the Abbey Theatre – a tragedy, say, a merry comedy and a serious comedy. Farce is too easy and sets our young writers on a false track. I do not think that a group of players from Dublin or elsewhere, going down to some villages in holiday time, would achieve the object proposed. The actors should be well trained and should form a professional company, playing again and again in each village. The method of Molière is the true method, and brings drama home at last to the house of Molière. A folk movement in the Gaedhealtacht would certainly have given us a distinctive literature: now this touring company would stir the waters.

To this it may be objected that in our age literature is metropolitan – that it will have its centre not only in the drama but in the city playhouse. But if we are seeking the expression in Gaelic literature of the Gaelic ways of thought and life we shall have to draw it from the Gaedhealtacht. It will, as I have said, come home to the city playhouse after. The necessity for drawing speedily what we can of that expression now is clear to those of us who know at first hand how the old oral tradition is dying, who have known poets and shanachies full of Gaelic lore to die with all their treasures in their hearts, leaving no records and no succession.

Some years ago in West Cork I spent a day with such a one, an old man who knew more poems, more hero-tales, more biographical tales of the Munster Bards than he ever had a chance of saying or telling. When I brought him a copy of the works of Eoghan Ruadh Ó Súilleabháin, he was able to explain passage after passage, reference after reference, in terms of this tradition of his. He was able to detect the passages and poems wrongly attributed to the poet. 'That's not by Eoghan Ruadh. That was written by Mary O'Shea, from Carriganimy beyond. I learned it for a wedding forty years ago. This is it, isn't it?'[6] He sang the poem, many verses of it, to a monotonous tune, marking the emphatic points by slapping my knee. My knowledge of Irish at the time and my patience of the music were soon exhausted, and I fear I discouraged the splendid old man, whom I never saw again. His children, though interested in the revival of the Irish language, are not heirs to his tradition. With him has died a whole store of literature and idiom.

As to the value of such a store I have no doubt. The Irish writer who is probably greatest of our time, that strong, self-sufficing, humorous, wise, old priest, whose prose I have quoted, has told me that in his version of the New Testament he was aided by his memory of sermons and impromptu translations made by Irish-speaking priests of half a century ago. Irish recently tended to meet English half way. The order of phrases tended to change. Writers tended to express things in the English order rather than in the Irish – worse still, tended to translate the English or French words for a thought rather than to express the thought in the different Gaelic way. Their prose resembled a certain kind of schoolboy Latin, a close translation, phrase by phrase of an English passage, possible phrase by phrase in another sense, but not a Latin rendering of the thought, not Latin prose. These tendencies were bad. By Canon O'Leary and others they have been checked. Writers have been sent back to the well of tradition and of the living speech. Drama must go to that well too. And it will go.

For all that I have written of the wreck and ruin going on so rapidly, I am confident of the future. Many of us are good lives for the language, though some of us still write in English. A number of us are better, writers already in the old tradition, though expressing

something of the life of our time. If I were asked to cite a perfect
example of such expression, the natural, almost casual, utterance in
sincere, inevitable words of some simple thought or emotion, I should
think first of one of the Old Irish poems, like that little poem about
the blackbird (*Domfarcai*), and then of a little poem written by a
friend of mine, in an autograph album of all the places in the world.

Autograph albums I do not like. I have been asked a few times in
my life to write in them, and have always done so with reluctance.
The verses found in them are rarely poetry. Copies of good poems
you will sometimes meet, but they are then copies in a double sense.
They suffer incongruity. All things are against them – the handwriting
of the copyist, sometimes even of the author – the little pansies and
forget-me-nots hand-painted round the pages. They suffer nicety and
prettiness.

But in one autograph album that I know there is one true poem,
right in its context, right in what I hold to be the essential qualities of
poetry. This album has been on the rounds for some years, and has
accumulated poems by some of the modern masters, drawings by
some of the best artists – an unusually choice and well-filled album.
One feels in good company when writing in it. At the request of the
owner I sent it some time ago to the Irish writer, Pádraig MacSuibhne,
for a contribution. He is not known to be a poet, yet it is he who
wrote the one true poem in the book. Before I sent it, I looked through
it and admired the gracious little poems, with the good Irish fragrance
in most of them. When I got it back I looked through it again – page
after page of such good verse, in English; then on the new page, this
Irish protest:

> A leabhráin, gabh amach fá'n saol,
> Is do gach n-aon dá mbuaileann leat
> Aithris cruinn go maireann Gael
> T'réis cleasa claon na nGall ar fad.

(Little book go forth into the world, and unto all that meet with thee,
duly relate that after the wiles of all the Gall, still live the Gael.)

It is the accent of the best of Dante's *tornate*: it is the accent of
true poetry, simple, sincere, due.

This little poem serves here as an example of what, to use Arnold's phrase, may be called the note of the new literature – a note of pride, of self-reliance, almost of arrogance. The Gaelic revival has given to some of us a new arrogance. I am a Gael and I know no cause but of pride in that. *Gael mé agus ní h-eol dom gur náir dom é.* My race has survived the wiles of the foreigner here. It has refused to yield even to defeat, and emerges strong to-day, full of hope and of love, with new strength in its arms to work its new destiny, with a new song on its lips and the word of the new language, which is the ancient language, still calling from age to age. The adorable delicacy, the shrinking sensibility, the paralysing diffidence which has its root in charity, the qualities which make for temporary defeat and yet, being of their nature joined with the unwavering conviction of truth and right, for ultimate victory – these live on. Now with them, in the same breasts with them, lives this too: its day is come.

This arrogance is a sign of energy, of vitality, and so here is good. The Gaelic movement is a revival. Though, through changes of methods and modes of advance, the exhaustion of old methods and the need for new movements, it may seem to-day that the central movement has lost force, it still goes forward. Of a tide of thought, drawn by the inspiration of an ancient cause, there is no ebb. This will have a voice, a literature, to-morrow, the voice of a people new to such a way of speech, the literature of a fresh people. To be a poet one must look with fresh eyes on life; to produce poets a nation must be fresh.

Ireland has already produced a great literature of old: the fragments that remain prove that. But, as we are now, we are a fresh people, fresh to literature. We have begun to produce a literature in English, a foreign tongue. This will not injure or delay the progress of Gaelic literature, which must be the work of other writers. Most of the Anglo-Irish poets – and it is almost all poetry still – have spent in attaining their knowledge and mastery of their craft all the resources of learning and acquirement in them. In the matter of technique – and this is all but supremely necessary in modern poetry – one language only will one poet master. Whether our people go forward in Anglo-Irish literature or not, some of our poets and writers of the next generation will certainly continue the production of a new literature in Irish.

As I have said, we are fresh in other senses too – fresh from the natural home of man, the fields and the country. We have not all grown up in streets amid the artificialities of civilization, with traditional memories of brick and plaster. The influences of nature will be felt by us as by the true poets of all tongues. Our nature poetry will owe nothing to the botanical observations of city dwellers; it will be no sham pastoral imitation; it will be natural and spontaneous, and our own.

But above all we are fresh in language, which the most city-hating English lover of nature cannot be. We are the children of a race that, through need or choice, turned from Irish to English. We have now so well mastered this language of our adoption that we use it with a freshness and power that the English of these days rarely have. But now also we have begun to turn back to the old language, not old to us. The future poets of the country will probably be the sons and daughters of a generation that learned Irish as a strange tongue; the words and phrases of Irish will have a new wonder for them; the figures of speech will have all their first poetry. Carlyle says of Imagination: 'Metaphors are her stuff; examine language – what, if you except some primitive elements, what is it but metaphors, recognised as such or no longer recognised, still fluid and florid, or now solid-grown and colourless?' The metaphors of Irish will not be colourless to the fresh eyes of the next generation, though the language be their native idiom.

Perhaps the temporary abandonment of Irish has not been an unmitigated disaster, now that its revival is assured. A language that transmits its literature mainly by oral tradition cannot, if spoken only by thousands, bequeath as much to posterity as if spoken by millions. The loss of idiom and of literature is a disaster. But, on the other hand, the abandonment has broken a tradition of pedantry and barren conventions; and sincerity gains thereby. The *aisling*[7] is now at last dead; the simple beautiful folk-songs in which recent Irish literature is richer perhaps than any other, are more likely to serve as models than the vain word-weaving of the bards. The writers of the *dán díreach*[8] became at last, to use a mis-translated phrase, mere 'schoolmen of condensed speech',[9] but their verse at worst had the high virtue of restraint. Their successors became fluent, eloquent craftsmen of skilful word-music.

The poets of the next age will learn from the faults of both schools; they will make restraint a canon of their art, not a pedantry; they will know that the too facile use of the adjective is a vice, and verse-music a snare.

Let us postulate continuity, but continuity in the true way.

Poems of the Irish Mode

Introductory

Translations from the Irish

Ballads and Street Songs

Original Poems

Poems of the Irish Mode

O F THE IRISH MODE which has been the subject of preceding studies, example is the best definition. I am putting together here a number of poems that are unmistakably of this mood.[1] My selection is, of course, nothing in the nature of an anthology; the poems are printed here to serve as examples and indications, ready at hand, of my meaning. I print no poem that has not good, and indeed evident, warranty. One can easily say of a poem like Mangan's *My Dark Rosaleen* that it is essentially Irish, that it has some indefinable quality not found elsewhere. Frankly, I am afraid to rely on those indefinable qualities. If I included *My Dark Rosaleen,* it would be because it is in part a translation of an Irish poem and is full of images and allusions found in Irish poetry. I prefer to take only poems which show one or another of those three influences dealt with in one of my studies: the influence of Irish versification, the influence of the Irish way of speech, the influence of Irish music.

This narrows my choice of course, and endangers my criticism. In spite of all that I say here, it may seem as if I were denying to some poems, omitted from this selection, their Irish claim. Some of them are indeed Irish in all but the marks I look for. *The Little Black Rose,* by Aubrey de Vere, is as good an example of these as Mangan's great poem:

> The Little Black Rose shall be red at last;
> What made it black but the March wind dry,
> And the tear of the widow that fell on it fast?
> It shall redden the hills when June is nigh!
>
> The Silk of the Kine shall rest at last;
> What drove her forth but the dragon fly?
> In the golden vale she shall feed full fast,
> With her mild gold horn and her slow, dark eye.

The wounded wood-dove lies dead at last!
The pine long bleeding, it shall not die!
This song is secret. Mine ear it passed
In a wind o'er the plains at Athenry.

Some poems which lack also these marks are even more surely Irish, being translations of Gaelic poems, but translations from syllabic into a form of accentual verse which has not medial assonances or other graces distinctly Gaelic. Such is Dr Sigerson's beautiful *Blackbird of Daricarn*:

Sweet thy song, in Dari grove,
No sweeter song from east to west;
No music like thy voice of love –
And thou beneath thy nest!

A strain the softest ever heard,
No more shall come its like to men.
O Patrick! list the wondrous bird –
Thou'lt chant thy hymn again.

If thou, as I, but knew the tale
It sings to all the ancient isle,
Thy tears would rise, and thou wouldst fail
To mind thy God a while.

In Norroway beyond the wave,
Its forest glades and streams among,
That bird was found by Fionn the brave,
And still we hear its song.

'Tis Daricarn yon western wood –
The Fianna huntsmen loved it best,
And there, on stately oak and good
Lost Fionn placed its nest.

The tuneful tumult of that bird,
The belling deer on ferny steep –
This welcome in the dawn he heard,

These soothed at eve his sleep.

Dear to him the wind-loved heath,
The whirr of wings, the rustling brake,
Dear the murmuring glens beneath,
And sob of Droma's lake.

The cry of hounds at early morn,
The pattering o'er the pebbly creek,
The cuckoo's call, the sounding horn,
The sweeping eagle's shriek.

The mountain, not the cell, they sought,
Great Fionn and the Fianna fleet;
Than tinkle of the bells they thought
The blackbird's song more sweet!

There is still another kind of poem which I cannot use, a poem
which is distinctively of this Irish Mode when sung to its air or spoken
to the rhythm of its air, but capable of being spoken quite naturally
in quite another way. To my ear the lines of this song of Robert Dwyer
Joyce's, which I quote here, have the slow, sweet rhythm of the lovely
air, *An Droighneán Donn* (The Blackthorn), or of the Irish poem of
the name that goes to it; but I have heard them riddled off in another
way which has shown me the difference that the association with the
music makes for me:

By road and by river the wild birds sing,
O'er mountain and valley the dewy leaves spring,
The gay flowers are shining, gilt o'er by the sun,
And fairest of all shines the *Droighneán Donn.*

The rath of the fairy, the ruin hoar,
With white silver splendour it decks them all o'er;
And down in the valleys, where merry streams run,
How sweet smells the bloom of the *Droighneán Donn*!

Ah! well I remember the soft spring day,
I sat by my love 'neath its sweet-scented spray;

The day that she told me her heart I had won,
Beneath the white blossoms of the *Droighneán Donn.*

The streams they were singing their gladsome song,
The soft winds were blowing the wild woods among,
The mountains shone bright in the red setting sun,
And my love in my arms 'neath the *Droighneán Donn.*

'Tis my prayer in the morning, my dream at night,
To sit thus again by my heart's dear delight,
With her blue eyes of gladness, her hair like the sun,
And her sweet loving kisses, 'neath the *Droighneán Donn.*

On the other hand I use Mangan's *Vision of Connacht in the Thirteenth Century* as showing the influence on the poet's ear of the rich tolling, in the verse which he studied, of that Gaelic assonance of wider range than any in other languages, broad vowels assonating with other broad and slender with slender, consonants alliterating with others of their class. Read the poem slowly, lingering on the stressed syllables and you will hear the full, rich music.

My examples are largely drawn from the earlier writers. This is, of course, natural; we trace the river to its springs. I am debarred, moreover, from using here the copyright work of contemporary authors. A few of them are finer poets in this mode and out of it than all but one or two of their predecessors, possibly greater poets than any before them here. Douglas Hyde certainly surpasses all his predecessors as a translator. His influence is probably the most potent felt by the younger poets of the Mode; the Irish lyrics of Padraic Colum read like other Love-Songs of Connacht omitted from Hyde's book by some extraordinary mishap – they are so good. The work of George Sigerson, of which I have given above an example, though not a typical one, is unique of its kind. It is of the Irish Mode mainly by virtue of its versification, which, in his translations, is always modelled on his originals.

The work of W. B. Yeats may stand with the greatest Anglo-Irish poetry. It may be surpassed by the work of one of his younger contemporaries. His work and theirs would supply me with examples, indeed the best examples, of poetry in this mode influenced by our way of speech and by our music. Professor J. W. Mackail, being asked to make an anthology of Latin Lyric Poetry limited to a hundred pieces, said that it might be plausibly argued that room could be found in such a selection for none but the work of Horace and Catullus. If I had to make an anthology of poems of the Irish Mode limited as is this selection, I could find room only for a small number of pieces by the earlier authors. And that perhaps is the best praise of those authors, paradoxical as it may seem. It is their seed that has flourished in the land.

I deal in one of my studies with some anthologies of Anglo-Irish verse. I wish to close this prosing with a reference for readers to other poets than those already mentioned. The work of Seumas O'Sullivan, Moira O'Neill, Joseph Campbell, Patrick J. McCall, and W. M. Letts is constantly of this mode. Some poems of Æ, Dora Sigerson, J. H. Cousins, Alice Furlong, Hon. Emily Lawless, Thomas Boyd, T. W. Rolleston, and, I think, of Thomas MacDonagh, are of it. The work of some young Irish Poets, of Joseph Plunkett and Peter McBrien, of Susan Mitchell and James Stephens, may well stand to posterity as more Irish, if one may say so, than any of this – as being most representative of the Irish gifts of fervour and vision which yet may save the world, now being devastated. Their work may so stand in the future; with such rare exceptions as *Your Fear,* which I print, it does not show the marks I look for, and, as I have already said, I fear suggesting more than I can prove.

The list of poets here is not, of course, intended to be complete, but some omissions and the inclusion of some of those mentioned may seem strange, even in view of the limitations I have set. I shall deal with a few typical cases. Dr John Todhunter (born 1839), an admirable poet, has written some poems of this mode. *Aghadoe* is in most of the anthologies:

> I walked to Mallow town from Aghadoe, Aghadoe,
> Brought his head from the gaol's gate to Aghadoe,
> Then I covered him with fern, and I piled on him the cairn.
> Like an Irish king he sleeps in Aghadoe.

Yet, living, as he has been, out of Ireland for many years, he is unknown to the present generation, as an influence nothing like Dr Sigerson, for instance, even though he too has translated many of the ancient Irish poems.

T. W. Rolleston who has done much Irish work, I include principally for the value of his beautiful version of O'Gillan's poem *The Dead at Clonmacnois*:

> In a quiet water'd land, a land of roses,
> Stands Saint Kieran's city fair;
> And the warriors of Erin in their famous generations
> Slumber there.   ...
>
> Many and many a son of Conn the Hundred-Fighter
> In the red earth lies at rest;
> Many a blue eye of Clan Colman the turf covers
> Many a swan-white breast.

Thomas Boyd, of whom we have heard nothing since the publication of his *Poems* in 1906 (Dublin: Gill), seems to me a poet sure to return and attain power. The twenty-five poems collected and published by Mr O'Donoghue in the volume mentioned are all Irish, though of many modes. No one can read the *Leanan Sidhe* or *An Donn Cuailgne* without seeing a poet in them; and they are not better than others in the book.

The work of Ethna Carbery is not as fine as that of Thomas Boyd, though some of her historical ballads will live:

> I am Brian Boy Magee –
> My father was Eoghan Ban –
> I was wakened from happy dreams
> By the shouts of my startled clan;
> And I saw through the leaping glare
> That marked where our homestead stood
> My mother swing by her hair
> And my brothers lie in their blood.   ...

It is not of the Irish Mode, at all events; it is ended (more's the pity), and it has not shed seeds. So with the work of others of whom I have made no mention in the text. It is not a glory of this Mode now and it does not seem to me destined for a better fortune. It is possible, of course, that I may have forgotten some writer of real power. Throughout I have had to depend mostly on my own reading and memory. No literary movement of equal importance has received so little notice from critics and historians, though the elder writers of the present time have had a world-wide vogue for years now.

[Among the translations which follow, these changes have been made to their original, 1916 edition's presentation:
• the original Irish versions of MacDonagh's own translations have been incorporated. In four cases, each English verse follows its Irish counterpart. That has not been done with *An Bunnán Buidhe/The Yellow Bittern*, because in that case MacDonagh took extensive liberty with the sequence of his verses and lines vis-a-vis the original Irish;
• the full set of MacDonaghs's verses of *The Stars Stand up in the Air* (partly quoted on p. 64) and its Irish original have been added for this edition;
• Mangan's *Song of Gladness* has been re-positioned to follow his other translations and to leave MacDonagh's together, except for MacDonagh's *Isn't it Pleasant for the Little Birds* which has been left in a prior position as in tune with its neighbours;
• as indicated in respect of Irish poems in the text, Roman script and modern spelling has been used; the original spelling of titles has, however, been unaltered.]

Translations From The Irish

Ceann Dubh Dílis

Put your head, darling, darling, darling,
Your darling black head my heart above;
Oh, mouth of honey, with the thyme for fragrance,
Who, with heart in breast, could deny you love?
Oh, many and many a young girl for me is pining,
Letting her locks of gold to the cold wind free,
For me, the foremost of our gay young fellows;
But I'd leave a hundred, pure love, for thee!
Then put your head, darling, darling, darling,
Your darling black head my heart above;
Oh, mouth of honey, with the thyme for fragrance,
Who, with heart in breast, could deny you love?

Samuel Ferguson

Cashel Of Munster

I'd wed you without herds, without money, or rich array,
And I'd wed you on a dewy morning at day-dawn grey;
My bitter woe it is, love, that we are not far away
In Cashel town, though the bare deal board were our marriage bed
    this day!

Oh, fair maid, remember the green hill-side;
Remember how I hunted about the valleys wide.
Time now has worn me; my locks are turned to grey,
The year is scarce and I am poor – but send me not, love, away!

Oh, deem not my blood is of base stain, my girl,
Oh, think not my birth was as the birth of the churl;
Marry me, and prove me, and say soon you will,
That noble blood is written on my right side still!

My purse holds no red gold, no coin of the silver white,
No herds are mine to drive through the long twilight;
But the pretty girl that would take me, all bare though I be and lone,
Oh, I'd take her with me kindly to the county Tyrone.

Oh, my girl, I can see 'tis in trouble you are,
And, oh, my girl, I see 'tis your people's reproach you bear.
– I am a girl in trouble for his sake with whom I fly,
And, oh, may no other maiden know such reproach as I!

Samuel Ferguson

Have you been at Carrick?

Have you been at Carrick, and saw my true-love there?
And saw you her features, all beautiful, bright, and fair?
Saw you the most fragrant, flowering, sweet apple-tree? –
Oh! saw you my loved one, and pines she in grief like me?

I have been at Carrick, and saw thy own true-love there;
And saw, too, her features, all beautiful, bright and fair;
And saw the most fragrant, flowering, sweet apple-tree –
I saw thy loved one – she pines not in grief, like thee!

Five guineas would price every tress of her golden hair –
Then think what a treasure her pillow at night to share,
These tresses thick-clustering and curling around her brow –
Oh, Ringlet of Fairness! I'll drink to thy beauty now!

When seeking to slumber, my bosom is rent with sighs –
I toss on my pillow till morning's blest beams arise;
No aid, bright Beloved! can reach me save God above,
For a blood-lake is formed of the light of my eyes with love!

Until yellow Autumn shall usher the Paschal day,
And Patrick's gay festival come in its train alway –

Until through my coffin the blossoming boughs shall grow,
My love on another I'll never in life bestow!

Lo! yonder the maiden illustrious, queen-like, high,
With long-flowing tresses adown to her sandal-tie –
Swan, fair as the lily, descended of high degree,
A myriad of welcomes, dear maid of my heart, to thee!

Edward Walsh

The Outlaw of Loch Lene

Oh, many a day have I made good ale in the glen,
'That came not of stream or malt, like the brewing of men.
My bed was the ground; my roof, the greenwood above,
And the wealth that I sought one far kind glance from my love.

Alas! on that night when the horses I drove from the field,
That I was not near from terror my angel to shield.
She stretched forth her arms – her mantle she flung to the wind,
And swam o'er Loch Lene, her outlawed lover to find.

Oh, would that a freezing sleet-wing'd tempest did sweep,
And I and my love were alone, far off on the deep;
I'd ask not a ship, or a bark, or pinnace to save, –
With her hand round my waist, I'd fear not the wind or the wave.

'Tis down by the lake where the wild-tree fringes its sides,
The maid of my heart, my fair one of Heaven resides –
I think as at eve she wanders its mazes along,
The birds go to sleep by the sweet wild twist of her song.

J. J. Callanan

Pastheen Finn[2]

Oh, my fair Pastheen is my heart's delight;
Her gay heart laughs in her blue eye bright;
Like the apple blossom her bosom white,
And her neck like the swan's on a March morn bright!

Then, Oro, come with me! come with me! come with me!
Oro, come with me! brown girl, sweet!
And, oh! I would go through snow and sleet
If you would come with me, brown girl, sweet!

Love of my heart, my fair Pastheen!
Her cheeks are as red as the rose's sheen,
But my lips have tasted no more, I ween,
Than the glass I drank to the health of my queen!
Then, Oro, come with me! come with me! come with me!
Oro, come with me! brown girl, sweet!
And, oh! I would go through snow and sleet
If you would come with me, brown girl, sweet!

Were I in the town, where's mirth and glee,
Or 'twixt two barrels of barley bree,
With my fair Pastheen upon my knee,
'Tis I would drink to her pleasantly!
Then, Oro, come with me! come with me! come with me!
Oro, come with me! brown girl, sweet
And, oh! I would go through snow and sleet
If you would come with me, brown girl, sweet!

Nine nights I lay in longing and pain,
Betwixt two bushes, beneath the rain,
Thinking to see you, love, once again;
But whistle and call were all in vain!
Then, Oro, come with me! come with me! come with me!
Oro, come with me! brown girl, sweet!
And, oh! I would go through snow and sleet
If you would come with me, brown girl, sweet!

I'll leave my people, both friend and foe;
From all the girls in the world I'll go;
But from you, sweetheart, oh, never! oh, no!
Till I lie in the coffin, stretched cold and low!
Then, Oro, come with me! come with me! come with me!
Oro, come with me! brown girl, sweet!
And, oh! I would go through snow and sleet
If you would come with me, brown girl, sweet.

Samuel Ferguson

The Coolun

Oh, had you seen the Coolun,
Walking down by the cuckoo's street,
With the dew of the meadow shining
On her milk-white twinkling feet.
My love she is, and my *cailin óg*
And she dwells in Bal'nagar;
And she bears the palm of beauty bright
From the fairest that in Erin are.

In Bal'nagar is the Coolun,
Like the berry on the bough her cheek;
Bright beauty dwells for ever
On her fair neck and ringlets sleek;
Oh, sweeter is her mouth's soft music
Than the lark or thrush at dawn,
Or the blackbird in the greenwood singing
Farewell to the setting sun.

Rise up, my boy! make ready
My horse, for I forth would ride,
To follow the modest damsel,
Where she walks on the green hill-side:
For ever since our youth were we plighted,
In faith, troth, and wedlock true –
Oh, she's sweeter to me nine times over
Than organ or cuckoo!

For ever since my childhood
I loved the fair and darling child;
But our people came between us,
And with lucre our pure love defiled:
Oh, my woe it is, and my bitter pain,
And I weep it night and day,
That the *cailín bán* of my early love
Is torn from my heart away.

Sweetheart and faithful treasure,
Be constant still, and true;
Nor for want of herds and houses
Leave one who would ne'er leave you.

I'll pledge you the blessed Bible,
Without and eke within,
That the faithful God will provide for us,
Without thanks to kith or kin.

Oh, love, do you remember
When we lay all night alone,
Beneath the ash in the winter storm,
When the oak wood round did groan?
No shelter then from the blast had we,
The bitter blast or sleet,
But your gown to wrap about our heads,
And my coat round our feet.

Samuel Ferguson

Pulse of my Heart

Before the sun rose at yester-dawn,
I met a fair maid adown the lawn:
The berry and snow
To her cheek gave its glow,
And her bosom was fair as the sailing swan –
Then, pulse of my heart! what gloom is thine?

Her beautiful voice more hearts hath won
Than Orpheus' lyre of old had done;
Her ripe eyes of blue
Were crystals of dew,
On the grass of the lawn before the sun –
And, pulse of my heart! what gloom is thine?

Edward Walsh

Nach Aoibhinn do na hÉiníní
Isn't it Pleasant for the Little Birds[3]

Nach aoibhinn do na héiníní
éiríos go hárd,
's bhíos a' ceiliúr le chéile
ar aon chraoibh amháin;
ní mar sin dom féin
's dom chéad míle grá;
is fada ón a chéile orainn
éiríos gach lá.

Isn't it pleasant for the little birds
That rise up above,
And be nestling together
On the one branch, in love?
Not so with myself
And the darling of my heart –
Every day rises upon us
Far, far apart.

Is báine í ná 'n lile
is deise í ná 'n scéimh,
is binne í ná 'n veidhlín
's is soilsí ná an ghréin;
is fearr ná sin uile
a h-uaisleacht 's a méin –
's a Dhia atá sna flaithis,
fuascail dom phéin!

She is whiter than the lily,
Than beauty more fine.
She is sweeter than the violin,
More radiant than the sunshine.
But her grace and her nobleness
Are beyond all that again –
And, O God Who art in Heaven,
Free me from pain!

Thomas MacDonagh from an anonymous original

Pearl of the White Breast[4]

There's a colleen fair as May,
For a year and for a day
I've sought by every way – Her heart to gain.
There's no art of tongue or eye,
Fond youths with maidens try,
But I've tried with ceaseless sigh – Yet tried in vain.
If to France or far-off Spain,
She'd cross the watery main,
To see her face again – The sea I'd brave.
And if 'tis Heaven's decree,
That mine she may not be,
May the Son of Mary me – In mercy save!

Oh, thou blooming milk-white dove,
To whom I've given true love,
Do not ever thus reprove – My constancy.
There are maidens would be mine,
With wealth in hand and kine,
If my heart would but incline – To turn from thee,
But a kiss, with welcome bland,
And a touch of thy dear hand,
Are all that I demand, – Wouldst thou not spurn;
For if not mine, dear girl,
Oh, Snowy-breasted Pearl!
May I never from the Fair – With life return!

George Petrie

The County of Mayo

On the deck of Patrick Lynch's boat I sat in woful plight,
Through my sighing all the weary day, and weeping all the night;
Were it not that full of sorrow from my people forth I go,
By the blessed sun! 'tis royally I'd sing thy praise, Mayo!

When I dwelt at home in plenty, and my gold did much abound,
In the company of fair young maids the Spanish ale went round –
'Tis a bitter change from those gay days that now I'm forced to go,
And must leave my bones in Santa Cruz, far from my own Mayo.

They are altered girls in Irrul now; 'tis proud they're grown and
    high,
With their hair-bags and their top-knots, for I pass their buckles by –
But it's little now I heed their airs, for God will have it so,
That I must depart for foreign lands, and leave my sweet Mayo.

'Tis my grief that Patrick Loughlin is not Earl of Irrul still,
And that Brian Duff no longer rules as Lord upon the hill:
And that Colonel Hugh MacGrady should be lying dead and low,
And I sailing, sailing swiftly from the county of Mayo.

George Fox from the original by Thomas Flavell[5]

The Fair Hills of Ireland

A plenteous place is Ireland for hospitable cheer,
    Uileacan dubh O!
Where the wholesome fruit is bursting from the yellow barley ear;
    Uileacan dubh O!
There is honey in the trees where her misty vales expand,
And her forest paths in summer are by falling waters fanned;
There is dew at high noontide there, and springs i' the yellow sand,
    On the fair hills of holy Ireland.

Curled he is and ringleted, and plaited to the knee,
    Uileacan dubh O!
Each captain who comes sailing across the Irish sea;
    Uileacan dubh O!
And I will make my journey, if life and health but stand,
Unto that pleasant country, that fresh and fragrant strand,
And leave your boasted braveries, your wealth and high command,
    For the fair hills of holy Ireland.

Large and profitable are the stacks upon the ground;
    Uileacan dubh O!
The butter and the cream do wondrously abound;
    Uileacan dubh O!
The cresses on the water and the sorrels are at hand,
And the cuckoo's calling daily his note of music bland,
And the bold thrush sings so bravely his song i' the forests grand,
    On the fair hills of holy Ireland.
Samuel Ferguson

Lamentation of Mac Liag of Kincora

Oh, where, Kincora! is Brian the Great?
And where is the beauty that once was thine?
Oh, where are the princes and nobles that sate
At the feast in thy halls, and drank the red wine?
    Where, O Kincora?

Oh, where, Kincora! are thy valorous lords?
Oh, whither, thou Hospitable! are they gone?
Oh, where are the Dalcassians of the Golden Swords?
And where are the warriors Brian led on?
    Where, O Kincora ?

And where is Murrough, the descendant of kings –
The defeater of a hundred – the daringly brave –
Who set but slight store by jewels and rings –
Who swam down the torrent and laughed at its wave?
    Where, O Kincora?

And where is Donogh, King Brian's worthy son?
And where is Conaing, the Beautiful Chief?
And Kian, and Corc? Alas! they are gone –
They have left me this night alone with my grief!
    Left me, Kincora!

And where are the chiefs with whom Brian went forth,
The ne'er-vanquished son of Evin the Brave,
The great King of Onaght, renowned for his worth,
And the hosts of Baskinn, from the western wave?
    Where, O Kincora?

Oh, where is Duvlann of the Swift-footed Steeds?
And where is Kian, who was son of Molloy?
And where is King Lonergan, the fame of whose deeds
In the red battle-field no time can destroy?
    Where, O Kincora ?

And where is that youth of majestic height,
The faith-keeping Prince of the Scots? – Even he,
As wide as his fame was, as great as was his might,
Was tributary, O Kincora, to thee!

Thee, O Kincora!

They are gone, those heroes of royal birth,
Who plundered no churches, and broke no trust,
'Tis weary for me to be living on earth
When they, O Kincora, lie low in the dust!
    Low, O Kincora!

Oh, never again will Princes appear,
To rival the Dalcassians of the Cleaving Swords!
I can never dream of meeting afar or anear,
In the east or the west, such heroes and lords!
    Never, Kincora!

Oh, dear are the images my memory calls up
Of Brian Boru! – how he never would miss
To give me at the banquet the first bright cup!
Ah! why did he heap on me honour like this?
    Why, O Kincora?

I am MacLiag, and my home is on the Lake;
Thither often, to that palace whose beauty is fled,
Came Brian to ask me, and I went for his sake.
Oh, my grief! that I should live, and Brian be dead!
    Dead, O Kincora!

James Clarence Mangan

A Farewell to Patrick Sarsfield, Earl of Lucan[6]

Farewell, O Patrick Sarsfield, may luck be on your path!
Your camp is broken up, your work is marred for years;
But you go to kindle into flame the King of France's wrath,
Though you leave sick Eire in tears –
    Och, ochone!

May the white sun and moon rain glory on your head,
All hero as you are, and holy man of God!
To you the Saxons owe a many an hour of dread
In the land you have often trod –
    Och, ochone!

The Son of Mary guard you, and bless you to the end!
'Tis altered is the time when your legions were astir,
When at Cullen you were hailed as conqueror and friend,
And you crossed Narrow-water, near Birr –
    Och, ochone!

I'll journey to the north, over mount, moor, and wave;
'Twas there I first beheld drawn up, in file and line,
The brilliant Irish hosts; they were bravest of the brave,
But, alas, they scorned to combine –
    Och, ochone!

I saw the royal Boyne when his billows flashed with blood;
I fought at Graine Og, when a thousand horsemen fell;
On the dark empurpled plain of Aughrim, too, I stood,
On the plain by Tubberdonny's well –
    Och, ochone!

To the heroes of Limerick, the City of the Fights,
Be my best blessing borne on the wings of the air;
We had card-playing there o'er our camp fires at night,
And the Word of Life, too, and prayer –
    Och, ochone!

But for you, Londonderry, may plague smite and slay
Your people! May ruin desolate you stone by stone!
Through you there's many a gallant youth lies coffinless to-day
With the winds for mourners alone –
    Och, ochone!

I clomb the high hill on a fair summer noon,
And saw the Saxons muster, clad in armour blinding bright:
Oh, rage withheld my hand, or gunsman and dragoon
Should have supped with Satan that night! –
    Och, ochone!

How many a noble soldier, how many a cavalier,
Careered along this road, seven fleeting weeks ago,
With silver-hilted sword, with matchlock and with spear,
Who now, *mo bhrón!* lieth low –
    Och, ochone!

All hail to thee, Beinn Eidir! but ah, on thy brow
I see a limping soldier, who battled and who bled
Last year in the cause of the Stuart, though now
The worthy is begging his bread –
 Och, ochone!

And Diarmid! oh, Diarmid! he perished in the strife;
His head it was spiked upon a halberd high;
His colours they were trampled: he had no chance of life
If the Lord God Himself stood by! –
 Och, ochone!

But most, oh, my woe! I lament and lament
For the ten valiant heroes who dwelt nigh the Nore,
And my three blessed brothers they left me and went
To the wars, and returned no more –
 Och, ochone!

On the bridge of the Boyne was our first overthrow;
By Slaney the next, for we battled without rest;
The third was at Aughrim. O Eire! thy woe
Is a sword in my bleeding breast –
 Och, ochone!

Oh, the roof above our heads, it was barbarously fired,
While the black Orange guns blazed and bellowed around!
And as volley followed volley, Colonel Mitchel inquired
Whether Lucan still stood his ground? –
 Och, ochone!

But O'Kelly still remains, to defy and to toil,
He has memories that hell won't permit him to forget,
And a sword that will make the blue blood flow like oil
Upon many an Aughrim yet! –
 Och, ochone!

And I never shall believe that my fatherland can fall
With the Burkes, and the Dukes, and the son of Royal James,
And Talbot, the captain, and Sarsfield above all,
The beloved of damsels and dames –
 Och, ochone!

James Clarence Mangan

Kathaleen Ny Houlihan

Long they pine in weary woe, the nobles of our land,
Long they wander to and fro, proscribed, alas! and banned;
Feastless, houseless, altarless, they bear the exile's brand;
    But their hope is in the coming-to of Kathaleen Ny-Houlahan!

Think her not a ghastly hag, too hideous to be seen,
Call her not unseemly names, our matchless Kathaleen;
Young she is, and fair she is, and would be crowned a queen,
    Were the king's son at home here with Kathaleen Ny-Houlahan!

Sweet and mild would look her face, oh! none so sweet and mild,
Could she crush the foes by whom her beauty is reviled;
Woollen plaids would grace herself, and robes of silk her child,
    If the king's son were living here with Kathaleen Ny-Houlahan!

Sore disgrace it is to see the Arbitress of thrones,
Vassal to a Saxoneen of cold and sapless bones!
Bitter anguish wrings our souls – with heavy sighs and groans
    We wait the young Deliverer of Kathaleen Ny-Houlahan!

Let us pray to Him who holds life's issues in His hands –
Him who formed the mighty globe, with all its thousand lands,
Girdling them with seas and mountains, rivers deep, and strands,
    To cast a look of pity upon Kathaleen Ny-Houlahan!

He who over sands and waves led Israel along –
He who fed, with heavenly bread, that chosen tribe and throng –
He who stood by Moses, when his foes were fierce and strong –
    May He show forth His might in saving Kathaleen Ny-Houlahan!

James Clarence Mangan from the original by William Heffernan[7]

The Song of Gladness[8]

It was on a balmy evening, as June was departing fast,
That alone, and meditating in grief on the times a-past,
I wandered through the gloomsome shades
Of bosky Aherlow,
A wilderness of glens and glades,
When suddenly a thrilling strain of song

Broke forth upon the air in one incessant flow;
Sweeter it seemed to me (both voice and word)
Than harmony of the harp, or carol of the bird,
For it foretold fair Freedom's triumph, and the doom of Wrong.

The celestial hymns and anthems, that far o'er the sounding sea
Come to Erin from the temples of bright-bosomed Italy;
The music which from hill and rath
The playful fairy race
Pour on the wandering warrior's path,
Bewildering him with wonder and delight,
Or the cuckoo's full note from some green sunless place,
Some sunken thicket in a stilly wood,
Had less than that rich melody made mine Irish blood
Bound in its veins for ecstasy, or given my soul new might!

And while as I stood I listened, behold, thousand swarm of bees,
All arrayed in gay gold armour, shone red through the dusky trees;
I felt a boding in my soul,
A truthful boding, too,
That Erin's days of gloom and dole
Will soon be but remembered as a dream,
And the olden glory show eclipsèd by the new.
Where will the Usurper then be? Banished far!
Where his vile hireling henchmen? Slaughtered all in war!
For blood shall rill down every hill, and blacken every stream.

I am Heffernan of Shronehill: my land mourns in thraldom long;
And I see but one sad sight here, the weak trampled by the strong,
Yet if to-morrow underneath
A burial-stone I lay,
Clasped in the skeleton arms of death.
And if a pilgrim wind again should waft
Over my noteless grave the song I heard to-day,
I would spring up revivified, reborn,
A living soul again, as on my birthday morn,
Ay! even though coffined, over-earthed, tombed-in, and epitaphed!

James Clarence Mangan from the original by William Heffernan

Eamonn an Chnuic[9]

Cé hé sin amuigh
a bhfuil faobhar ar a ghuth
ag réabadh mo dhorais dúnta?
Mise Éamon an Chnuic
atá báite fuar fliuch
ó shíor-shiúl sléibhte is gleannta.

– Who is that out there still
With voice sharp and shrill,
Beating my door and calling?
– I am Ned of the Hill,
Wet, weary and chill,
The mountains and glens long walking.

A laogh ghil 's a chuid,
cad a dhéanfainn-se dhuit,
muna gcuirinn ort binn dem ghúna,
's go bhfuil púdar go tiubh
á shíor-shéideadh leat
's go mbeimís araon múchta.

– O my dear love and true!
What could I do for you
But under my mantle draw you?
For the bullets like hail
Fall thick on your trail,
And together we both may be slaughtered.

Is fada mise amuigh
faoi shneachta 's faoi shioc
's gan dánacht agam ar éinne;
mo sheisreach gan scor,
mo bhranar gan chur,
is gan iad agam ar aon chor.

– Long lonely I go,
Under frost, under snow,
Hunted through hill and through hollow.
No comrade I know:
No furrow I sow:
My team stands unyoked in the fallow:

Níl caraid agam;
is dánaid liom san,
do ghlacfadh mé moch ná déanach
's go gcaithfidh mé dul
thar farraige soir,
ós ann nach bhfuil aon dem ghaolta.

No friend will give ear
Or harbour me here –
'Tis that makes the weight of my sorrow!
So my journey must be
To the east o'er the sea
Where no kindred will find me or follow!

Original by Eamon Ó Riain; translation by Thomas MacDonagh[10]

A Dhruimfhionn Donn Dílis

A Dhruimfhionn donn dílis,
a shióda na mbó,
cá ngabhann tú san oiche
's cá mbiónn tú sa ló?
bím-se ar na coillte
's mo bhuachaill im chomhair,
agus d'fhág sé siúd mise
ag sileadh na ndeor.

– O Druimfhionn Donn Dílis!
O Silk of the Kine!
Where goest thou for sleeping?
What pastures are thine?
– In the woods with my gilly
Always I must keep,
And 'tis that now that leaves me
Forsaken to weep.

Níl fearann, níl tíos agam,
níl fíonta ná ceol,
níl flatha am choímhdeacht,
níl saoithe ná sló;
ach ag síor-ól an uisce
go minic sa ló
agus beath-uisce 's fíon
ag mo naimhde ar bord.

Land, homestead, wines, music:
I am reft of them all!
Chief and bard that once wooed me
Are gone from my call!
And cold water to soothe me
I sup with my tears,
While the foe that pursues me
Has drinking that cheers.

Dá bhfaghainnse cead aighnis
nó radharc ar an gcoróin,
Sasanaigh do leidhbfinn
mar do leidhbfinn sean-bhróg
tré chnocaibh, tré ailltibh
's tré ghleannta dubha ceo
agus siúd mar a bhréagfainnse
an Druimfhionn donn óg.

– Through the mist of the glensides
And hills I'll return:
Like a brogue beyond mending
The Sasanach I'll spurn:
If in battle's contention
I have sight of the crown,
I'll befriend thee and defend thee,
My young Druimfhionn Donn!

Thomas MacDonagh – *ón mbéaloideas*

Stuairín Na mBachall mBreágh Réidh
The Stars Stand Up in the Air

Táid na réalta 'na seasamh ar an spéir,
An ghréin is an ghealach 'n-a luí;
Tá an fharraige tráite gan braon,
'S níl réim ag an eala mar bhíodh;
Tá an cuaichín i mbarra na ngéag
'Ghá shíor-rá gur éalaigh sí uainn,
A stuairín na mbachall mbreá réidh
D'fhág Éire faoi fhadthuirse chruaidh!

The stars stand up in the air,
    The sun and the moon are gone,
The strand of its waters is bare,
    And her sway is swept from the swan.

The cuckoo was calling all day,
    Hid in the branches above,
How my stóirín is fled far away –
    'Tis my grief that I give her my love !

Trí ní do chím trés an ngrá,
An peacadh, an bás, is an phian,
Is m'intinn á inseann gach lá dhom
M'aigne, gur chráigh sí le ciach.
A mhaighdean do mhill tú im' lár mé,
Is m'impí óm' lámh chughat-sa 'niar,
Mo leigheas ó na saighdte im' lár-se,
'S go bhfaighe tú na grása ó Dhia.

Three things through love I see,
    Sorrow and sin and death –
And my mind reminding me
    That this doom I breathe with my breath.

But sweeter than violin or lute
    Is my love, and she left me behind –
I wish that all music were mute,
    And I to all beauty were blind.
Thomas MacDonagh from an anonymous original

An Bunnán Buí

A bhunnáin bhuí, 'sé mo léan do luí
'S do chnámha sínte tar éis do ghrinn;
Ní easpa croí ach díobháil dí
A d'fhág 'do luí thú ar chúl do chinn;
Is measa liom féin ná scrois na Traí,
Tú bheith gan bhrí ar leaca lom
'S nach dearnais díth ná dola 'on tír
'S nárbh fhearr leat fíon ná uisce poill!

A bhunnáin álainn 'sé mo mhíle crá
Tú id chúl ar lár amuigh rómham sa tslí
'S gur moch gach lá a chluininn do ghrág
Thíos ar an láib is tú ag ól na dí;
'Sé an ní deir cách led bhráthair Cathal
Go bhfaighidh mé bás mar siúd, má's fíor,
Acht ní hamhlaidh tá, siúd an préachán breá
Chuaidh a dh'éag ar ball de easpa dí.

A bhunnáin óig sé mo mhíle brón
Tú bheith gan treoir i measc na dtonn
'S na lucha móra ag triall ar do thorramh
Ag déanamh spóirt agus ceiliúr ann;
Dá gcuirfeá scéala fá mo dhéin-se
Go raibh tú i ngéibheann gan bhrí fá bhroid,
Do bhrisfinn béim mhór ar an loch sin Vesey
A fhliuchfadh do bhéal is do chorp istigh.

Dúirt mo stór liom ligean den ól –
Nach mbeinn-se beo ach seal beag gearr;
'Sé duirt mé léi go dtug sí a h-éitheach –
Go mb' fhad ar mo shaol an deoch a fháil;
An bhfaca sibh éan an phíopáin réidh
Ag dul in éag den tart ar ball?
A chomharsain chléibh, fliuchaidh bhur mbéal,
Ní bhfaighidh sibh braon i ndiaidh bhur mbáis!

Ní hiad bhur n-éanlaith atá mé ag éagcaoin,
An lon, an smaolach ná an chorr ghlas
Ach mo bhunnán buí bhí lán de chroí
'S gur cosúil liom féin é i snua 's i ndath;
Ní bhíodh sé choiche ach ag síor-ól na dí

'S deir siad go mbím-se ar an nós sin seal,
Níl braon dá bhfaighead nach ligfead síos
Ar cheist go bhfaighinnse bás den tart!

The Yellow Bittern[11]

The yellow bittern that never broke out
In a drinking bout, might as well have drunk;
His bones are thrown on a naked stone
Where he lived alone like a hermit monk.
O yellow bittern! I pity your lot,
Though they say that a sot like myself is curst –
I was sober a while, but I'll drink and be wise
For fear I should die in the end of thirst.

It's not for the common birds that I'd mourn,
The black-bird, the corn-crake or the crane,
But for the bittern that's shy and apart
And drinks in the marsh from the lone bog-drain.
Oh! if I had known you were near your death,
While my breath held out I'd have run to you,
Till a splash from the Lake of the Son of the Bird
Your soul would have stirred and waked anew.

My darling told me to drink no more
Or my life would be o'er in a little short while;
But I told her 'tis drink gives me health and strength
And will lengthen my road by many a mile.
You see how the bird of the long smooth neck
Could get his death from the thirst at last –
Come, son of my soul, and drain your cup,
You'll get no sup when your life is past.

In a wintering island by Constantine's halls
A bittern calls from a wineless place,
And tells me that hither he cannot come
Till the summer is here and the sunny days.
When he crosses the stream there and wings o'er the sea
Then a fear comes to me he may fail in his flight –
Well, the milk and the ale are drunk every drop,
And a dram won't stop our thirst this night.

***Original above by Cathal Buidhe Mac Giolla Ghunna; translation
by Thomas MacDonagh***

Ballads and Street Songs

Shule Aroon[12]
A BRIGADE BALLAD

I wish I were on yonder hill,
'Tis there I'd sit and cry my fill
Till every tear would turn a mill,
Is go dtéidh tú, a mhuirnín, slán!

> *Siubhail, siubhail, siubhail, a rúin!*
> *Siubhail go socair, agus siubhail go ciuin,*
> *Siubhail go dtí an dorus agus éulaigh liom,*
> *Is go dtéidh tú, a mhuirnín, slán!*

I'll sell my rock, I'll sell my reel,
I'll sell my only spinning-wheel,
To buy for my love a sword of steel,
Is go dtéidh tú, a mhuirnín, slán!

I'll dye my petticoats, I'll dye them red,
And round the world I'll beg my bread,
Until my parents will wish me dead,
Is go dtéidh tú, a mhuirnín, slán!

I wish, I wish, I wish in vain,
I wish I had my heart again,
And vainly think I'd not complain,
Is go dtéidh tú, a mhuirnín, slán!

But now my love has gone to France,
To try his fortune to advance;
If he e'er come back 'tis but a chance,
Is go dtéidh tú, a mhuirnín, slán!

Anonymous

The Croppy Boy[13]

It was very early in the spring,
The birds did whistle and sweetly sing,
Changing their notes from tree to tree,
And the song they sang was Old Ireland free.

It was early in the night,
The yeoman cavalry gave me a fright;
The yeoman cavalry was my downfall
And taken was I by Lord Cornwall.

'Twas in the guard-house where I was laid
And in a parlour where I was tried;
My sentence passed and my courage low
When to Dungannon I was forced to go.

As I was passing by my father's door,
My brother William stood at the door;
My aged father stood at the door,
And my tender mother her hair she tore.

As I was walking up Wexford Street
My own first cousin I chanced to meet:
My own first cousin did me betray,
And for one bare guinea swore my life away.

My sister Mary heard the express,
She ran upstairs in her mourning-dress –
Five hundred guineas I will lay down,
To see my brother through Wexford Town.

As I was walking up Wexford Hill,
Who could blame me to cry my fill?

I looked behind and I looked before,
But my tender mother I shall ne'er see more.

As I was mounted on the platform high,
My aged father was standing by;
My aged father did me deny,
And the name he gave me was the Croppy Boy.

It was in Dungannon this young man died,
And in Dungannon his body lies;
And you good Christians that do pass by
Just drop a tear for the Croppy Boy.

Anonymous

The Streams of Bunclody[14]

Oh, was I at the moss-house where the birds do increase,
At the foot of Mount Leinster or some silent place
Near the streams of Bunclody, where all pleasures do meet,
And all I'd require is one kiss from you, sweet.

If I was in Bunclody I would think myself at home,
'Tis there I would have a sweetheart, but here I have none.
Drinking strong liquor in the height of my cheer –
Here's a health to Bunclody and the lass I love dear.

The cuckoo is a pretty bird, it sings as it flies,
It brings us good tidings and tells us no lies,
It sucks the young bird's eggs to make its voice clear,
And it never cries cuckoo till the summer is near.

If I was a clerk and could write a good hand,
I would write to my true love that she might understand,
I am a young fellow that is wounded in love,
That lived by Bunclody, but now must remove.

If I was a lark and had wings, I then could fly,
I would go to yon arbour where my love she doth lie,
I'd proceed to yon arbour where my love does lie,
And on her fond bosom contented I would die.

The reason my love slights me, as you may understand,
Because she has a freehold, and I have no land,
She has a great store of riches and a large sum of gold,
And everything fitting a house to uphold.

So adieu, my dear father, adieu, my dear mother,
Farewell to my sister, farewell to my brother;
I'm going to America, my fortune for to try;
When I think upon Bunclody, I'm ready for to die!

Anonymous

The Groves of Blarney[15]

The groves of Blarney they look so charming,
Down by the purling of sweet, silent streams,
Being banked with posies that spontaneous grow there,
Planted in order by the sweet rock close.
'Tis there's the daisy and the sweet carnation,
The blooming pink and the rose so fair,
The daffadowndilly, likewise the lily,
All flowers that scent the sweet, fragrant air.

'Tis Lady Jeffers that owns this station;
Like Alexander, or Queen Helen fair,
There's no commander in all the nation,
For emulation, can with her compare.
Such walls surround her, that no ninepounder
Could dare to plunder her place of strength;
But Oliver Cromwell her he did pommel,
And made a breach in her battlement.

There's gravel walks there for speculation
And conversation in sweet solitude.
'Tis there the lover may hear the dove, or
The gentle plover in the afternoon;
And if a lady would be so engaging
As to walk alone in those shady bowers,
'Tis there the courtier he may transport her
Into some fort, or all under ground.

For 'tis there's a cave where no daylight enters,
But cats and badgers are for ever bred;
Being mossed by nature, that makes it sweeter
Than a coach-and-six or a feather bed.
'Tis there the lake is, well stored with perches,
And comely eels in the verdant mud;
Besides the leeches, and groves of beeches,
Standing in order for to guard the flood.

There's statues gracing this noble place in –
All heathen gods and nymphs so fair;
Bold Neptune, Plutarch, and Nicodemus,
All standing naked in the open air!
So now to finish this brave narration,
Which my poor genii could not entwine;
But were I Homer, or Nebuchadnezzar,
'Tis in every feature I would make it shine.

R. A. Milliken

Original Poems[16]

At the Mid Hour of Night

At the mid hour of night, when stars are weeping, I fly
To the lone vale we loved, when life shone warm in thine eye;
And I think oft, if spirits can steal from the regions of air,
To revisit past scenes of delight, thou wilt come to me there,
And tell me our love is remembered, even in the sky.

Then I sing the wild song it once was rapture to hear
When our voices, commingling, breathed like one on the ear;
And as Echo far off through the vale my sad orison rolls,
I think, O my love! 'tis thy voice from the Kingdom of Souls,
Faintly answering still the notes that once were so dear.

Thomas Moore

The Starling Lake

My sorrow that I am not by the little dún
By the lake of the starlings at Rosses under the hill,
And the larks there, singing over the fields of dew,
Or evening there and the sedges still.
For plain I see now the length of the yellow sand,
And Lissadell far off and its leafy ways,
And the holy mountain whose mighty heart
Gathers into it all the coloured days.

My sorrow that I am not by the little dún
By the lake of the starlings at evening when all is still,
And still in whispering sedges the herons stand.
'Tis there I would nestle at rest till the quivering moon
Uprose in the golden quiet over the hill.

Seumas O'Sullivan

The Irish Peasant to his Mistress[17]

Through grief and through danger thy smile hath cheered my way,
Till hope seemed to bud from each thorn that round me lay;
The darker our fortune, the brighter our pure love burned,
Till shame into glory, till fear into zeal was turned.
Oh! slave that I was, in thy arms my spirit felt free,
And blessed e'en the sorrows that made me more dear to thee.

Thy rival was honoured, while thou wert wronged and scorned;
Thy crown was of briars, while gold her brows adorned;
She wooed me to temples, while thou layst hid in caves;
Her friends were all masters, while thine, alas! were slaves;
Yet cold in the earth at thy feet I'd rather be
Than wed what I loved not, or turn one thought from thee.

They slander thee sorely who say thy vows are frail;
Hadst thou been a false one, thy cheek had looked less pale;
They say, too, so long thou hast worn those lingering chains,
That deep in thy heart they have printed their servile stains –
Oh! do not believe them, no chain could that soul subdue:
Where shineth thy spirit, there liberty shineth too.

Thomas Moore

A Vision of Connaught in the Thirteenth Century

I walked entranced
Through a land of Morn:
The sun, with wondrous excess of light,
Shone down and glanced
Over seas of corn
And lustrous gardens aleft and right.

Even in the clime
Of resplendent Spain,
Beams no such sun upon such a land;
But it was the time,
'Twas in the reign,
Of Cahal Mór of the Wine-red Hand.

Anon stood nigh
By my side a man
Of princely aspect and port sublime
Him queried I –
'O, my Lord and Khan,
What clime is this, and what golden time?
When he – 'The clime
Is a clime to praise,
The clime is Erin's, the green and bland;
And it is the time,
These be the days,
Of Cahal Mór of the Wine-red Hand!'

Then saw I thrones
And circling fires,
And a Dome rose near me, as by a spell,
Whence flowed the tones
Of silver lyres,
And many voices in wreathèd swell;
And their thrilling chime
Fell on mine ears
As the heavenly hymn of an angel-band –
'It is now the time
These be the years,
Of Cahal Mór of the Wine-red Hand!'

I sought the hall,
And, behold! – a change
From light to darkness, from joy to woe!
King, nobles, all,
Looked aghast and strange;
The minstrel-group sate in dumbest show!
Had some great crime
Wrought this dread amaze,
This terror? None seemed to understand

'Twas then the time,
We were in the days,
Of Cahal Mór of the Wine-red Hand.

I again walked forth;
But lo! the sky
Showed fleckt with blood, and an alien sun
Glared from the north,
And there stood on high,
Amid his shorn beams, a skeleton!
It was by the stream
Of the castled Maine,
One Autumn eve, in the Teuton's land,
That I dreamed this dream
Of the time and reign
Of Cahal Mór of the Wine-red Hand!

James Clarence Mangan

Your Fear

I try to blame
When from your eyes the battle-flame
Leaps – when cleaves my speech the spear
For fear lest I should speak your name.

Your name, that's known
But to your heart, you fear has flown
To mine – You've heard not any bird,
No wings have stirred save yours alone.

Alone your wings
Have fluttered: half-forgotten things
Come crowding home into your heart,
Filling your heart with other Springs:

Springs when you've sung
Your secret name with happy tongue
Loudly and innocent as the flowers
Through hours of laughter proudly young.

Young is the year
And other wings are waking: near
Your heart my name is knocking loud –
Ah, be not proud! You need not fear.

Fearing lest I
Should wrest your secret from on high
You will not listen to my name –
I cannot blame you though I try.

Joseph Plunkett

The Fairy Thorn
AN ULSTER BALLAD

'Get up, our Anna dear, from the weary spinning-wheel;
For your father's on the hill, and your mother is asleep:
Come up above the crags, and we'll dance a Highland reel
Around the Fairy Thorn on the steep.'

At Anna Grace's door 'twas thus the maidens cried,
Three merry maidens fair in kirtles of the green;
And Anna laid the rock and the weary wheel aside,
The fairest of the four, I ween.

They're glancing through the glimmer of the quiet eve,
Away in milky wavings of neck and ankle bare;
The heavy-sliding stream in its sleepy song they leave,
And the crags in the ghostly air.

And linking hand-in-hand, and singing as they go,
The maids along the hill-side have ta'en their fearless way,
Till they come to where the rowan trees in lonely beauty grow
Beside the Fairy Hawthorn grey.

The Hawthorn stands between the ashes tall and slim,
Like matron with her twin grand-daughters at her knee;
The rowan berries cluster o'er her low head grey and dim
In ruddy kisses sweet to see.

The merry maidens four have ranged them in a row,
Between each lovely couple a stately rowan stem,
And away in mazes wavy, like skimming birds they go:
Oh, never carolled bird like them!

But solemn is the silence of the silvery haze
That drinks away their voices in echoless repose,
And dreamily the evening has stilled the haunted braes,
And dreamier the gloaming grows.

And sinking one by one, like lark-notes from the sky,
When the falcon's shadow saileth across the open shaw,
Are hushed the maidens' voices, as cowering down they lie
In the flutter of their sudden awe.

For, from the air above and the grassy ground beneath,
And from the mountain-ashes and the old Whftethorn between,
A Power of faint enchantment doth through their beings breathe,
And they sink down together on the green.

They sink together silent, and stealing side to side,
They fling their lovely arms o'er their drooping necks so fair,
Then vainly strive again their naked arms to hide,
For their shrinking necks again are bare.

Thus clasped and prostrate all, with their heads together bowed,
Soft o'er their bosoms' beating – the only human sound –
They hear the silky footsteps of the silent fairy crowd,
Like a river in the air gliding round.

Nor scream can any raise, nor prayer can any say,
But wild, wild the terror of the speechless three –
For they feel fair Anna Grace drawn silently away,
By whom they dare not look to see.

They feel their tresses twine with her parting locks of gold,
And the curls elastic falling, as her head withdraws;
They feel her sliding arms from their trancèd arms unfold,
But they dare not look to see the cause;

For heavy on their senses the faint enchantment lies
Through all that night of anguish and perilous amaze;
And neither fear nor wonder can ope their quivering eyes,
Or their limbs from the cold ground raise;

Till out of night the earth has rolled her dewy side,
With every haunted mountain and streamy vale below;
When, as the mist dissolves in the yellow morning tide,
The maidens' trance dissolveth so.

Then fly the ghastly three as swiftly as they may,
And tell their tale of sorrow to anxious friends in vain –
They pined away and died within the year and day,
And ne'er was Anna Grace seen again.

Samuel Ferguson

The Lark in the Clear Air

Dear thoughts are in my mind,
And my soul soars enchanted,
As I hear the sweet lark sing,
In the clear air of the day.
For a tender beaming smile,
To my hope has been granted,
And to-morrow she shall hear,
All my fond heart would say.

I shall tell her all my love,
All my soul's adoration,
And I think she will hear me,
And will not say me nay.
It is this that gives my soul
All its joyous elation,
As I hear the sweet lark sing,
In the clear air of the day.

Samuel Ferguson

May Day

I wish I were to-day on the hill behind the wood –
My eyes on the brown bog there and the Shannon river –
Behind the wood at home, a quickened solitude
When the winds from Slieve Bloom set the branches there a-quiver.

The winds are there now and the green of May
On every feathery tree-bough, tender on every hedge:
Over the bog-fields there larks carol to-day,
And a cuckoo is mocking them out of the woodland's edge.

Here a country warmth is quiet on the rocks
That alone make never a change when the May is duly come;
Here sings no lark, and to-day no cuckoo mocks:
Over the wide hill a hawk floats, and the leaves are dumb.

Thomas MacDonagh

The Triad of Things not Decreed

Happy the stark bare wood on the hill of Bree!
To its grey branch, green of the May: song after sigh:
Laughter of wings where the wind went with a cry
My sorrow! Song after sigh comes not to me.

Happy the dry wide pastures by Ahenree!
To them, in the speckled twilight, dew after drouth:
White clover, a fragrance in the dumb beast's mouth.
My sorrow! Dew after drouth comes not to me.

Happy Oilean Acla in the ample sea!
To its yellow shore, long-billowed flood after ebb:
Flash of the fish, silver in the sloak weeds' web.
My sorrow! Flood after ebb comes not to me.

Alice Furlong

Notes

Notes to Study 1

1. *The Triads of Ireland*: A collection of wise sayings made at the end of the ninth century. Examples: Three candles that illume every darkness: truth, nature, knowledge. Three rude ones of the world: a youngster mocking an old man, a robust person mocking an invalid, a wise man mocking a fool. *The Triads* have been edited and translated by Kuno Meyer in the Todd Lecture Series of the Royal Irish Academy, vol. xiii (Hodges, Figgis & Co., Dublin.)

2. *La Belle Dame Sans Merci*. In the *Life and Letters of John Keats,* Lord Houghton tells how the sheets on which Keats had written his *Ode to a Nightingale* were thrust away by the author 'as waste paper, behind some books', and the difficulty that his friend Brown had in putting together and arranging the stanzas of the ode. Among 'other poems as literally "fugitive", rescued in much the same way', he gives 'a ballad of much grace and tenderness and expressive of the feelings that were then growing fast within him.' It is *La Belle Dame Sans Merci*, the same version. with 'knight-at arms,' not 'wretched wight', which Keats quotes with such humorous notes in his letter of 28th April, 1819 to George and Georgiana Keats. Leigh Hunt in the *Indicator,* May 1820, published the 'wretched wight' version, which, though probably the revised second version, is judged inferior by most critics.

3. 'To us as to the ancient Irish, the half-said thing is dearest.' See Kuno Meyer's *Ancient Irish Poetry*: Introduction, and Study 8.1 of this volume.

4. 'Certainly I must confesse my own barbarousnes, I never heard the olde song of *Percy and Duglas*, that I found not my heart mooved more than with a Trumpet: and yet it is sung but by some blinde Crouder, with no rougher voyce, then rude stile: which being so evill aparrelled in the dust and cobwebbes of that uncivill age, what would it worke trymmed in the gorgeous eloquence of *Pindar*?' – Sir Philip Sidney: *An Apologie for Poetrie.*

    For two essays by Addison on *Popular Poetry: The Ballad of Chevy Chase*, see *Spectator*, Nos. 70 and 74.

5. Examples of the absolute construction with 'and' are found as early as Chaucer:
    > What couthe a stourdy housebonde more devyse,
    > To prove hir wyfhode and her stedfastnesse,
    > And he contynuyng ever in stourdynesse.

    – *Clerkes Tale,* iv. 91.
    There is another example in the same *Tale* at vi. 109.

6. *Is*. There are three distinct verbs in Irish corresponding to three senses of the verb to be. The examples in the text will show one use of the verb of identity.

7. A.C.H. of *Poetry,* a Chicago monthly. I use here and elsewhere what I find well said for my purpose, even when the thing is not daringly original.

8. *The Crown of Wild Olive*: War.

9.   A terrible and splendid trust
       Heartens the host of Innisfail:
   first lines of a poem by Lionel Johnson.
       The heritage to the race of kings:
   first line of Mr Joseph Plunkett's poem *Our Heritage.*
       I saw thee arise
       With the lure of God in thine eyes:
   from *Banba,* by Thomas Boyd.
       Poetry of Irish Opposition and Revolt is Chapter 12, Volume iv of Brandes'
   Main Currents.
10. *Eamonn an Chnuic, Druimfhionn Donn Dílis* and most of the other Irish and
    Anglo-Irish poems referred to in the text will be found in translation or in the
    original (English) among the *Poems of the Irish Mode* at the end of the book.
11. The greater works of St. John of the Cross are *The Ascent of Mount Carmel,*
    The Obscure Night of the Soul, A Spiritual Canticle between the Soul and Christ,
    The Living Flame of Love. These consist of mystical poems with explanations.
    He has left besides seventeen poems without commentary.

Notes to Study 2

1. 'The life and ways of the Gael.' The Gael largely assimilated the old Danes [a
   common misnomer for Vikings/Norsemen] and the Normans, who became *ipsis*
   Hibernis Hiberniores [= more Irish than the Irish themselves].
2. 'Certain Irishmen ... expressed English or European life.' These are here
   regarded altogether from the Gaelic standpoint. From the English point of view
   they seem to form a strong group, typical and expressive of Irish dissent and
   divergence. The term 'Hiberno-English,' recently coming into use, might be
   applied to these to distinguish them from those whose immediate inspiration is
   Irish.
       Among the Hiberno-English writers represented in the first volume of the
   Cabinet of Irish Literature are Sir John Denham, Richard Flecknoe, Wentworth
   Dillon, Earl of Roscommon, George Farquahar, Thomas Parnell, William
   Congreve. In the same work will be found accounts of some of the Irish writers
   who remained at home in body only.
3. 'George Darley's reference to Irish history, his use of clan names.' For instance,
   in *The Flight of the Forlorn: A Romantic Ballad Founded on the History of*
   Ireland, he has 'Shan-avon' for Shannon, 'Hi-dallan' as the name of an
   individual, and stanzas like this, full of errors:
           Clan Tir-oen! Clan Tir-conel!
           Atha's royal sept of Connacht!
           Desmond red! and dark O'Donel!
           Fierce O'More! and stout MacDonacht!
     Curran's Irish phrases.' One of his best known poems has these lines:
           Thou gem of the west, the world's *cushla ma chree!* ...
           Thy friendship is seen in the moment of danger
           And the wanderer is welcomed with *cushla ma chree!*
     Cuisle mo chroidhe means 'pulse of my heart.' Curran's lines are

nonsensical. He must have known some Irish, but he probably regarded it as fair game for any use.

William Drennan's poems. Compare, for instance, the first stanzas of his two best known poems: *When Eire first Rose from the Dark-swelling Flood* and the *Wake of William Orr*. Nothing in Anglo-Irish verse surpasses the solemn simplicity of the second-named:

> Write his merits on your mind –
> Morals pure and manners kind;
> In his head as on a hill
> Virtue placed her citadel.
>
> Why cut off in palmy youth?
> Truth he spoke, and acted truth –
> 'Countrymen, unite!' he cried,
> And died – for what his Saviour died.
>
> God of Peace and God of Love,
> Let it not Thy vengeance move!
> Let it not Thy lightnings draw –
> A Nation guillotined by law! ...
>
> Here we watch our brother's sleep;
> Watch with us, but do not weep;
> Watch with us through dead of night,
> But expect the morning light.

4. Charles MacLaughlin, who changed his name to Macklin, was born in 1690 and died in 1797. He became one of the greatest of English actors. He returned to Ireland on more than one occasion, but finally died in England, where he had played at Drury Lane chiefly, up to almost his hundredth year. 'This was the Jew that Shakespeare drew', in Shylock. The plays of his that seem to us of most interest are the *True-Born Scotchman* and *Love à la Mode*. The Theatre of Ireland revived some years ago *The Irish Fine Lady*, under the title of *The True-born Irishman*.

5. *English as We Speak it in Ireland* is the title of an interesting book by the late Doctor P. W. Joyce.

Notes to Study 3

1. For Carleton's letter from London see Mr D. J. O'Donoghue's Introduction to *The Black Prophet* (Laurence and Bullen).

2. 'The function of the conventional word-order.' In English, since the decay of inflexions word-order has the function of making clear the meaning. In Old English the order of words was nearly as free as that of Latin. (See Leon Kellner: *Historical Outlines of English Syntax* § 480.) But yet modern diction is not the only possible or the best. 'Modern syntax, fettered by logic, is artificial, the result of literary tradition, and therefore far from being a true mirror of what is going on in the mind.' (Ibid § 9.). Tennyson's line, 'Flashed all their sabres

bare', follows the right order and is better than 'All their bare sabres flashed.'
Naturalness is, of course, another matter, and my remarks here are no
contradiction to what I say at p. 100 and elsewhere in this volume.

3.   The stock example of Alfred's style is his Preface to the West Saxon version of
the *Cura Pastoralis* of Gregory the Great. It will be found in most Anglo-
Saxon readers (for instance in Sweet's), in some anthologies of English prose
and in such books as Kellner's *English Syntax,* cited elsewhere in these Notes
and recommended here for reference in connection with the development of
syntax. An interesting book more easily accessible (Kellner has been out of
print for some time) is Sweet's Temple Primer: *The History of Language.*

Most books on the growth and structure of the English language give many
examples of words that have come in from history and of the puns and the
blunders that have been ennobled – words like 'nap,' the card-game, from
Napoleon's way of war, 'tory' and 'boycott' from Irish ways of war. 'Derring-
do', a noun, is Spenser's misinterpretation of Chaucer's verb in the line 'In
dorrying don that longeth to a knyght.' (In daring to do what belongeth to a
knight.) In looking at a dictionary now for confirmation of this reference I
find, before 'derring-do': 'derrick, n. contrivance for moving or hoisting heavy
weights ... (obs. senses, *hangman, gallows,* from name of hangman c.1600).'
After 'derring-do' comes 'derringer, n. small-bore pistol (U.S. inventor's
name)'.

Notes to Study 4

1.   A few additional examples: *He went into fits of laughter* for *He laughed loudly.*
What's on you? They are after killing the little dog on me, (for *my little dog*). *I
was not going in under the table, and if I was itself, hadn't I the floor swept?*
These forms are all used in Anglo-Irish.
2.   See W. B. Yeats' *Poems* (1912 edition): Glossary and Notes.
3.   *Ingin Ni Murachu.* The correct Irish form would be *Inghean Ui Mhurchadha.*
If Mr Stephens spelled it *Inyan ee Vurachu,* he would have been near the right.
Inghin is the dative or prepositional case of *Inghean* (daughter). '*Ni,*
indeclinable, used in O surnames of females ... it is an abbreviation of *Ni Ui*
(from *Inghean Ui*).' (Dinneen's *Irish-English Dictionary*). *Murachu*
(*Murchadha*) has not its initial consonant aspirated as it should have. The cases
in the correct Irish form are, nominative, genitive, genitive: Daughter of the
descendant (grandson) of *Murchadh,* Daughter of O'Murrough.
4.   I have written on the metre of Ernest Dowson's poem in *Thomas Campion and
the Art of English Poetry.* [Dublin: Hodges, Figgis, and London: Simpkin,
Marshall, 1913.]

Notes to Study 5

1.   Lionel Johnson. Writing as I am of literature rather than of poets, I have not
been able to do honour due to some Irish writers who go without that honour.
Lionel Johnson was a great poet, different from the others of greatest name in
this book, but not surpassed in his art by any. His lyrics are deliberate, builded,
balanced, sonorous, full of dignity, but not the less spontaneous, not the less

the creatures of a passionate art than those of fine careless rapture, not the less
winged for other rapture and eyed for vision and for tears. To know fine poetry,
read his long poem *Ireland*. I take a stanza at random:

> Nay! we insult thee not with tears, although
> With thee we sorrow: not as for one dead
> We mourn for one in the cold earth laid low.
> Still is the crown upon thy sovereign head,
> Still is the sceptre within thy strong hand,
> Still is the kingdom thine:
> The armies of thy sons on thy command
> Wait, and thy starry eyes through darkness shine.
> Tears for the dear and dead! For thee *All hail!*
> Unconquered Inisfail!
> Tears for the lost: thou livest, O divine!

Read a poem on a subject that has been a net of poor prose to many poets,
Ninety-Eight:

> *Who fears to speak of Ninety-Eight?*
> He, who despairs of Ireland still:
> Whose paltry soul finds nothing great
> In honest failure: he, whose will
> Feeble and faint in days of gloom,
> Takes old defeat for final doom. ...

> *Who fears to speak of Ninety-Eight?*
> The renegade who sells his trust:
> Whose love has rottened into hate
> Whose hopes have withered into dust:
> He who denies, and deems it mad,
> The faith his nobler boyhood had.

2. Mr Clement Shorter is set down with the 'men of law' by a mistake, which I
   regret. His edition of Emily Brontë's *Complete Poems* (1910) contains one
   hundred and thirty-eight new pieces, including the poem I quote. Except that
   three stanzas which seem incongruous are printed with it, no fault can be found
   with his editing of this, or, to my knowledge, of the others.

3. Pádraic Ó Prunta, spelled Padruig ua Pronntuidh in a MSS. volume in Irish
   written by him in 1763, now in the possession of Douglas Hyde. See *The Brontës*
   by Clement Shorter, vol. i., p. 23.

4. For a popular account of the work of O'Donovan, O'Curry and Petrie, see *A
   Group of Nation Builders* by Rev. P. M. MacSweeney, M.A., Professor of
   English at Maynooth College, published by the Catholic Truth Society of
   Ireland.

Notes to Study 6

1. On quantitive and accentual verse and other technical matters the author has
   written fully in his book on English prosody: *Thomas Campion and the Art of
   English Poetry*.

2. *Accent and Rhythm explained by the Law of Monopressure*, published

anonymously in 1888.

3. In an admirable passage of the Introduction to his Selection of Spenser's Poems (The Golden Poet's Series: Jack) Mr Yeats has shown the difference between the 'marching rhythms, that once delighted more than expedient hearts' and the varied and troubled rhythms of a poetry that has 'learned ecstasy from Smart in his mad cell, and from Blake, who made joyous little songs out of almost unintelligible visions, and from Keats, who sang of a beauty so wholly preoccupied with itself that its contemplation is a kind of lingering trance.' He takes as example of this vaguely suggestive poetry a stanza of Shelley's *Laon and Cynthia,* which is in the Spenserian stanza; and shows that the lines which are in Spenser like bars of gold thrown ringing one upon another, are in Shelley's poem broken capriciously. Spenser's verse rushes, as he says, to some preordained thought with that marching rhythm; in Shelley's 'the meaning is an inspiration of the indolent muses, for it wanders hither and thither at the beckoning of fancy.' Rhythms do express emotions, and mingled rhythms express mingled emotions, in verse as in music.

4. *Deibhidhe* is one of the forms of Irish *dán direach* or straight verse. For a sample see text p. 55. It is impossible here to explain the technicalities of the *dán direach.* Students are referred to Meyer's *Primer of Irish Metrics.*

5. 'The ancient pitch.' That even the Romans marked pitch in their copies of poems is known from the fact that in the earliest codex of Virgil's works, a manuscript of the fourth century, in the Laurentian Library at Florence, are neumes as guides to the reciter. Neumes, derived from the Greek accents, were used to represent the degrees of the scale.

6. I do not know that I should call the inversion 'candles three' a forced phrase. It is entirely justified and it is not at all of the same order as:
    > What will ye more of your guest and sometime friend?

    At all events, in the matter of word-order poetry has other rights. See p. 24, and note thereon.

7. On the subject of music and metre, see the author's *Thomas Campion and the Art of English Poetry*, Chapter VII.

8. My keeping of the incorrect spellings of Irish words in the titles of poems, *Lene* for *Léin, Pastheen* for *Páistín*, must seem inconsistent with my claim for justice to Irish. I do not, however, feel myself justified in altering an author's constant spelling of a title, though I am willing to correct his spelling of Irish words which have not assumed pseudo-English forms.

9. See the author's *Thomas Campion and the Art of English Poetry*, Chapter VI.

10. 'Three things through love I see.' From a translation of an Irish poem, *Táid na Réalta 'na Seasamh ar an Aer.* [That is in fact the first line of a poem titled *Stuairín Na mBachall mBreágh Réidh* – literally, the handsome woman of the fine, smooth ringlets; the entire poem in both languages seems to deserve a reproduction in this 1996 edition – see p. 126.]

Notes to Study 7

1. *Dán Direach.* See Note 4 to Study 6, *Deibhidhe.*
    [Eve. MacDonagh's note relating to this poem in *Lyrical Poems* has been

incorporated with his footnote from p. 84 of the 1916 edition of *Literature in Ireland,* as a paragraph in the text, in this edition, immediately following the poem.]

2. In *The Irish Review*, February, 1914.
3. 'The Old Days of "Unknowing" in the fourteenth century.' The fourteenth century is one of the golden ages of Mysticism. In England it produced *The Cloud of Unknowing* and other profound works. So well were mystical works appreciated at the time that when a translation *(Dionise Hid Divinite)* of a work of Dionysius the Areopagite, was made, probably by the same author as *The Cloud of Unknowing*, it 'ran across England like deere.' See Appendix to *Mysticism* by Evelyn Underhill (Methuen). For a discussion of the language of the mystics, see the same work. 'No direct description of spiritual experience is or can be possible to man. It must always be symbolic, allusive, oblique: always suggest, but never tell, the truth.' This itself suggests, but does not tell, the truth. That the words of a living language may have double use is certain. 'In Chinese poetry', says Ernest Fellonosa, 'every character has at least two shades of meaning, its natural and its spiritual – or the image and its metaphorical range.' *(Epochs of Chinese and Japanese Art)*
4. The passage by Lord Dunsany is from *The Gods of Pegana.*
5. Coventry Patmore to Francis Thompson. See Everard Meynell's *Life of Francis Thompson,* p. 221. This I have from Father George O'Neill, S.J., M.A., Professor of English Language at University College, Dublin, who knew Father Hopkins here, and still has some unpublished music composed by him. Patmore has a single poem (published) entitled *Sponsa Dei.*
6. Ronsard. The reference, of course, is to the famous *Sonnets pour Hélène.*
7. A translation of 'that untranslateable *Eamonn an Chnuic'* will be found on pp. 142-3.. Judging from the attempts of Mangan and others, and from my own failure before to make anything like an adequate version, I wrote this sentence in the text. Since, in making my selection of Poems of the Irish Mode, I have, I hope, disproved it. As in the case of *Is Truagh gan Mise i Sasana,* pp. 106-7, I have omitted stanzas which I believe to be mere accretions to the true poem.
8. *'Cueillez des aujourdhui les roses de la vie.'* Ronsard.

Notes to Study 8.1

1. *Urbanitas, curiosa felicitas, ego postera crescam laude recens,* 'marvellous boy,' 'sleepless soul', 'Criticism disdains to chase a school boy to his common places.' Doctor Johnson: *Life of the English Poets: Thomas Gray.*
2. Dr Sigerson. See Introduction, *Bards Of the Gael and Gall.*
3. John Eglinton. In his book of literary criticism *Pebbles from a Brook* (published at Kilkenny by Standish O'Grady in 1901) and in the earlier *Literary Ideals in Ireland (Daily Express* Office, Dublin, and Fisher Unwin, London, 1899) to which he contributed with W. B. Yeats, Æ and the late William Larminie, readers will find (if they can find the books) interesting discussions of many of my subjects. It is a pity that John Eglinton has not collected his critical studies.
4. *The Three Sorrows of Story-Telling: Deirdre,* by Douglas Hyde.
5. 'The Golden Age of Irish Civilization'. Ireland was then indeed an island of

Saints and Scholars. The Science of the Saints was known and revered as it never has been since in any whole nation.

6. *Duanaire Finn* is the 1908 volume of the Irish Texts Society.

The Ulidian Cycle includes the great *Táin Bó Cuailnge* with its attendant tales, among them the Deirdre Saga (*Oidhe Chloinne Uisnigh*: The Fate of the Sons of Uisnech). The Fenian Cycle is that of Finn and the Fiana (generally now spelt Fianna), of the great poet Oisín (son of Finn and father of Oscar), of Diarmuid Donn and Gráinne.

7. The Standish O'Grady referred to is Standish James, author of *The Bardic History of Ireland, The Coming of Cuculain* and other romantic retellings of Irish story, not Standish Hayes of the *Silva Gadelica* and of the *Catalogue of the Irish MSS. in the British Museum,* the most wonderful catalogue ever made, being a great work in itself. Standish Hayes edited his first Irish text, *The Pursuit of Diarmuid and Gráinne* in 1855, and died the 18th October, 1915, two days before I wrote these words. Standish James still walks the earth. I saw him do it this morning. 'Years ago', wrote Æ in the *United Irishman*, discussing a statement of O'Grady's in his *All Ireland Review*,

years ago, in the adventurous youth of his mind, Standish O'Grady found the Gaelic tradition like an antiquated dún with the doors barred. Listening, he heard from within the hum of an immense chivalry, and he opened the doors and the wild riders went forth to work their will ... The wild riders have gone forth, and their labours in the human mind are only beginning. They will do their deeds over again, and now they will act through many men and speak through many voices.

8. Matthew Arnold's 'touchstones' will be found in the General Introduction to *The English Poets*, edited by T. H. Ward (first published 1880). The introduction is republished as the first of *Essays in Criticism,* second series (*The Study of Poetry*).

9. *I sing of a maiden*: 'makeless', matchless; 'ches', chose; 'al so', as.

10. For the utterly uninitiated (these notes in general are for the uninitiated) I must explain that *An Craoibhín Aoibhin* is the poet name of Douglas Hyde. It means 'The Pleasant Little Branch'.

11. Translation in Kuno Meyer's *Ancient Irish Poetry*.

12. *Domfarcai*. This little poem was discovered on the margin of one of the ancient manuscripts of St. Gall by Cavaliere Nigra. 'While translating these verses', wrote the discoverer,

I love to imagine the poor monk who, more than a thousand years ago, was copying the manuscript and, taken off for a moment by the song of the blackbird, saw through the casement of his cell the green crown of woods which surrounded his monastery in Ulster or in Connacht; and having heard the quick trilling of the bird, he wrote these verses and returned more lightly to his interrupted labours.

See *Bards of the Gael and Gall*, Introduction.

13. [MacDonagh's note to accompany 'Grange House Lodge' in *Lyrical Poems* reads: 'Marbhan (pronounced approximately Mauravaun), the brother of Guaire, King of Connacht in the seventh century, is the hermit of the Old-Irish poem known as *King and Hermit*.']

14. Some species of birds.
15. *Thomas Campion and the Art of English Poetry*, Chapter IX.
16. Atkinson: *On Irish Metric* (Dublin: Ponsonby, 1884).
17. Eoin MacNeill is professor of Early and Mediæval Irish History, Osborn Bergin of Early and Mediæval Irish Language and Literature, Douglas Hyde of Modern Irish, and R.A.S. Macalister of Celtic Archæology at University College, Dublin. The work of Professor Macalister in the region of Irish art is of as great interest and importance as that of any of his colleagues in literature and language. George Sigerson, M.D., is also a professor of University College, but of a different faculty. [McNeill's and Hyde's careers are in brief, summary form at the end of these Notes.]

Notes to Study 8.2

1. Comparisons like those I institute between the diction of Wordsworth and of the Anglo-Irish poets are generally unfair, as being of unlikes. Mine is not so; the poems compared are similar in situation.
2. For an account of the three harpstrings see *Duanaire Finn* xvii.
3. [MacPiarais/Pearse himself also translated the poem, with the title 'Renunciation'. That appears in *The 1916 Poets* (1963, 1995) whose editor Desmond Ryan gives the original Irish in full on p. 3 and comments thus on the MacDonagh translation: ' ... a version as with all the others from *Suantraidhe Agus Goltraidhe* more accurate and musical and faithful than Pearse's own'.]
4. [The translation is again by Thomas MacDonagh, as indicated by his note 3 of 'Poems in the Irish Mode'.]
5. This same passage from *Séadna* is translated in *A Talk about Irish Literature* by An Gae Bolga (Dublin: Gill, 1907).
6. Father Dinneen in his edition of Eoghan Ruadh acknowledges that the poem has been attributed to *Maire Ní Sheadha,* but holds that the style is clearly Eoghan Ruadh's. The poem is *Maidean fhuar fhliuc ag eighre suas dam.*
7. The *Aisling* describes a vision of Ireland. 'A popular air', says Father Dinneen, was seized upon and wedded to a poetic vision of Erin as a virgin endowed with every grace of mind and with all loveliness, who appears to the poet and enthralls him with her beauty. The vision takes place either as he lies in bed, weary and oppressed, or as he saunters by some lonely river in melancholy mood, sorrowing over his country's ills. The poet, lost in wonderment at the queenly figure, reverently inquires of the virgin who she is, whether she is a human being or a goddess, whether Helen or Diana, or Deirdre or Cearnait, or the lady who brought over the Normans to our shores. The queen replies that she is none of these, but the spouse of the banished Stuart. Then she recounts her woes ... There is the inevitable announcement of a speedy deliverance.

No fewer than eighteen of the forty-four poems of Eoghan Ruadh collected by Father Dinneen are *aislingí,* and the proportion in the work of others is as great. Like the Elizabethan sonnet in England, of which many thousands were published between Sidney and Shakespeare, the Irish *aisling* became a craze.

8. *Dán direach.* See Note 4 to Study 6.

9. 'Schoolmen of condensed speech' is a mistranslation of a line in the Lament
    for the Bardic Schools by the great poet O'Gnive [Ó Gnímh] written in the
    beginning of the seventeenth century. The two words at the end of the first line
    of:

    > *Ni clos sgoluidhe, sgeal tinn,*
    > *D'Uibh nDalaigh na d'Uibh nUiginn.*

    were taken to be *sgeil teinn*; so instead of 'There are not (heard) scholars, a
    sore tale! of the O'Dalys or of the O'Higgins', it was read 'There are no
    schoolmen of condensed speech, etc.'

Poems of the Irish Mode

1. Poems of the Irish Mode. The great majority of these poems are songs with
    very beautiful old Irish airs. Almost all the Translations are so, and of course
    all the Ballads. I should print with the Translations the original Irish poems,
    but that I think it well to send students of Irish to the original sources. To print
    them for others would be useless. If any readers of these versions are prompted
    to begin their study of Irish by a study of these originals, I would refer them to
    the sixpenny booklets, *Ceol Sidhe,* published by the Irish Book Company,
    Dublin. Mangan's *Poets and Poetry of Munster* (Duffy) and Edward Walsh's
    Irish Popular Songs (Gill) give Irish and English on opposite pages. [With the
    advent of greater bilingualism, the publishers of this edition have compromised
    by including the original Irish ones which MacDonagh himself translated.]
2. Pastheen Finn. *An Páistín Fionn* means the fair-haired child, not brown girl
    sweet. Ferguson takes other liberties with his original, but in general reproduces
    the rhythm and effect of the song excellently.
3. The unsigned poems and verse translations here and through the book are the
    author's own. [This device has been modified by attributing the five MacDonagh
    poems among 'Translations from the Irish' to him.]
4. *Pearl of the White Breast* is perhaps the least satisfactory translation used here,
    as it does not turn into beautiful poetry, and as it needs to a degree its air to set
    it in this mode; yet as it is a faithful version, and by Petrie, I have let it stand.
5. Flavell's name is written also Lavelle. George Fox was an early friend of
    Ferguson's. He left Ireland and was lost sight of by the poet, who long after, in
    1880, dedicated his poems to him. Lady Ferguson, in her *Life* of her husband,
    says that Ferguson was the writer of this translation, but that as it had been
    attributed to Fox, who had helped him with it, he refused later to claim it. All
    editors respect Ferguson's generosity with their right hands, but add a note like
    this with their left. The original reads to one like a poor translation into
    unidiomatic Irish. But it is in Hardiman's book, published in 1831, long before
    this version appeared, so it must be all right. Such wrong may a poet suffer at
    the hands of a translator!
6. In a note to his edition of Mangan's Poems, Mr D. J. O'Donoghue, generally
    most accurate of commentators, says that *A Farewell to Patrick Sarsfield* only
    distantly resembles the original. Except that it is not a complete translation,
    omitting some stanzas, it is wonderfully close to the Irish poem. Students can
    compare the version with the original in *The Poets and Poetry of Munster*

(Dublin: Duffy).

7. 'William Heffernan [c.1720-1803] more usually called *Uilliam Dall* or Blind William [actually Liam Dall Ó hIffearnáin], a native of Shronehill in Co. Tipperary, was born blind, and spent the greater part of his life, a poor houseless wanderer, subsisting upon the bounty of others.' (Edward Walsh) He lived in the first half of the eighteenth century. His poems have never been collected. [They were since published by the Government Stationery Office in 1939, twenty-four in number, with a life and notes by the editor, Risteárd Ó Foghludha: *Ar Bruach na Coille Muaire.*]

8. *The Song of Gladness.* The vision of the bees seems wonderful in the work of a poet blind from birth, till we find that Heffernan barely mentions a swarm without a chief, the rest being Mangan's. Critics who would reduce the themes of lyric poetry to a small number, and find them appearing independently in many languages might find interesting parallels to the last stanzas of this poem. As Mr D. J. O'Donoghue has pointed out, Fanny Parnell's fine poem *After Death* practically repeats it. Edward Walsh has translated this, as most of the other poems done also by Mangan and Ferguson. His versions are more literal but in general inferior. He gives the original in his *Irish Popular Songs.* [See p. 126]

9. *Eamonn an Chnuic* and *Druimfhionn Donn Dílis* are both in the form of dialogue, the former between Ireland and the Rapparee (though with its long tail of verses it assumed the form of an ordinary love poem), the latter between the Stuart and Ireland, the white-backed, brown, true, silk of the kine.

   It will be noticed that assonance of final syllables in the original *(cnuic, fliuch)* is represented in the translation by rime, assonance of penultimates *(déanach, gaolta)* by assonance.

   [See Note to Study 7.]

10. [Eamon an Chnuic (literally, Ned of the Hill) – Edmond O'Ryan (died 1724) was a native of either Knockmeale or Atshanboe, Upperchurch, near Thurles, Co. Tipperary. He was a son of a substantial landowner and was educated abroad. Having shot a tax collector in defence of a neighbouring widow's property, he became a classic Tory or outlaw. He served in or assisted the Jacobite forces. He was murdered for the reward of £200 on his head. He was buried at Curraheen, Hollyford, near Thurles.]

11. Mr J. H. Lloyd, who discovered and published *An Bunán Buidhe* (The Yellow Bittern), has told me that he suppressed some inferior stanzas. These I have never known. Mr Lloyd wrote of Cathal Buidhe in *Irisleabhar na Gaedhilge* on more than one occasion, and in his book, *Duanaire na Midhe.* The poem, the song of a drinker, is certainly symbolical. I have authority for my translation of *Hallaí Chuinn* by 'Constantine's halls'. [MacDonagh's note to 'The Yellow Bittern' in *Lyrical Poems* reads: 'All my translations are very close to the originals. In my version of this poem I have changed nothing for the purpose of elucidation. I have even translated the name of *Loch Mhic an Ein*, a lake in the North-west of Ireland. Some of the references must be obscure to all but students of Irish literature; I think, however, that the poem does not suffer too much from the difficulty of these.' [But see p. 126]

12. *Shule Aroon.* I have kept the title used in the broad-sheets and in all editions of

this street song; but have spelled correctly the Irish refrain. The translation is:

Walk, walk, walk, my (secret) love!
Walk, so quiet, and walk so soft,
Walk to the door and elope with me –
And may you go safe, my darling!

An Craoibhín Aoibhinn (Douglas Hyde) has an Irish version of this song which some day may be translated into English verse of the Irish Mode and so send this, like the Irish heroes in Æ's phrase, to do its deeds again and speak through many voices. To start it, I translate in prose the first verse of Dr Hyde's version:

O pleasant, handsome, youthful boy!
Wide was your heart, sweet was your kiss.
I wish that I were yours for life –
And may you go safe, my darling!
Walk, walk, walk, my love!
There's no cure to get but the cure of death.
Since you have left me, poor is my case –
And may you go safe, my darling!'

13. *The Croppy Boy.* This is one of several versions of this famous ballad. It is chosen by me as being more interesting metrically than the others. The variant nearest to it, used by Padraic Colum in his *Broad-sheet Ballads* (Dublin: Maunsel) has obviously been worked over. The second line becomes:

When the small birds tune and the thrushes sing,

The second stanza:

It was early, early, on Tuesday night
When the yeoman cavalry gave me a fright,
To my misfortune and sad downfall
I was taken prisoner by Lord Cornwall.

On the other hand I am sorry to miss the two stanzas that take the place of the second last of this version:

I choose the black and I choose the blue,
I forsook the red and orange too,
I did forsake them and did them deny,
And I'll wear the green like a Croppy Boy.

Farewell, father, and mother too,
And sister Mary, I have none but you;
And for my brother, he's all alone,
He's pointing pikes on the grinding stone.

Of course Carroll Malone's version is practically a different poem. Though it is now more commonly sung, it is full of absurdities: 'a vested priest', *'Nomine Dei,* the youth begins', and then the whole confession. Perhaps its preference is due to the two fine lines:

I bear no hate against living thing,
But I love my country above my king.

14. The Librarian of University College, Dublin, Mr D. J. O'Donoghue, referred to frequently above, who knows more about Anglo-Irish literary history and publications than anyone else, has told me that this version of *The Streams of*

Bunclody is a redaction by Halliday Sparling, editor of *Irish Minstrelsy* (Canterbury Poets Series) made from several variants. Readers will acknowledge that it has been well made. The lovely precision of 'proceed', three stanzas from the end, and the wistful rambling of the closing line, might have been spoiled by a hand less true.

15. I defy the malediction of Sam Lover against editors who omit the stanza added to *The Groves of Blarney* by Father Prout. Readers who are afraid to share my fate and think it their duty to read it, will find it in Prout's *Reliques,* or in any of the collections of the timid editors.

16. Original Poems. I have to thank Alice Furlong, Seumas O'Sullivan and Joseph Plunkett for permission to use poems of theirs which they were able to give me without asking the permission of publishers. I decided when making this selection not to ask for copyright poems. Now that I am come to the end of my work, I am half tempted to regret not having broken my rule in some instances in order to secure other good poems which would introduce to my readers other authors with whose work I could not deal here. Again one instance must suffice for all. Dora Sigerson Shorter has written some of the best modern ballads, poems very distinctively Irish. Her work has a breath of romance all its own, that 'breath of flowers' that she feared to leave behind in Ireland. Beautiful lyrics of hers, such as *Ireland* and *Can Doov Deelish,* may be read in the anthologies. I should like to have printed these and others. I comfort myself with the thought that my book may send some to her *Complete Poems,* where they will find them in a better atmosphere, as to the works of other good poets barely mentioned in this book. The published works of most of the Anglo-Irish poets of the time are within easy reach of everyone.

17. *The Irish Peasant to his Mistress* is addressed to the Irish Catholic Church which suffered under the Penal Laws, not yet quite removed, persecution unparalleled.

[The following abbreviated notes on the principal contemporaries of whom MacDonagh treats in these Studies may sketch their context for newcomers to the history of the era. Some are also referred to in the MacDonagh Profile, p. 179 onwards.]

Pádraic (1881-1972) **and Mary** (1885-1957) **Colum** married shortly after her rejection of MacDonagh's proposal. They co-authored *Our Friend James Joyce,* published in 1959 after her death. She wrote an autobiography and published essays; his sixty-one books included a biography of Arthur Griffith, the founder of Sinn Féin, poetry, plays, criticism, folklore and travel. His *She Moved Through the Fair* is best known as a song. See Zack Bowen, *Pádraic Colum: A Biographical Critical Introduction* (Illinois, 1970).

Douglas Hyde (1863-1947) wrote more than thirty books – poetry, translations, plays and an autobiography. The first President of Ireland, 1938-45, he had co-founded literary societies in Dublin and London with Yeats, and the Gaelic League with MacNeill, but resigned from its presidency in 1915 when Pearse and others politicised it – 'the sword' versus 'the dove of peace'. He led successful campaigns to have Irish accepted by the Post Office, the secondary schools curriculum and for university matriculation. See Janet Egleson Dunleavy, *Douglas Hyde, A Maker of Modern Ireland* (California, 1991); Dominic Daly *The Young Douglas Hyde* (IUP, 1974).

Eoin MacNeill (1867-1945) wrote four seminal books on early Irish history and laws. Essays of his led to the foundation of both the Gaelic League and the Irish Volunteers of which he became Chief-of-Staff. Misled by its military council as to plans for the Easter Rising, he countermanded Pearse's orders. He became Minister for Finance, Industries, and Education in successive Dáil, 1919-1925. He resigned from the (Northern Ireland-Irish Free State) Boundary Commission upon differing with the Chairman's interpretation of a governing clause in the Treaty and a newspaper 'leak' of indications that the Commission would leave the border virtually intact. See F. X. Martin & F. J. Byrne eds., *The Scholar Revolutionary* (IUP, 1973); F. X. Martin ed., Michael Tierney, *Eoin McNeill: Scholar and Man of Action* (Clarendon, 1981).

Kuno Meyer (1858-1919) wrote numerous books of Irish interest. These included *The Irish Odyssey* (1885), *The Voyage of Bran* (1895), *Early Relations between Gael and Brython* (1896), *Liadan and Cuirthir* (1902) and *Ancient Irish Poetry* (1913). He was born in Hamburg, Germany and having read Celtic Philosophy at University he developed a passionate interest in the Celtic languages and literatures.

Patrick Henry Pearse (1879-1916) wrote some twenty volumes of poetry, plays and pamphlets. St. Enda's School implemented his radical ideas on bi-lingual, child-centred education. Director of Military Organisation for the Irish Volunteers and a member of the Irish Republican Brotherhood, he was president and Commandant-General of the Provisional Government of the Irish Republic whose Proclamation he read at the GPO. His and the other leaders' executions ensured that the blood sacrifice he had advocated in violent language bore fruit as the War of Independence. See Ruth Dudley Edwards, *Patrick Pearse: The Triumph of Failure* (London, 1977).

Joseph Mary Plunkett (1887-1916) wrote a book of poetry, edited *The Irish Review*, and founded the Irish Theatre with MacDonagh and Edward Martyn. Director of Operations for the Irish Volunteers, he drew up the Rising's military plans. He married Grace Gifford, Muriel MacDonagh's sister, on the eve of his execution. See W. I. Thompson, *The Imagination of an Insurrection: Dublin, Easter 1916* (New York-Oxford, 1961), pp. 131-9; Sydney Czira, *The Years Flew By* (Dublin, 1974).

George William Russell (Æ) (1867-1935) published over a dozen books of poetry, essays and internationally-lauded works on the economics of the co-operative movement (he was assistant secretary of the Irish Agricultural Organisation Society) and employer-worker relations (following his appeal to the Dublin employers in an open letter during the 1913 Lock-Out). See Henry Summerfield, *That Myriad–Minded Man: A Biography of G. W. Russell* (New Jersey, 1975). Robert B. Davis, *George William Russell* (Boston, 1977).

Dr George Sigerson (1836-1925) published work on medicine, biology, history and land tenure, and the anthology of translated verse acclaimed by MacDonagh. He was Professor of Biology at UCD, and a Senator of the Irish Free State, 1922-5. See J. B. Lyons, 'Medicine and Literature in Ireland' in *Journal of the Irish College of Physicians and Surgeons, 3, No. 1* (1973), pp. 3-9.

Francis (1878-1916) and Hanna (1877-1946) Sheehy Skeffington worked together for womens' rights until his murder for which she refused British Army compensation. He wrote *The Life of Michael Davitt* and a novel, and was the first auditor of the revived L. & H. Society UCD. She became a judge of the Dáil courts during the War of Independence, supported the anti-Treaty campaign, and was a founder of the Womens' Social and Progressive League. See Maria Luddy, *Hanna Sheehy Skeffington* (Dun Dealgan, 1995); L. Leveson & J. H. Natterstad, *Hanna Sheehy Skeffington: Irish Feminist* (Canada, 1986); C. P. Curran, *Under the Receding Wave* (Gill & Macmillan, 1977), pp. 111-18.

James Stephens (1882-1950) published several works of fiction and verse, notably the *Crock of Gold*, as well as an eye-witness account, *The Insurrection in Dublin*. He wrote the introduction to MacDonagh's collected *Poetical Works*. He became a BBC broadcaster. See Augustine Martin, *James Stephens, A Critical Study* (Gill & Macmillan, 1977).

John Millington Synge (1871-1909) took Yeats's advice to study Irish life on Aran. He also studied ordinary people's lives in Wicklow. The resulting plays featured an enhancement of common speech. They also drew protests, notably against *The Playboy of the Western World*, from Colum, Pearse and Arthur Griffith as denigrating the character of Irish people, particularly women. See David Kiely, *J. M. Synge: A Biography* (Gill & Macmillan, 1994).

William Butler Yeats (1865-1939) was the first of four Irishmen to be awarded the Nobel Prize for Literature (1923). Added to his prolific output of poetry were plays, a novel, essays and autobiography. He was a founder of the Irish Literary Theatre-Abbey Theatre and a promoter of Synge's and playwright Sean O'Casey's work. See A. Norman Jeffares *W. B. Yeats: A New Biography* (Hutchinson, 1989).

Bibliography

In the text and in notes I have named many books, recommending some and censuring others. I can give here only a general guidance to readers for whom these Studies are an introduction to the literatures with which I deal. Books of reference in the subject are few, and, by comparison with those of other literatures, unsatisfactory. This study is still too new to have its histories and its appreciations complete. As there is really no knowing Anglo-Irish without some knowledge of Irish work, even at second hand, I would recommend readers to look into editions of Irish classics such as those of the Irish Texts Society (which has now published fourteen volumes); into the *Thesaurus Palæohibernicus* of Whitley Stokes and John Strachan, the Introduction to the first volume and all the end of the second; into the *Silva Gadelica* of Standish Hayes O'Grady, and into numbers or volumes of *Eriu* (published by the School of Irish Learning, Dublin), *Gadelica* (Hodges, Figgis), *Celtic Review,* Scottish (London: Nutt), *Irisleabhar na Gaedhilge (The Gaelic Journal)* now dead, of the French *Revue Celtique*, and the German *Irische Texte* and *Zeitschrift für Celtische Philologie*. The *Proceedings* of the old Ossianic Society are now, like many of these, hard to get, and, like them, fascinating. To mention editions and translations of individual classics, even of the *Tain,* would draw me aside from the main track. In the second volume of *The Irish Review* (1912-1913), Doctor Osborn Bergin edited for the first time a series of very interesting early Modern Irish poems. In the first and third volumes, Mr P. H. Pearse edited the beginning of an Irish Anthology, Lyric Poems and Poems of Irish Rebels. To many of us the great treasure-house of Irish poetry is still James Hardiman's *Irish Minstrelsy* in two volumes (published 1831). It is rivalled in our days by Douglas Hyde's *Love Songs of Connacht* and *Religious Songs of Connacht.* Doctor Sigerson's *Bards of the Gael and the Gall* (Unwin) and Eleanor Hull's *Poem Book of the Gael* (Chatto and Windus) do not give the originals like the others, but refer readers to the sources, as does Kuno Meyer's *Ancient Irish Poetry* (Constable), a book of prose versions. Latterly, of course, there has been a constant stream of editions of Gaelic Poetry and Prose, known to all students.

The histories of Gaelic Literature are Douglas Hyde's large *Literary History of Ireland* and small *Story of Early Gaelic Literature* (Unwin) and Eleanor Hull's *Text Book of Irish Literature* in two volumes (Gill). They have to be read with caution.

Of Anglo-Irish Anthologies I have written at some length in the text. The Introductions to the Brooke-Rolleston *Treasury of Irish Poetry* (1890) and to W. B. Yeats' *Book of Irish Verse* (1895) and the notes on the life and work of the poets in the former work, are good. Anthologies not mentioned in the text are the first of all. Charlotte Brooke's *Irish Poetry* (1789) and Halliday Sparling's useful little *Irish Minstrelsy* (Scott: Canterbury Poets).

Doctor P. W. Joyce's *English as we Speak it in Ireland* is published by Messrs. Gill, Dublin. Professor Mary Hayden and Professor Marcus Hartog contributed to the *Fortnightly Review,* April and May, 1909, a study, *The Irish Dialect of English.* For an interesting list of books on the subject see Maurice Bourgeois' *John Millington Synge and the Irish Theatre,* pages 223 and 224, footnote.

It is impossible here to add much to what has been written in Study 5 by way of guidance to Anglo-Irish prose. The works of the authors there mentioned form the main bulk of the literature that is fixed. In our days we have had a considerable dramatic literature, written by Edward Martyn, W. B. Yeats, J. M. Synge, Padraic Colum, Lady Gregory and by a host of other authors who cannot yet be definitely placed. Their works are published mostly by Messrs Maunsel, Dublin. We have had a great body of stories, sketches and essays. Most of the poets are also writers of prose. The most characteristically Anglo-Irish are Douglas Hyde again, Padraic Colum again, whose uncollected short stories are better than anything of their kind that I know, William Boyle, Emily Lawless, Lady Hartley (May Laffan), Jane Barlow, Seamus MacManus, Miriam Alexander, Shan Bullock and William Buckley. James Stephens has attained a very great contemporary reputation and deserves it. The early works of the late Canon Sheehan are among the best Anglo-Irish novels. W. B. Yeats is as great a master of prose as of verse and distinctively Irish, too, though his work, in the main critical and philosophic, is far apart from that of all the others mentioned here. His *Complete Works* are published by A. H. Bullen, Stratford-on-Avon.

All the poets that matter I hope I have mentioned in the text or in notes, A few of some fame I have omitted because I do not think their work good. The principal Dublin publishers of verse are Maunsel and Hodges, Figgis and Co. The catalogues of these houses contain lists of the authors and their works.

The best encyclopaedias of the subject are *The Cabinet of Irish Literature,* in four volumes (Gresham Publishing Company), which can easily be got, and the far finer but rare *Irish Literature,* in ten volumes (Philadelphia: John D. Morris Company: 1904). In *Every Irishman's Library* the Talbot Press (Dublin) is issuing a series of anthologies of verse and prose and editions of masterpieces of Anglo-Irish literature. For the rest, go to the compilations and editions of D. J. O'Donoghue: *The Poets of Ireland* (Hodges, Figgis), his *Life* and complete edition of Mangan, his complete works of Lover, his editions of some works of Carleton. Father S. J. Brown has just published a large book of reference, *Ireland in Fiction,* an extension of his *Reader's Guide to Irish Fiction.* He has also made a *Guide to Books on Ireland.* To end with what I began and therewith to assuage the learned who have forgotten that this Bibliography is not for them, I give the name of the great list of Gaelic books: *Bibliography of Irish Philology and of Printed Irish Literature,* made by R. I. Best and published by the National Library of Ireland.

A Profile of Thomas MacDonagh

A Select Chronology

1878 Born at Cloughjordan, Co. Tipperary.
1896 Joined the Holy Ghost Congregation at Rockwell College, Co. Tipperary.
1901 Released from the Congregation at his request.
     Taught English and French in Kilkenny and Fermoy colleges.
     Joined the Gaelic League and taught Irish classes.
1902 *Through the Ivory Gate*, poems, published.
1903 *April and May*, poems, published.
1905 *The Golden Joy*, poems, published.
1908 Assistant headmaster, St. Enda's School, Dublin.
     When the Dawn Is Come, a three-act play, produced.
1910 *Songs of Myself*, poems, published.
1911 Assistant lecturer in English, UCD.
     A director of *The Irish Review* journal.
1912 Married Muriel Gifford; their son Donagh born.
     Metamphsycosis, a one-act play, produced.
1913 *Lyrical Poems* published.
     Committee member of the Irish Volunteers, formed 25 Nov.
1914 *Thomas Campion and the Art of Poetry* (his M.A. thesis) published.
     Appointed Director of Training of the Irish Volunteers – the minority group after the movement had split.
1915 *Pagans*, a one-act play, produced.
     Their daughter Barbara born.
     Joined Irish Republican Brotherhood.
1916 Co-opted to the secret military committee of the Irish Volunteers.
     One of the seven signatories of the Proclamation of the Irish Republic and Commandant of Jacob's Factory garrison during the week-long armed rising which commenced on Easter Monday, 24 April.
     Court-martialled on 2 May and executed 3 May.

Thomas MacDonagh's life was a comparatively short one. He was less than three months past his thirty-eighth birthday when he faced a firing squad at 3.30 a.m. on 3 May 1916 for his lead role in the Easter Rising and as one of the signatories of the Proclamation of the Irish Republic. It is only when one realises that his literary, academic and political achievements were accomplished in fifteen years that his intellect, ability and enormous energy can be fully appreciated.

He was born on 1 February 1878 in the village of Cloughjordan in north-west Tipperary close to the border of Co. Offaly. Both parents were teachers and had come as such to the first Catholic school which opened there the previous year. His father Joseph McDonagh was son of 'Red' Pat McDonagh of Rooskey, Co. Roscommon, who was listed in the 1851 Census as a 'hedge schoolmaster'. His mother, Mary Louise Parker, was born in Dublin, daughter of an English-born printer of Greek with Trinity College Press. She had converted to Roman Catholicism from Unitarianism.[1] They had met and married in Cloghan, Co. Offaly, where they both taught before the move of twenty miles or so to the neighbouring Co.Tipperary.

Family Talent

Mary McDonagh wrote poems, short stories and essays and these survive in the MacDonagh papers in the National Library of Ireland.[2] Some have amendments and corrections in Thomas's writing. Many of her stories relate to life in a small village and to emigration. A poem, 'Child of the Wandering Poor', deals with the plight of the itinerant mother and her child and their rejection by society. A few of her stories were published by the Catholic Truth Society. She also gave piano lessons locally. She was widowed in 1894 when her youngest child was eleven years old. She had already discontinued teaching.

Thomas and his three brothers, John, Joseph and Jim, received their primary education in their father's classroom, while his two sisters, Mary and Eleanor (known as Nell),[3] were taught by their mother in the adjoining girls' room. Music and singing were amongst

Thomas's pastimes and he was an avid reader. Mary became a Sister of Charity.[4] The artistic talent in the family was also evidenced in John (Jack), as actor, singer, playwright, broadcaster and film-maker, and in Jim, who became a musician in England. Joseph was the second political activist – Sinn Féin MP for North Tipperary in 1918.[5]

Rockwell College

Thomas spent nine years in Rockwell College, a boarding school of the Holy Ghost congregation near Cashel in south Tipperary. After two years as a pupil he joined the congregation. His period as a seminarian is reflected in some of his spiritual poems. He matriculated through the Royal University of Ireland in 1896 and thereafter taught classes in the college. The earliest appearance in print of a literary effort was in September of that year when his essay entitled 'The Iron Bracelet' shared the one guinea prize in an English publication called *The Golden Penny*.[6] He was then eighteen years old.

'Tod' Ryan who was in senior class at Rockwell when MacDonagh, four years older, was teaching the juniors, recalled in 1966 'that he was very keen on rugby, playing in the forwards. He would get in there with the two Ryans, Mick and Jack – they were internationals. Tom was small, but a handy little fellow.'[7]

In 1901 he was released at his own request from the Holy Ghost congregation. MacDonagh now ventured into the world at large for the first time as an adult. Two of his early poems relate to this period – 'The House In The Wood By The Lake' and 'The Parting,' subtitled 'on leaving a long-loved place'. Personal emotional experiences figure as themes in much of his poetry.

The Ireland he re-entered had changed considerably since his boyhood. Major influences had included the formation of the Land League, of the Gaelic Athletic Association, and of the Gaelic League, the introduction of representive local government in the counties, and the centenary commemoration of the 1798 rebellion.

To Work

MacDonagh's first job was in St. Kieran's College, Kilkenny, where he taught English and French. While in that city he formed a friendship with Francis Dominick Hackett which endured after Hackett's emigration to the USA. MacDonagh's letters to him, as quoted by his first biographers, Edd Winfield Parks and Aileen Wells

Parks, are the prime revelation of his ambitions, values and opinions.

He shared rooms with a young Cavan man, Francis Skeffington (1878-1916), a teacher in the city's Protestant seat of learning, Kilkenny College. It was in Kilkenny that he joined the Gaelic League – allegedly 'for a lark', but he became an immediate convert and went on to become branch secretary and organiser of its first Feis.

Pádraig Ó Dubthaigh, who met him in the Aran Islands in 1902, writing in *The Record* after 1916 had these observations:

> ... reserved on personal topics, but when some social, national or literary issue was raised he spoke out of a full-stored mind ranging over a wide field of allusions ... never dogmatic.

His sister-in-law, Sydney Gifford Czira, described him as 'sturdily built with curly brown hair and large grey eyes', 'a most witty and fascinating talker' with a 'mischievous sense of humour', and 'He loved to poke fun at solemn people, and I remember him criticising some members of the Gaelic League who couldn't take a joke by saying, in exasperation, "Ah, those people are always on their oath" '.[8]

Novice Poet

Even at this early stage of his secular career MacDonagh showed the confidence, energy and competence which were to become his hallmarks. Seeking advice on the poems he now intended publishing, he sent the manuscript at the end of 1901 to none other than William Butler Yeats, some thirteen years his senior, by then an established writer and a leading figure in the Irish Literary Revival. Yeats replied:

> ... a thousand is far too large an edition for a first book of verse. ... Now about the verses themselves. They show you have a thoughtful and imaginative mind – but you have not yet got a precise musical & personal language. ... If you are young, & if you feel you have something you must give expression to, I strongly advise you not to publish for the present – but (1st) to read the great old masters of English, Spenser, Ben Jonson ... perhaps Chaucer – until you have got our feebler modern English out of your head. ... (2nd) I will advise you to translate a great deal from the Irish – to translate literally, preserving as much of the idiom as possible. ...[9]

He certainly took to studying the old masters and translating, as is particularly evident in *Literature in Ireland*. But he rejected the poet's advice to postpone publication; his volume of fifty-five poems appeared at the end of 1902, dedicated to Yeats. The title, *Through The Ivory Gate*, is taken from Virgil's *Aenead*, where the gate of ivory leads one into the land of false dreams and the gate of horn into the land of true dreams. The final poem in the book is entitled 'Through The Gate Of Horn'.

His affinity with his native Cloughjordan and in particular with his havens, Scott's Hill and Knocknacree wood which overlook the village, is evident in many of the poems, notably in 'Summer Joys' and one simply titled 'Knocknacree.'[10]

He was unhappy with the finished product and with the reviews. He wrote to his later publisher, Denis O'Donoghue: '… If anything could have turned my hair grey, the worry of that first book would have done it.'[11] A year later he wrote to Hackett: 'My days of niggling and selling are over; only 113 copies of 'Ivory Gate' are sold yet! Soon shall the homes of the solvent know me not'.[12] One hopes that at least he had taken Yeats's advice to reduce the print run.

Activist

In September 1901 MacDonagh went to St. Colman's College, Fermoy, where he was to remain for five years. He again taught senior English and French. Outside of school he became Vice-President of the town's branch of the Gaelic League and taught Irish classes twice weekly. In a letter to Hackett in 1906 he reported he was now 'a pretty fluent speaker of Irish' and that he had learned 'to sing traditionally' and had 'appeared at some pretty big concerts'.[13]

It was in St. Colman's that MacDonagh and a teaching colleague Patrick J. Kennedy, also from Cloughjordan and ex-Kilkenny, set in motion steps to found the Association of Secondary Teachers of Ireland. Kennedy became its first President.[14]

Undaunted by his first publishing experience he brought out another collection of twenty-two poems in 1903. These, entitled *April and May,* were dedicated to Rev. E. Crehan, CSSP, Rockwell College. Many had nationalist or religious themes. Again, the fruits of Yeats's advice was demonstrated in his precise, musical translation from Irish of 'A Dhruimfhionn Donn Dílis'. One poem, 'To William Rooney,' commemorated the associate of Arthur Griffith who had written 'The

Men of the West,' 'Ninety-Eight', and 'An tSean Bhean Bhocht,' and who died in 1901 at twenty-seven years of age. Eleven years later MacDonagh published a revised version. The change of title to 'Of A Poet Patriot' put the focus on the universal rather than a particular hero. Indeed he may well have intended it to be interpreted as a self-epitaph – as it was perceived after his death.

Two years later, 1905, he published his third volume of poems, *The Golden Joy*. Nationalist and religious themes predominate. Many concern his own spiritual experiences and doubts. An obscurity of language in parts was commented on by reviewers and by friends in letters to him.

The previous year he had entered and won a special competition in the Feis Ceoil which entailed translating from Italian into English the text of a cantata entitled *The Exodus*.The music was written by Bendetto Palmieri whose brother had written the original text.[15]

'A Grand Success'

In 1908, now thirty years old and with some seven years of worldly living behind him, he left Fermoy and St. Colman's and went to Dublin. MacDonagh became assistant headmaster at St. Enda's School, then in Oakley Road, Ranelagh, and the Pádraic Pearse-MacDonagh partnership began. Founded by Pearse, the school was described as 'an adventure in a new method of education, bi-lingual and geared to Irish needs'. An advertisement promised it would be 'Irish-Ireland in atmosphere'. MacDonagh was to teach French and English. His mother, writing to 'My dearest Tom' from Cloughjordan in August 1908, concluded: 'I suppose St. Enda's is getting ready to receive boarders. I am sure it will be a grand success, please God ...'

Mrs McDonagh died three months later and was buried in Grawn graveyard on the outskirts of Cloughjordan.[16]

The contrast between MacDonagh's confident and gregarious personality and Pearse's is portrayed by Ruth Dudley Edwards:

> P. H. Pearse, headmaster, who met his new pupils in the hall of St. Enda's, was an imposing figure. The shyness of the youth had given way to the aloofness of his maturity ... But the boys were quickly put at ease by the ebullient, laughing man who swept quickly on the scene and had the apprehensive newcomers feeling at home within ten minutes – Thomas MacDonagh.[17]

However, MacDonagh's commitment to this new school was not as total as Pearse's, for he revealed in a letter to Hackett in November that he was applying for an Inspectorship of Schools. He was not successful. He attributed this to the lack of a University degree – a shortcoming he set about remedying in the following year. He was to remain on St. Enda's staff during its most successful years, 1908-10. He left to study for his degree but returned for a short time in 1911-12.

Playwright
In October 1908 his three-act play, *When the Dawn Is Come*, was produced by the Abbey Theatre. The title of the play is adapted from the last line of his 'To William Rooney'. It had four performances with Abbey greats Sara Allgood playing the heroine and J. M. Kerrigan the principal male role. The Yeats patronage had continued. He had written to MacDonagh at Fermoy that January: 'Do come and see me when you come to Dublin but meanwhile I wish you would send on the altered version of the play – the sooner the better'.[18]

The theme of the play is the liberation of Ireland, and it was written, according to himself, in 'rhythmic verse' but which reads as very turgid prose indeed. The plot deals with seven men and two women who form a Supreme Council of Ireland and the action is set fifty years in the future. Thurlough McKiernan, a poet, has been elected Captain of the Army to take supreme command for one week – the remaining captains to assume command in rotation. A crisis, founded on suspicions, is averted when the enemy attacks and Thurlough leads the army to victory, but is fatally wounded.

In the hindsight of MacDonagh becoming one of the seven leaders of the 1916 Easter Rising, three of them poets, the play is endowed with extraordinary prescience. Its conflicts have shades of their deception of Eoin McNeill and the later all-or-nothing versus compromise Treaty debates.

Some reviews of the play were favourable. He spent considerable time revising it during the next six years. He changed the name to 'Freedom', but the revised version had no public performance.[19]

Frenetic Activity
Correspondence with Hackett gives an account of MacDonagh's academic and literary activities during 1909 and 1910 – articles, reviews and poems for Dublin and London magazines, school

textbooks for St. Enda's, and reading for his own Bachelor of Arts examination. He was a frequent theatre-goer and socialised with Arthur Griffith, journalist and founder of the political party, Sinn Féin; pacifist Francis Skeffington (who on his marriage in 1903 to Hannah Sheehy endorsed his commitment to women's rights by changing his name to Sheehy Skeffington), writers Pádraic Colum, George Russell (Æ), James Stephens, and

> I have been a good deal with Yeats of late. … I like him very much and he talks freely to me. He is thinking of going to live in Italy. It is a great pity. He cannot go on giving his time to the Abbey, away from his own work, for no reward, but abuse … I have also a private pupil for Irish, a son of Count Plunkett.[20]

He spent the summer of 1910 in Paris in preparation for his B.A. examination and graduated later that year in French, Irish and English. He demonstrated his continued development as a poet with the publication of *Songs Of Myself* late in 1910.[21] These poems are very personal. Some relate to anguish suffered by the ending of a love affair. The girl in question was Mary Maguire, a teacher in St. Ita's, the school for girls adjoining St. Enda's. She married Pádraic Colum in 1912.[22] The book's two translations from Irish, 'Is Truagh gan Mise i Sasana' and 'Táid na Réalta 'na Seasamh ar an Aer' are in keeping with the theme of some of his own compositions – unrequited love, estrangement and separation.

John-John

One of the poems in *Songs Of Myself* and the most frequently reproduced of his writings is 'John-John'. This has the universal theme of lovers drawn together from societies which are distinct, adapted to an Irish setting of a tinker or itinerant tinsmith and a settled woman.

> … Oh, you're my husband right enough,
> But what's the good of that?
> You know you never were the stuff
> To be the cottage cat,
> To watch the fire and hear me lock
> The door and put out Shep –

The interest in the life-style of itinerants/travellers which was evident in Mrs McDonagh's 'The Child of the Wandering Poor' was to continue to a third generation via his son Donagh's ballad opera, 'God's Gentry'.

Multiple Roles

As well as writing, teaching and socialising, MacDonagh continued to be a serious student. By the end of 1911 his academic career had begun to take shape. His thesis on Thomas Campion, the Elizabethan poet, gained him an M.A. with first-class honours and the post of assistant lecturer in English in University College, Dublin. The book version of the thesis was published in 1914.[23]

In 1911 he became a director of *The Irish Review*, a journal of literature and politics launched in March. He did sub-editing and contributed articles and poems.

A co-founder of that journal, Pádraic Colum, supplies this portrait as of this period:

> ...Those who saw Thomas MacDonagh in his university robe and noted his flow of speech and his tendency to abstractions might have carried away an image of one of those adventurous students who disputed endlessly in a medieval university. But MacDonagh was far from being a pedant – he was a wonderfully good comrade, an eager friend, a happy-hearted companion. He had abundance of good spirits and a flow of wit and humour remarkable even in a Munster man. He had too an intimate knowledge of the humours of popular life in the country and the country town – a knowledge which he seldom put into his writing, but which has become vivid in that unique poem 'John-John'.[24]

The university position enabled him to marry Muriel Gifford in January 1912. Muriel, of Protestant Unionist stock, was one of twelve children. Her sisters included Grace, an artist, who would marry Joseph Plunkett (MacDonagh's private pupil) prior to his execution, and Sydney (Czira), who, under the pen name of 'John Brennan' was a highly-regarded journalist. He wrote of his forthcoming marriage in a joint letter to his brother Jack, then touring with an opera company in America, and Dominick Hackett:

... Muriel and I are of the same religion, which is neither
Catholic or Protestant nor any form of dogmatic creed, neither
of us ever go to church or chapel, but for the sake of several
things and people are willing to conform for a marriage
ceremony.[25]

Their son Donagh was born in November 1912 and their daughter
Barbara in 1915.

Lyrical Poems, his last book of verse, appeared in 1913. He
described the collection in the foreword as containing the lyrical
poems written by him since the publication of *Songs of Myself* in
1910 and 'all that I wish to preserve of my previous work ...'.

The publication included two poems originally published in *The
Irish Review*, 'The Man Upright' (1911) and 'The Night Hunt' (1913).
Both are redolent of Cloughjordan atmosphere, and, like 'John-John',
have appeared in notable anthologies.

The former, though beautifully crafted, is an unkind and rather
hostile view of his native village, uncomplimentary to its residents
and to people engaged in trades. This was merely an expression of
the widespread outlook and reality that pliers of crafts and trades,
and manual labourers, were subordinate to the white collar worker –
a view which obtained well into the 1960s. MacDonagh's 'Man
Upright' was Denis Costello, the local schoolteacher. [26]

In contrast, The Night Hunt' celebrated sights and sounds of things
rural.

Another of the major poems in the collection is his translation of
'An Bunnán Buidhe/The Yellow Bittern'. His is the best-known
translation, having preference in anthologies over those of Daniel
Corkery and Tom McIntyre.

Though 'Wishes For My Son' in the collection was inspired by
Donagh's birth, there is much that is subjective in it – acknowledge-
ment that he had attempted and achieved many things; desire for
more action in his life; regret that opportunity to do glorious deeds
had evaded him. Such opportunities he wished for Donagh:

Wild and perilous holy things
Flaming with a martyr's blood,
And the joy that laughs and sings
Where a foe must be withstood ...

But his immediate wishes were:

> Simple Joys: the natural growth
> Of your childhood and your youth,
> Courage, innocence, and truth:

Lyrical Poems did not include one effort which had appeared in *The Irish Review* in 1912 and re-appeared only in the miscellaneous section of *The Poetical Works* – the collection published in September 1916. It contains the solitary input of a personal characteristic which was otherwise absent from his verse, as noted by Pádraic Colum: 'We may keep one regret about MacDonagh and it is that he has left us so little of the happy-hearted and humourous part of his nature in his poetry'.[27] The poem is 'Dublin Tramcars II'.

> Calvin and Chaucer I saw today
> Come into the Terenure car:
> Certain I am that it was they,
> Though someone may know them here and say
> What different men they are,
> I know their pictures – and there they sat,
> And passing the Catholic church at Rathgar
> Calvin took off his hat
> And blessed himself, and Chaucer at that
> Chuckled and looked away.

His interest in the theatre extended to a joint directorship with Edward Martyn and Joseph Plunkett, of Hardwicke Street Theatre. They specialised in producing plays rejected by the Abbey Theatre and works by the Russian Chekov and the Norwegian Ibsen, each hugely influential and only recently deceased.

In 1915 they staged his own play, *Pagans,* which had some echoes of 'John-John' in a different milieu. The main characters are an incompatible husband and wife. He is a writer, bohemian, returning home after a three-year disappearance. She is a conventional Edwardian. The re-union ends: 'Your way of life is not my way of life … you may go, John, quite free this time'. A one-act play of his, *Metempsychosis: Or A Mad World*, had one performance by the New Theatre of Ireland in 1912. The language of the characters obscured for most of the audience the allegory of Ireland's reincarnation.

Volunteer

Though he was not involved in the Home Rule movement, MacDonagh monitored its impact and progress and wrote to Hackett in 1911: ' ... Ireland is all expectancy of Home Rule. Sinn Féin has fallen quite in the background ... In the 'Irish Review' we are going to have a series of articles on it.'[28]

As the Irish Parliamentary Party's drive for Home Rule approached a climax the Ulster Unionist reaction to this probable achievement led to the formation of the Ulster Volunteer Force in January 1913. Nationalist Ireland reacted by forming the Irish Volunteers. The initiative was taken by a colleague of MacDonagh's at University College, Dublin, Eoin MacNeill, Professor of History and a well-known Gaelic scholar. A public meeting on 25 November saw the new movement launched, to engage in 'defensive and protective activities', according to MacNeill's manifesto. MacDonagh enrolled on the night and became a member of the Central Committee.

The movement drew forth from him that rare combination of a profusion of ideas (the 'high talk' recalled by Æ) and executive competence, already manifest in his literary and academic careers. Early in 1914 Hackett was given a glimpse of the literary man turned political strategist.

> ... We have already gone a good way towards fusing existing organisations. ... A.O.H. men, Sinn Feiners, Gaelic Leaguers, Irish Freedom men, Parliamentarians, G.A.A., and the University men. ... at present we are only at the drill stage. The movement is spreading. We have against us, of course, a good part of the old generation, all those who think it our business to fight not England but Ulster.
>
> We know no more here than you do about the prospects of Home Rule. Some of us are prepared for whatever happens. If it passes, good, we shall be in a better position to stand for the full right. If not, we shall have a splendid opportunity of getting a strong feeling in the demand for the full right. We should be able to get Redmond and the others to withdraw from Westminister and set up government here. If only they had the courage they could do it successfully.[29]

Notwithstanding his support for the constitutional path, he co-organised with Belfast-born Bulmer Hobson, a leading figure in the Volunteer movement and a vice-President of Sinn Féin, the march of a group of Volunteers to Howth in July 1914 to receive arms landed there by the yacht, *Asgard* – a move influenced by the importation of arms for the Ulster Volunteer Force the previous April.

The outbreak of the Great War in August had brought conscription in England and many Irishmen domiciled there returned to Ireland to avoid being called up. MacDonagh organised an employment office for them on Volunteer premises. The movement split in September over the issue of John Redmond's call upon Volunteers to serve 'not only in Ireland itself but wherever the firing line extends in defence of right, of freedom, and religion in this war'[30] (against Germany). MacDonagh was amongst the minority who sided with Eoin McNeill versus Redmond. They retained the name, Irish Volunteers, and adopted an anti-conscription policy.

Front Rank

His appointments to the General Council and as Director of Training and propagandist in speech and writing followed. He was now a part-time military officer organising week-end training camps and giving practical instruction in the handling of weapons. Though Home Rule was on the statute books since September 1914 its implementation had been suspended due to the outbreak of the war. The Volunteers were soon formed into a disciplined body to meet any contingency such as their suspension, or threatened conscription of the country as a whole.

The Irish Review became their platform. MacDonagh's strongly-worded anti-conscription propaganda in the Sept-Nov. issue led to its suppression under the Defence of the Realm Act and its ultimate demise.

His daughter Barbara was born in March 1915 and his poem titled by her name appears to be his last personal one. It is a very sophisticated composition, in which domestic, religious and nationalist themes are entwined with classical allusions and a consciousness of Europe at war. He forecast for her:

> The greater glory you shall see
> And the greater peace, beyond these wars.

His letter to Hackett in May 1915 reveals how entrenched he was in the military movement.

> ... I have found a great thing to do in and with life outside of the very real and wonderful interest that a wife and two children give me. ... I am Director of Training for the whole country and have to keep a staff working to keep that department. But the work, half like that of a Cabinet Minister and half like that of a regular military officer, is wonderfully interesting and exhilarating. I am ten years younger than when you saw me last – or rather than I was a little before you saw me last, for half of it is due to my marriage. ... Of course none but the best metal has stood the test. Men like Æ write for the *London Times*. My friend David Houston, the founder of *The Irish Review*, a splendid good man, has been shocked by the *Lusitania* affair into going into the British Army ... Remain those who under all circumstances at all times will be and must be Irish rebels. Zealous martyrs, and so saviours and ... liberators, for I am confident we shall win this time, through peace, I hope, but if necessary by war.[31]

'Militarism'

Peace and War were the topics of a debate at a meeting organised by the Irish Women's Franchise League to protest at government action which prevented an Irish delegation attending a Women's International Peace Congress at The Hague. MacDonagh attended the Irish Women's meeting and seconded a resolution approving the objectives of that Congress. His speech raised deep and searching questions which were noted and answered point by point by his old Kilkenny room-mate, Francis Sheehy Skeffington, now a leading pacifist and campaigner for women's rights. The format of reply was a four-page 'Open Letter' in the *Irish Citizen*.

He acknowledged that MacDonagh spoke at the meeting 'with unmistakeable sincerity in advocacy of peace. You traced war, with perfect accuracy, to its roots in exploitation ... in the same speech you boasted of being one of the creators of a new militarism in Ireland'. He adverted to MacDonagh's description of bayonet fighting and the hope he had expressed 'to have a better opportunity than voting ...' Skeffington said he was 'not blind to the movement's merits ... But it is militarism. It is organised to kill'.

'Can you not conceive an organisation' ... (proceeding to suggest in outline the equivalent of a civil rights movement of more recent times, with an overriding consideration:) 'an organisation that will not lay it down as its fundamental principle, "we will prepare to kill our fellowmen?" ' He concluded, 'Think it over, before the militarist current draws you too far from your humanitarian anchorage'.[32]

The Easter Rising

MacDonagh's organisational skills were drawn on for the funeral of the veteran Fenian, Jeremiah O'Donovan Rossa, in July 1915. He was in charge of all the arrangements.[33]

A secret military committee within the Irish Volunteer movement had been set up in May 1915. It included Pádraic Pearse, Joseph Plunkett, Eamon Ceannt, Sean McDermott and Tom Clarke. All were members of the secret Irish Republican Brotherhood (IRB) and committed to, indeed planning, an armed uprising. It did not include the Volunteers' Chief-of-Staff, Eoin MacNeill. Though MacDonagh was sworn in to the IRB around September he was co-opted to the military committee only in April 1916, James Connolly of the Irish Citizen's Army having been added in January.

Though not actually published until after his death, the date of January 1916 appended to *Literature in Ireland* is confirmation that his military and literary commitments were running in tandem during the last months of his life. His University colleague, Michael Hayes, and others, observed that he gave no intimation of the forthcoming insurrection.

> To those of us who knew MacDonagh and saw him daily, even in the rising, he seemed quite different from Pearse; ... he did not appear to have the idea that he was going to sacrifice his life to restore the soul of Ireland. He never lost his interest in literature, in teaching, in poetry, in drama. Up to the very end when he knew the rising was coming he was helping his brother in the production of a play at the Hardwicke Theatre ... He had made conscious, and very arduous, preparations to fit himself for a university post. He was not a dabbler in literature or criticism. ... He hoped to succeed Robert Donovan as professor of English here at University College.[34]

We know from Muriel's statement made after his execution that he had not slept at their home, 29 Oakley Road, Ranelagh, for two weeks prior to the outbreak of the rising – he would call in each morning. She also revealed that he had a bodyguard. Her husband did not, apparently, tell her of the planned rising when he left her on Easter Sunday night.[35]

MacDonagh was very involved in the confrontations and conferences which occupied the leaders on Good Friday, Easter Saturday and Sunday, following the discovery of the planned insurrection by Chief-of-Staff, Eoin MacNeill, and his issue of a countermanding order.[36]

But the rising did go ahead, a day later than planned by the military committee. Easter Monday evening, 24 April, saw Thomas MacDonagh with the rank of Commandant in command of Jacob's biscuit factory, Bishop Street. The garrison, which included his brother Jack, were never subjected to a full-scale attack but did encounter sporadic sniping to which they responded.[37] Presumably MacDonagh was appraised of the fate of Francis Sheehy Skeffington who, shocked by the extent of civilian looting, had gone on to the streets in an effort to stop it. He was arrested by a British patrol, taken to Portabello barracks, court-martialled and shot dead in the early hours of Wednesday morning on the orders of Capt. Bowen-Colthurst who was later adjudged guilty of murder but held to be insane.[38]

Surrender

The pacifist was one of the 450 killed and 2,614 wounded in the week's fighting, over three-quarters of them civilians and insurgents combined.[39] Pearse ordered a surrender on the Saturday, 'In order to prevent the further slaughter of Dublin citizens, and in the hope of saving the lives of our followers now surrounded and hopelessly outnumbered …'.[40] The physical reality of 1916 was a painful irony set against Pearse's written exhortations of 1913: 'We may make mistakes in the beginning and shoot the wrong people; but bloodshed is a cleansing and sanctifying thing … [41]

After the surrender on the Saturday, and the arrest of Pearse and Connolly, MacDonagh was in supreme command of the insurgents still in action. He surrendered to General Lowe reluctantly on Sunday, after consultations with Lowe and with his own second-in-command, Eamon Ceannt. He was taken to Richmond Prison initially and later to Kilmainham Jail where he was court-martialled and sentenced to death. Messengers taking the news of his impending execution to Muriel were unable to get through but Mary/Sr Francesca did see him for a short time. By then he and Pearse had already made their confessions and received Holy Communion from Fr Aloysius, a Capuchin. MacDonagh, Pearse and Tom Clarke were executed at 3.30 a.m. on Wednesday, 3 May.

Sheehy Skeffington's 'Open Letter' had said, 'We are all in the same tangle'. MacDonagh had now joined his friend as a victim of the militarism on which they disagreed, at the hands of one the most practised militarist empires of recent centuries – its militarism cruel, callous, yet crass as to the political and cultural fall-out.

Tributes came from MacDonagh's peers, Yeats, Stephens, Colum, Æ. Francis Ledwidge wrote an elegy which echoed themes in MacDonagh's own compositions – the yellow bittern, Ireland and Spring – and is written in the 'Irish Mode' identified in *Literature in Ireland.*

Ledwidge had responded to the call to defend small nations in Europe. He wore the same uniform as those who shot MacDonagh. He himself was killed in action the following year.

Yeats's immediate summary was that MacDonagh

> was coming into his force;
> He might have won fame in the end,
> So sensitive his nature seemed,
> So daring and sweet his thought'.[42]

Last Letter

The revolutionary was in conflict with the writer, teacher and family man. There are disturbing echoes in that real-life drama of the climax of the fictional 'John-John' and *Pagans*, elevated to the level of terrible tragedy by the involvement of great love, high ideals and the utter finality of death.

The awesome choice made by MacDonagh is underlined in his last written words – from Kilmainham at the midnight before his execution. That letter, his public apologia and private testament, is a document of inexpressible poignancy. Having outlined his financial situation, named his executors, and expressed hope that his wife and children would be cared for, he concluded:

... It is a great and glorious thing to die for Ireland ... When my son Don was born I thought that to him and not to me would this be given. God has been kinder to me than I hoped ... My dearest love, Muriel, thank you a million times for all that you have been to me ... Good bye, my love, till we meet again in heaven ... I kiss this paper that goes to you ... God help and sustain you, my love. But for your suffering this would be all joy and glory.[43]

The Family

Muriel and the chldren lived for a short while in Thurles with her brother-in-law Joe and his family. They returned to Dublin to a Plunkett-owned house in Marlboro Road, Donnybrook. She was involved in the preparation and proof reading of *The Poetical Works* which came out in September 1916 and was reprinted in November. Her father died around that time and she was a beneficiary in his will.

She converted to Catholicism some months before she died of 'heart failure due to exhaustion' during a long-distance swim from Skerries to Lambay Island on 9 July 1917.[44] She was aged 31 years.

In the aftermath of the fifteen executions, and the imprisonment of surviving participants, public opinion which had ranged from condemnation of the armed rising to indifference now changed to support for the concept of a republic. At the time of her death Muriel was on a holiday provided by the Prisoners Dependents fund which had enjoyed widespread support. Her funeral to Amiens Street station and thence to Marlboro Road was huge and ran hours late. Emotions were high as polling was about to take place in the historic Clare by-election for the Westminister parliament. Eamon de Valera, the Irish Volunteer Commandant whose sentence of death for his part in the Easter Rising had been commuted to life imprisonment, was contesting the seat for Sinn Féin. De Valera, accompanied by Joe MacDonagh who was also in Clare helping with the canvass, made the journey to Dublin. Muriel was buried in Glasnevin.

The two children, then aged four and a half years and two years and four months, spent some time with Jack MacDonagh and with their aunt Eleanor Bingham in Broadford, Co. Clare, before going to boarding schools. Both graduated in Arts from University College, Dublin in the 1930s. Donagh qualified as a barrister and became a district justice on the Western Circuit. Alongside his legal career he was a poet, playwright, and broadcaster. He died in 1968. Barbara/ Bairbre married Liam Redmond, actor and film maker.

Literary Memorial

Literature in Ireland, completed by MacDonagh in January, was published in June 1916, reprinted in July with a 'Literary Introduction' added by Pádraic Colum, again reprinted that November, all by The Talbot Press. It got an American publication towards the end of the year. T. Fisher Unwin, London, took it up and published it in 1918. Its sales and that of *The Poetical Works* in September 1916, reprinted November, alleviated Muriel's financial difficulties somewhat.[45]

Literature in Ireland earned continuing critical acclaim, sampled here in the quotations on the cover of this edition.[46] It is identified as a 'classic' with 'literary historical significance' (p. xi, this edition). There are sections in the book which are very heavy going, some which are great debating fodder, some – with eight decades of reflection – capable of being dismissed. Johann Norstedt, for instance, in a close analysis in 1980 spotlit 'a needless diversion'; 'this contradictory position'; 'overtones of his concern with the charge of obscurity frequently levelled at his own poetry'.

But the central thesis of Study 5, brought forward in its three elements to MacDonagh's Preface, stands up, and Norstedt concludes with a favourable endorsement as quoted on the cover.

MacDonagh's thesis is illustrated by a minor and hugely enjoyable anthology, not just the selection of translations, ballads and original songs at the end. The generous supply of verse examples to support his argument throughout the text are similarly entertaining.

A generosity of friendship is apparent in the extensive space he devotes to Plunkett's work of criticism and Pearse's poems. On the other hand, he is not loath to tax both Yeats and Stephens severely with misuse in their work of his beloved Irish language. There is a proud patriotism evident in the very undertaking of the whole analysis of what he defines as Anglo-Irish literature, in his exposition in Study 3 of the effects of nationalism, in the proclamation: 'The Gaelic revival has given to some of us a new arrogance. I am a Gael and I know no cause but of pride in that'.

Informed by the character sketches by his contemporaries which are quoted above, one can envisage his relish in translating the powerful passage from Canon O'Leary's *Séadna* and its delicious *dénouement*. He creates memorable phrases – what would nowadays be called one-liners or write bytes: 'A Molière that cannot interest his washerwoman will not interest the passers by'; 'he who makes music for his little clan makes music for all the world'. He telescopes two experiences and finds 'a blackbird with a Cork accent'.

Perhaps the last word in regard to the book should be left to Pádraic Colum, both loyal friend and percipient critic:

> These studies, written after the writer's life had been committed to a cause, carry something more than literary knowledge and a literary doctrine: they have personality and a prophetic outlook. *Literature in Ireland* is Thomas MacDonagh's testament: by it he leaves to the Irish generations his knowledge and his discoveries, and, above all, his proud hopes for the resurgent Ireland that he knew. It is one of the few proud books that have been written for us: Thomas MacDonagh, scholar and critic, has taken Ireland for granted: he decries nothing, dispraises nothing, denies nothing of what another people possesses: he has full knowledge of Ireland's achievement in literature and he says 'it is good', he has full belief in her destiny and he says 'it is brave'.[47]

Commemoration

In addition to his writings, the deposit of his personal papers, and two biographies, MacDonagh is commemorated by his national costume in the National Museum's 1916 Room, an Oisín Kelly bust in UCD library, his name on Kilkenny railway station and memorabilia in its Rothe House museum, a plaque in Fermoy College, a portrait and essay medal in Rockwell College. His native county has affixed his name to streets in most of its towns, to a Templemore pipe band, to a Séamus Murphy bust in Golden, to the Gaelic Athletic Association's parks in Nenagh and Cloughjordan, to two of its trophies and all of its North divisional medals since 1934.

> Perhaps the most apt of all the memorials: a rose tree in the former playground of the school where he learned and his parents taught, outside a library which now has a collection of his and his son Donagh's books donated by his nephew Joe

and grandson Breffni and fronted by a tasteful plaque carrying the words of his wish in the 'Singer's Grave' (1902):

If in my life I shall have sung or done some thing,
For which mankind may praise me when I'm gone,
Then bring a rose-tree to my grave, and plant it in the Spring.[48]

The library in Cloughjordan was erected in 1966 to mark the jubilee of the Easter Rising by Tipperary Joint Libraries Committee and dedicated to his memory. His daughter, Mrs Bairbre Redmond, performed the unveiling. In the context of this volume, an extract from her address seems an appropriate way to conclude this profile.

In speaking here today I hope that I may speak for my father, who was first a poet and then an educationist. In another kind of Ireland than that into which he was born he could have devoted himself to those twin parts of one profession. When he died it was for them …

I wish he were here in person to speak of those things. He would say, I'm sure: This, if anything, is what I hoped might happen to me after my death, that the young growing up can have their nutriment from the great minds of the world, and can be larger people with greater understanding of the world they live in.[49]

Another thirty years and several waves of students later, this re-publication of his major work of criticism, following on that of his poems[50] may provide further 'nutriment'.

And as a bonus overleaf – a 'tilly', as one with 'an intimate knowledge of the humours of popular life' would have said – here is Ledwidge's elegant elegy, honouring the man and, in its crafting, the immortality of the best of MacDonagh's creative work. And, interwoven, a complementary tribute to MacDonagh the translator from Irish into English, by way of a translation from Ledwidge's English into Irish – crafted, exquisitely apposite, by an educationist from MacDonagh's own country whose literary output, to adapt MacDonagh's phrase, turned back to the old language.[51]

Nancy Murphy

Thomas MacDonagh
Caoineadh Thomáis

He shall not hear the bittern cry
In the wild sky, where he is lain,
Nor voices of the sweeter birds
Above the wailing of the rain.

Ní chloisfidh sé an bunnán buí
Go dubhach ag caoi os cionn a chré,
Ná ceiliúr lon is céirseach donn
Ar chraobha crann tráth fuine lae.

Nor shall he know when loud March blows
Thro' slanting snows her fanfare shrill,
Blowing to flame the golden cup
Of many an upset daffodil.

Ní bhraithfidh sé ar theacht don Mháirt
An ghaoth go hárd ag fógairt fás,
Ag adú blaidhm i gceannaibh crom
Na mbleachtán seang nár ghéill don bhás.

But when the Dark Cow leaves the moor,
And pastures poor with greedy weeds,
Perhaps he'll hear her low at morn
Lifting her horn in pleasant meads.

Ach nuair a thréighfidh Síod' na mBó
An cimín móinteach lom gan féar,
Músclófar é arís, tá seans,
Ag ciúinghéim seanfaí i móinéar.

Original by Francis Ledwidge; translation by Máirtín Ó Corrbuí

Notes to the Profile

1. MS 20,646, MacDonagh Papers, NLI, biographical notes compiled by George Bingham, Thomas's nephew. In this Mary Louise McDonagh's surname is given as Burroughs-Parker but it appears only as Parker on the birth records of her children. Thomas commenced spelling his name MacDonagh in the early 1900s.

2. MS 10,858, MacDonagh Papers, NLI.

3. Helen is used in the civil record of her marriage to Sergeant Daniel Bingham, RIC, then stationed in Ballina, Killaloe, in 1897. She appears variously as Ellen/Eleanor in the birth records of her children. Daniel later retired from the RIC and became Petty Sessions Clerk in Broadford, Co. Clare. After his death she emigrated to her children in New York and died there.

4. MS 10,585, MacDonagh Papers, NLI. Mrs McDonagh recorded her profession on 23 April 1895 in a copy book. Her name in religion was Francesca.

5. Jack, who died in 1961, made the historic *Irish Loan* film which was later incorporated into *Mise Éire*. His most notable play was *The Irish Jew* which was performed on Broadway. He was productions director with Radio Éireann. Jim, who died in 1931, played the oboe professionally. He had two daughters and a son, Terry, who became Professor of Music in the Royal College of Music, London, and first oboist with the BBC Symphony Orchestra.

    Joe was an excise officer who then became headmaster at St. Enda's school after the 1916 rising. While MP for North Tipperary he became an alderman of Dublin Corporation upon moving residence from Thurles, Co. Tipperary, where two of his three children were born. He and W. T. Cosgrave founded an insurance firm, now MacDonagh & Boland. He was jailed as an anti-Treatyite during the Civil War, developed peritonitis in jail, and died in hospital on Christmas Day 1922. His three children were Mary (Moll) who married Frank Lemass, later General Manager of CIE, Thomas who stood as a Fianna Fáil candidate in North Tipperary in a general election, and Joe who managed the insurance firm.

    In 1924 Mary/Sr Francesca compiled for publication her personal selection of Thomas's poems. In the preface she refers to 'little brochures of poems which he presented to friends at festivals'. One of these, inscribed 'Ninth Number of The Irish Melodies for ML', is MS 8,093 in the MacDonagh Papers.

6. MS 20,645 MacDonagh Papers, NLI, a page from *The Golden Penny,* 19 Sept 1896. The other winner was from Oxford.

7. Memories of 'Tod' Ryan quoted by G. V. Oakley in the *Midland Tribune Jubilee Supplement,* 1966.

8. Sydney Gifford Czira, *The Years Flew By* (Dublin, 1974), p. 19.

9. Edd Welland Parks & Aileen Wells Parks, *Thomas MacDonagh* (University of Georgia Press, USA, 1967), p. 7.

10. Verses from both those poems and also the complete 'An Staicín Eorna' – which latter poem conforms perfectly to his lauding of simplicity: 'that clear, sincere, colloquial statement' – appear in 'Thomas MacDonagh: His Early Verse' in *Tipperary: A Treasure Chest* (RELAY, 1995), pp. 188-9. All three were unjustifiably omitted by him from his *Lyrical Poems,*

11. Parks and Parks, p. 76.

12. Parks and Parks, p. 10. One suspects he would have been wryly amused to find that a copy of that first publication – which was priced at one shilling (5p) with a cloth edition at two shillings – was on sale a few years ago in Dublin for the sum of £105 – its inflated price influenced no doubt by his own corrections and annotations in the margins.

13. Parks and Parks, p. 11.

14. Records of the founding of ASTI in July 1909 do not survive but the September 1916 issue of the *Journal of Education* states that MacDonagh was a former member of the Association and 'indeed instrumental in giving it some vitality and recalling it from the torpor into which it had been allowed to sink' (W. J. Williams).

15. The Parks' biography, p. 82, gives the impression that MacDonagh wrote the original words, but MS 20,646, MacDonagh Papers. NLI, is an envelope signed by John MacDonagh, 10.9.1958, which apparently contained a copy of *The Exodus*. On the envelope is a note stating that Thomas translated the text from the Italian by Palmieri's brother. The note stated that it had to be done by an Irish man or woman in order to enter. The envelope was empty when I examined it in 1980.

16. In 1993 Cloughjordan guild of the Irish Countrywomen's Association sponsored the erection of a gravestone in Grawn cemetery to commemorate herself and Joseph. Hitherto their burial place was unmarked. Their grandchild Mrs Moll Lemass – Joe's daughter – attended the ceremony.

17. Ruth Dudley Edwards, *Patrick Pearse: The Triumph of Failure* (London, 1977), p. 118.

18. MS 13,663-2,452 MacDonagh Papers, NLI. Yeats had opened the letter with the comment, 'I would have replied to you long ago but I couldn't read your writing ...'

19. A typescript of acts 1 and 3 survive in the MacDonagh papers in the NLI.

20. Parks and Parks, cited above, pp. 20-1. Count Plunkett, Director of the National Museum and a writer, was elected MP in 1917 on an abstentionist ticket and became Minister for Foreign Affairs in the first Dáil. The son was Joseph, nine years younger than MacDonagh and needing to acquire Irish for university matriculation.

21. MS 20,645, MacDonagh Papers, NLI, 1,000 copies were printed, costing £11 2s 6d (£11.12p); the author got 12 copies, newspapers 41 and libraries 5.

22. Mary Colum, *Life and The Dream* (New York & London 1947), p. 174. 'At intervals one or another of my young men friends would propose to me but we would laugh it off. I had, as far as I remember no sentimental interest in them, only an interest in the causes we were all working for and in the plays and poems they wrote ... I did not have any taste for exchanging the independent and interesting life I was living for pottering around a kitchen, planning meals, hanging curtains and so on and I let my young men friends know my sentiments about this. One of them, however, declined to listen to me and kept assuring me that he was the person Heaven had destined me to marry and that I could not escape my fate ...' The subject is also dealt with in Parks' *Thomas MacDonagh*, pp. 25-6. The Colums later went to live in the United States. Mary died in 1957 and Pádraic in 1972.

23. MS 20,645 MacDonagh Papers, NLI. 1,124 copies were printed.

24. Pádraic Colum, 'Literary Introduction', *Literature in Ireland* (2nd edition), p. xviii.

25. Parks cited above, p. 28. Sidney Gifford Czira, recounts in her *The Years Flew By* that Pearse, who was to be the best man, did not turn up and the services of a man who was trimming the hedge outside the church had to be called upon. A year later when Donagh was being christened in Rathgar church Pearse happened to drop in to say a prayer and MacDonagh greeted him with the words, 'Well, you got here for the christening, anyway'.

26. *The Irish Times,* 18 Dec. 1976, General Michael Joseph Costello in an interview with Michael Finlan.

27. Colum, p. 326, in Joy ed, *The Irish Rebellion of 1916* and Its Martyrs (New York, 1916).

28. Parks and Parks, p. 25.

29. Parks and Parks, cited above, p. 6.

30. T. W. Moody & F. X. Martin eds, *The Course of Irish History* (Dublin, 1984), p. 439.

31. Parks and Parks, cited above, pp. 51-3.

32. *Irish Citizen,* 22 May 1915.

33. A detailed map of the route and the arrangement of Units is preserved in the MacDonagh Papers, NLI.

34. Michael Hayes,'Thomas MacDonagh and the Rising', in *The Easter Rising and University College, Dublin,* F. X. Martin, OSA, gen. ed, 1966, p. 48.

35. There is a printed copy of a statement made by Muriel in the MacDonagh Papers. In it she stated that she last saw Thomas about 10 o'clock Easter Sunday night 'in the presence of friends who were with us' and that she got one written message from him from Jacob's factory mid-week which went, 'I have never been better and happier than now'.

36. The various steps taken and the people involved in them are well set out in Ruth Dudley Edwards, cited above.

37. The *Irish Independent 1916-66 Supplement,* pp. 7-8, has a memoir by Bill Stapleton, one of the Jacob's factory garrison. A cookhouse was established in the factory bakehouse where regular hot meals were made by members of the Cumann na mBan unit. Barricades in the vicinity of the factory were manned all day. The third floor of the high-rise building had look-out points with a continuous roster of volunteers deployed for two-hour stints of guard duty. On Thursday MacDonagh, responding to a request from Commandant Eamon de Valera under seige in Boland's Mills, sent a detachment of eighteen men off on bicycles to create a diversion in the vicinity of the mills. This they did with reasonable success and all but one returned unharmed. The injured man died later – the only casualty out of the 185-man garrison.

38. D. J. Hickey & J. E. Doherty, *A Dictionary of Irish History Since 1800,* p. 532.

39. F. S. L. Lyons, *Ireland Since the Famine* (London, 1971), p. 374.

40. Ruth Dudley Edwards, cited above, p. 308.

41. Lyons, pp. 335-6.

42. W. B. Yeats, 'Easter 1916', *The Collected Poems of W. B. Yeats* (New York, 1957), p. 178.

43. Parks and Parks, cited above, the full letter is quoted on pp. 70-2.

44. *Weekly Freeman,* 14 July 1917.

45. Johann Norstedt, *Thomas MacDonagh: A Critical Biography* (Virginia, 1980), pp. 136-7,

46. Parks, cited above; Norstedt cited above, pp. 108-117; Gerald Dawe, *The*

Irish Times, 29 April 1995; Robert Farren, 'The Gaelic Voice in Anglo-Irish Poetry' in Sean Lucy ed, *Irish Poets in English* – the Thomas Davis Lectures (Cork, 1972), pp. 132-3; John Jordan, *Hibernia*, 17 Dec. 1976. See also Patrick C. Power, *The Story of Anglo-Irish Poetry (1800-1922)* (Cork, 1967), pp. 78-9, 174.

47.　　　Pádraic Colum, 'Literary Introduction', *Literature in Ireland* (2nd edition), p. xv.

48.　　　Donal A. Murphy, 'Commemorating Thomas MacDonagh' in *Centenary Special Programme*, North Tipperary GAA Hurling Final, 1984, Tomás Ó Ciarba ed, pp. 40-1.

49.　　　*Nenagh Guardian,* 16 April 1966.

50.　　　Desmond Ryan ed, *The 1916 Poets* (Gill and Macmillan, 1995).

51.　　　*Wordsnare*, No. 2, 1974 (Nenagh).

Francis Ledwidge (1891-1917), wrote three books of poems which were collected and published in 1919 by his patron Lord Edward Dunsany, himself a prolific writer who made 'mystery in a gracious way about plain things' (p. 70). Ledwidge joined the same British regiment as Dunsany, the Royal Iniskilling Fusiliers. He was killed in Flanders, Belgium, by shell-fire while preparing an assault roadway – he had been a County Council road ganger before enlisting. See Alice Curtayne, *Francis Ledwidge: A Life of the Poet* (London, 1972); Alice Curtayne ed, *The Complete Poems of Francis Ledwidge* (London, 1974).

Máirtín Ó Corrbuí (1912-), was born in Carney, fourteen miles from Cloughjordan. He is the author of some thirty books, all but four in Irish, embracing biography, children's, detective and adventure, and historical incidents woven into fiction. He has won thirty-two awards in the annual Oireachtas literary competitions. His books in English include *Kenry*, a history of that barony in Co. Limerick (he taught in Pallaskenry), and *Tipperary* (Brandon, 1991), a travelogue with an historical eye over its shoulder. He has had eight one-act plays in Irish and a three-act play in English broadcast by RTE.

Index

This index does not repeat the directions of the Table of Contents: it does not give references to the Poems of the Irish Mode. It gives reference to Notes only when new names and new matter are introduced in these. Otherwise, references will be taken to include notes. It does not cover the Bibliography, [nor the 1996 Introduction, nor the 1996 Profile.]

A leabhráin, gabh amach fá'n saol 116
A Mhuire na nGrás 88
A.C.H. of *Poetry* 161
Abbey Theatre 114
absolute construction with And, 7
Addison 7
Æ 124, 167, 168
Affliction of Margaret, The 24
aisling 118
Alfred, King 27
Allingham, William 41
American literature 101
Ancient Irish literature, 76 et seq.
Ancient Irish Poetry 77, 168
Andersen, Hans 86
Anglo-Irish (the term) 18
Anglo-Irish authors 41
Anglo-Irish dialect 7, 8, 18, 25, 28, 33
Anglo-Irish literature (essentials) 14, 40
anthologies 64 et seq., 124
Arnold, Matthew 2, 38, 83, 87, 100, 116
Arthurian Epics 35, 77
Atkinson, Professor Robert 95
Austen, Jane 7
authority 4, 6
authors, Anglo-Irish 41 et seq.
authors, Hiberno-English 16, 17, 41, 162

Bacon, Francis 24
ballad, Irish street 17
ballads literature 7
Banims, the 43
Beaudelaire, Charles 32
Benson, A. C. 42
Bergin, Osborn 96, 169
Best, R. I. 96
Bible, the 7
Blackbird of Daricarn, The 121
Blake, William 3, 24, 28
Book of Irish Verse, A 64

Boyd, Thomas 124, 125, 162
Brandes, George 10
Bridges, Robert 53
Brontë, Charlotte 42
Brontë, Emily 42, 43
Brooke, Stopford 64, 65
Browning, Robert 3, 61
Buile Suibhne 96
Burns, Robert 43, 62, 112
Burns, Thomas 112
Butt, Isaac 43

Callanan, J. J. 6, 36, 37, 41, 129
Campbell, Joseph 124
Campion, Thomas 36, 38, 166, 169
Canterbury Tales 22
Carbery, Ethna 125
Carducci 112
Carleton, William 23, 43
Carlyle, Thomas 118
Cartesian philosophy 4
Catullus 87, 124
Celtic Literature, on the Study of 38
Celtic Note, the 4, 38
characteristics, Irish 8
Chaucer 2, 14, 15, 22, 23, 25, 26, 28, 72, 101, 102
Chesson, Nora 18, 41
Chesterton, G. K. 61
clarity 86
Classic Renaissance 7, 25, 77 et seq.
Coleridge, S. T. 67
colloquialism 24
Colum, Pádraic 68, 72, 100, 101, 102, 123, 172
Columbus 4
Confessio Amantis 22
Cooke, John 64, 65
Copernicus 4
Cousins, J. H. 124
criticism and literature 83, 99 et seq., 105
Curran, John Philpot 17, 43

dán díreach 60, 118
Dante 112, 116
Darley, George 17
Darwin 4
Davis, Thomas 41, 43
De Quincey, Thomas 32 et seq.
de Vere, Aubrey 41, 120
Deirdre 50, 80, 83
Dinneen, Rev. P. S. 100, 169
Domfarcai fidbaidae fál 89, 116
Douglas, Gavin 14
Dowson, Ernest 36
Drama 11, 111 et seq.
dramatic lyric, the 60 et seq.
Drennan, William 17
Droighneán Donn, An 122
Dhruimfhionn Donn Dílis, A 11
Drummond, William 52
Dryden, John 2, 14, 86
Duanaire Finn 81, 95, 96
Dublin Book of Irish Verse, The
    61, 64, 65
Dunbar, William 14, 15
Dunsany, Lord 69, 70

Eamonn an Chnuic 11, 72
Edgeworth, Maria 43
Eglinton, John 80
Elizabethan literature 4, 14, 72
Emmet, Robert 10, 43
English language 27
Eriú 60, 96

Famine, Irish 23
Fellonosa, Ernest 167
Fenian cycle, the 81
Ferguson, Samuel 35-7, 41, 43, 55-6,
    127, 128, 130, 132, 135, 159, 170
Finn's *Song of Summer* 55
Fitzgerald, Edward 42
Flavell, Thomas 135
Flood, Henry 43
folk literature 11
Fox, George 135
French literature 27, 40
French Revolution 4
Furlong, Alice 124, 160
futurists 3, 6

Gaedhealtacht 108, 111 et seq.
Gael and Greek 18, 77

Gaelic (language) 11
Gaelic influence 7, 24, 25, 78
Gaelic League 100, 111 et seq.
Gaelic literature 11, 16, 26
Gaelic Renaissance 73, 77 et seq.,
    117 et seq.
Gaelic symbolism 11
Gaelicisms 8
Galileo 4
Gilbert, W. S. 34
Goethe 112
Golden Age of Irish civilization 81
Golden Treasury of English Songs and
    Lyrics, The 61, 64
Goldsmith, Oliver 17, 41, 61, 62
Gower, John 22
Grattan, Henry 17, 43
Gray, Thomas 112
Greek and Gael 18, 77
Gregory, Pádraic 64, 65
Griffin, Gerald 41, 43

Hardbeck, Carl 38
Heffernan, William (Liam Dall Ó
    hIffearnáin) 140, 141
Heine 112
Henley, W. E. 62, 63
Hiberno-English authors 16, 17,
    41, 162
history and literature 81
history, Irish 26 et seq.
Homer 4
Hopkins, Father Gerard 71
Horace 49, 76, 77, 86, 124
Houghton, Lord 161
Housman, A. E. 105
Hull, Eleanor 65, 83, 89
hunger in Irish literature 10
Hyde, Douglas 41, 56, 65, 71, 86-8,
    95, 108, 111, 123, 167, 169, 172

I am Eve, great Adam's wife 60
I sing of a maiden 87
Ibsen 11, 112
Impressionism 5, 11
individual and collective 107
intellectualism 4
intonation, Irish 8, 36, 50, 51, 120
Irish and English languages 15, 27,
    30 et seq., 98, 117,
Irish characteristics 8

Irish intonation 8, 36, 50, 51, 120
Irish language 11, 31 et seq., 34
Irish Mode 4, 6, 18, 36, 38, 41, 55, 120 et seq.
Irish music 8, 15, 17, 36, 38, 50, 55, 120
Irish patriotism 9
Irish poetry, ancient 77
Irish prose 108
Irish Review, The 167
Irish scholars 43
Irish street ballads 17
Irish words in English 34 et seq.
Is Truagh gan Mise i Sasana 106

Jacobites 26
James I of Scotland 14, 18
Johnson, Lionel 18, 41, 162, 164
Johnson, Samuel 167
Jonson, Ben 14, 25, 52
Joyce, P. W. 18
Joyce, Robert Dwyer 122

Keating, Geoffrey 33
Keats, John 4, 5, 6, 40, 77, 113
Kellner, Leon 163, 164
King and Hermit 55, 90

La Belle Dame Sans Merci 5
Lake Isle of Inishfree 47
Lalor, James Fintan 43
Lament for the Makaris 14
Lament of the Old Woman of Beare, The 35, 55, 92 et seq.
Langland, William 22, 25
language and literature 22, 105 et seq.
language, English 27
language, Irish 11, 31 et seq., 34
Larminie, William 167
law of monopressures 46
Lawless, Emily 41, 124
Le Fanu, J. Sheridan 43
learning and literature 52
Lecky, W. H. 43
Les Regrets de la Belle Heaulmière 92
Letts, W. M. 124
Lever, Charles 43
literature, American 101
literature, Ancient Irish 76 et seq.
literature, ballad, 7
literature and criticism 83, 99 et seq.

literature and language 22, 105 et seq.
literature and learning 52
literature and nationality 27, 40
literature, Anglo-Irish, (essentials) 14 et seq., 40 et seq.
literature, ballads 7
literature, Elizabethan 4, 14
literature, folk 11
literature, French 40
literature, Gaelic 11, 16, 26
literature, Restoration 14
literature, Scots 14
literature, themes of Irish 79, 80, 83 et seq.
Little Black Rose, The 120
Lloyd, J. H. 171
Lloyd, Seaghan 106
Love-Songs of Connacht, The 123
Lover, Samuel 43, 173

Mac Giolla Ghunna, Cathal Buidhe 147
Macalister, R.A.S. 169
MacDonagh, Thomas 57, 107, 124, 143, 144, 145, 147, 160
Mackail, J. W. 123
Macklin, Charles 17, 43
MacNeill, Eoin 81, 95, 96, 169
Macpherson, James 6, 24
MacPiarais, Pádraic (P. H. Pearse) 102 et seq., 108
MacSuibhne, Pádraig 116
MacSweeney, Rev. P. M. 165
Maguire, Hugh 53
Main Currents in Nineteenth Century Literature 10
Malone, Carroll 172
Mangan, James Clarence 6, 41, 42, 43, 53, 54, 56, 72, 120, 123, 137, 139, 140, 141, 156, 170
Mathurin, Charles 43
McBrien, Peter 124
McCall, Patrick J. 124
Mé Eba ben Adaimh uill 60
Meredith, George 80
Messe ocus Pangur ban 55
metaphors 71, 118
Meyer, Kuno 43, 60, 77, 90, 91, 93, 95, 168
Michael 24
Milligan, Alice 41, 54

Milliken, R. A. 152
Milton, John 2, 6, 53, 72
Mistral 23, 112
Mitchel, John 43
Mitchell, Susan 124
Modern Irish Poetry 64
Molière 23, 114
monopressures, the law of 46
Moore, George 112
Moore, Thomas 10, 17, 37, 41, 56, 153, 154
Munster bards 115
music and metre 50, 55 et seq.
music, Irish 8, 15, 17, 36, 38, 50, 55, 120
My Dark Rosaleen 120
mysticism 5, 11, 68 et seq.

Naomh ar Iarraidh, An 111
nationality and literature 27, 40
Newbolt, Henry 53, 54
Newman, Cardinal 85
Night before Larry was Stretched, The 17

obscurity 66 et seq.
O'Connell, Daniel 27, 43
O'Curry, Eugene 34, 43, 95
O'Donnell, Hugh 26
O'Donoghue, D. J. 125, 163, 170, 171, 172
O'Donovan, John 34, 43
O'Grady, Standish Hayes 43, 96, 168
O'Grady, Standish James 43, 84, 168
O'Hussey's Ode to the Maguire 53
Oireachtas 112, 113
O'Keeffe, J. G. 96
O'Leary, Canon Peter 108, 115
Omond, T. S. 47
O'Neill, Eoghan Ruadh 26
O'Neill, Father George 167
O'Neill, Hugh 26
O'Neill, Moira 124
Ó Prunta, Pádraic 43
Ó Riain, Eamon (Edmund O'Ryan, Eamonn an Chnuic) 143
O'Shaughnessy, Arthur 42, 86
Ó Súilleabháin, Eoghan Ruadh 115
O'Sullivan, Seumas 124, 154
Out of the night that covers me 62
Outlaw of Loch Lene, The 55

Oxford Book of English Verse, The 53
Pale, The 15, 17, 23, 111, 114
Palgrave, Sir Francis 61, 64
Parnell, Charles Stewart 10, 27
Parnell, Fanny 171
Pashteen Finn 55
Patmore, Coventry 56, 71
patriotism, Irish 9
Pearse, P. H. 102 et seq., 108
Pepy's Diary 7
Petrie, George 43, 134
philosophy, Cartesian 4
phonetics 8, 34
Plunkett, Joseph 66, 67, 124, 157, 162
Poe, E. A. 42
Poem Book of the Gael, The 65
Poet, The 23
Poetry (Chicago monthly) 161
poetry (interpretative) 64
poetry, Ancient Irish 77, 168
Pope, Alexander 2
Pride and Prejudice 7
printing 11
prose, Irish 108
Prout, Father 173
Prudhomme, Sully 86

qualities of Irish literature 79, 85, 90

Raftery, Anthony 72, 108
Religious Songs of Connacht, The 87
Renaissance, Classic 4 et seq., 7, 26, 77
Renaissance, Gaelic 73, 77 et seq., 117 et seq.
Restoration literature 14
Revolution, French 4
rhythm 49
rhythm and emotion 49
rime 95
Róisin Dubh 72
Rolleston, T. W. 64, 124, 125
Romance 5, 6, 7, 25
Ronsard 72, 167
Ruskin, John 10

Samhain 112
scholars, Irish 43
Scots literature 14
Séadna 108

sex in Irish literature 10
Shakespeare 2, 3, 6, 14, 26, 28, 33, 38, 72, 79, 86, 105, 112
Sheil, Richard Lalor 43
Shelley, P. B. 80
Sheridan, R. B. 17, 41
Shorter, Clement 165
Shorter, Dora Sigerson 124, 173
Sidney, Sir Philip 7
Sigerson, George 41, 78, 89, 95, 121, 123, 124, 169
Silva Gadelica 96
sincerity in literature 63
Sparling, Halliday 172
Spenser 25, 26
St. Guthlac 50
St. John of the Cross 12
standards (critical, literary) 2, 12, 41, 76 et seq., 80 et seq., 101, 113
Stars Stand Up in the Air, The 57
Stephens, James 35, 124
Stokes, Whitley 43, 89, 96
Strongbow 18
Stuairín Na mBachall mBreágh Réidh 57, 145
Suantraidhe agus Goltraidhe 102 et seq.
Sweet, Henry 164
Swift 17, 41
Swinburne, A. C. 106
syllabic verse 51, 55
symbolism, Gaelic 11
Synge, J. M. 10, 34

Tagore, Rabindranath 9
Táin Bó Cuailgne 77, 95
Tell me, tell me, smiling child 42
Tennyson, Alfred 3
The middle of the things I know 69
themes of Irish literature 79, 80, 83 et seq.
Thesaurus Palæohibernicus 89, 96
Thompson, Francis 67, 71, 73
Three Sorrows of Story-Telling, The 167
Three things through love I see 57
Tincéir agus an tSidheog, An 111
Times, The 42
'Tis a pity I'm not in England 107
Todhunter, John 124
Town of Passage, The 47

translation 8, 17, 86 et seq.
Treasury of Irish Poetry, A 64
Trench, Archbishop 22
Triads of Ireland, the 2
Tryst after Death, The 91

Ulidian Cycle, The 81 et seq.
Underhill, Evelyn 167
University College, Dublin 98

Verlaine, Paul 105, 106
vers libres 5
versification 8, 36 et seq., 46 et seq., 90, 94, 105, 120 et seq.
Villon 17, 77, 92, 113
Virgil 113
Vision of Connacht in the Thirteenth Century, A 123

Wagner 5
Wallace, Colm 108
Walsh, Edward 41, 129, 132, 170, 171
Wars of the Roses, The 26, 79
Watson, William 53
Weldon, Robert 108
whimsicality 8
Whitman, Walt 3
Wild Earth 102
Wind Among the Reeds, The 35
Wolfe, Charles 7
word-order 24
words 86
words, Irish, in English 34 et seq.
Wordsworth, William 6, 24, 80, 99, 100

Yeats, W. B. 24, 35, 41, 47, 50, 51, 56, 64, 72, 99, 101, 112, 123, 166

1916 Poets, The 169